Performance and Impact of Microfinance

DEVELOPMENT ECONOMICS AND POLICY

Series edited by Franz Heidhues and Joachim von Braun

Vol. 58

PETER LANG

Frankfurt am Main · Berlin · Bern · Bruxelles · New York · Oxford · Wien

Performance and Impact of Microfinance

Evidence from Joint Liability Lending Programs in Malawi

Franklin Simtowe

PETER LANG
Internationaler Verlag der Wissenschaften

Bibliographic Information published by the Deutsche Nationalbibliothek
The Deutsche Nationalbibliothek lists this publication in the Deutsche Nationalbibliografie; detailed bibliographic data is available in the internet at <http://www.d-nb.de>.

Zugl.: Hohenheim, Univ., Diss., 2006

Gedruckt mit Unterstützung
des Deutschen Akademischen Austauschdienstes.

D 100
ISSN 0948-1338
ISBN 978-3-631-57242-9

www.peterlang.de

DEDICATION

This dissertation is dedicated to my father Peter and my mum Evelyn, my brothers and sisters Elias, John, Stanly, Lilian, Charity, Estere, MacDonald and Moses.

Editorial Preface

Microfinance institutions (MFIs) aim at achieving the three objectives embedded in the triangle of microfinance, namely expanding the outreach to the poor, achieving impact on poverty reduction, and ensuring that the services are delivered in a manner that promotes the financial sustainability of the MFI.

In Malawi, almost all MFIs continue to face problems of low outreach, limited impact and lack of financial sustainability. The success of MFIs in addressing the three objectives, simultaneously, depends on the institutional and technological innovations they employ. Although group lending with joint liability is recommended as an institutional innovation that can potentially address these problems, moral hazard is a common occurrence among credit groups.

In view of these problems, this thesis investigates the performance and impact of group lending with joint liability in Malawi. The joint liability lending institutions are assumed to be out-performing the conventional lending institutions for two reasons. First, members of a community may know more about one another in terms of actions and states than outsiders of the moral community. Hence, in this way adverse selection, moral hazard and auditing problems are reduced. The second reason relates to the fact that a conventional bank cannot apply financial sanctions against poor people who default on the loan.

Joint liability lending institutions on the other hand are able to use poor people's neighbors and social networks to impose pecuniary sanctions on defaulting members at a low cost. In so doing, auditing costs and limited enforcement problems faced by conventional banks are administered in the non-conventional system through joint liability lending. The joint liability lending institutions give the poor incentives to collect information from their group members and use the information to apply non-financial sanctions to non-paying members.

This research focuses on credit groups from the Malawi Rural Finance Company (MRFC). It investigates the incidence and determinants of moral hazard and intra-group insurance and assesses the impact of credit access on the adoption of hybrid maize. The strength of this study is that it addresses both group level problems as well as household level impact. Group level data as well as household level data are used in the analysis. The results indicate that moral hazard remains a problem and that intra-group insurance occurs whenever groups face internal repayment problems. The findings further indicate that access to credit enables households to invest in high productivity technologies such as hybrid maize.

A key contribution of this study is the application of a household model under credit market failure. Very few empirical research efforts have employed this framework by especially taking into account the credit constraint status of a household. The household modeling approach provides a simple framework for assessing the impact of access to credit among households that differ in their credit constraints. In sum, this study provides interesting insights to researchers and students interested in understanding the performance and impact of joint liability lending in developing countries.

Prof. Dr. Dr. h.c. Franz Heidhues
University of Hohenheim
Stuttgart

Prof. Dr. Joachim von Braun
International Food Policy Research Institute (IFPRI)
Washington D.C.

Acknowledgements

A number of individuals and institutions provided me with technical, moral and financial support during the period of my research. I am greatly indebted to Professor Dr. Manfred Zeller of the Institute of Agricultural Economics and Social Sciences in the Tropics and Subtropics at the University of Hohenheim for his supervision, guidance and encouragement throughout my research period. His guidance was always constructive and inspiring. I also would like to thank Professor Dr. Dr. h.c. Jürgen Zeddies, a co-supervisor, for his kind acceptance to co-supervise my work. I am indebted to Professor Dr. Klaus Frohberg for his support throughout my PhD studies at the Center for Development Research (ZEF) of the University of Bonn.

I would further like to thank Dr. Peter Wobst of the Institute of Prospective Technological Studies, Professor Dr. Andrew Dorward of the Faculty of Life Sciences at the Imperial College of London and Dr. Alexander Phiri of the University of Malawi and Bunda College for their contributions in the early stages of proposal development. I thank Dr. Kennedy Bisani Lweya, Mr. Elias Simutowe and Mr. Felix Sikana for their support during my field research.

I extend my sincere thanks to Dr. Aliou Diagne of the West African Rice Development Institute for his encouragement and advice both before I enrolled for the PhD program as well as during the period of my PhD studies. Indeed, part of my success in research as well as my academic life is a result of his encouragement.

This study was conducted with financial support from DAAD through the Center for Development Research at the University of Bonn. Therefore, I would like to express my sincere gratitude to the DAAD for the financial support without which I wouldn't have enrolled for a PhD program in Germany.

I would also like to thank Dr. G. Manske, Mrs. R. Zabel and all those working in ZEF IDP secretariat for facilitating my studies at ZEF. I am deeply grateful to Dr. John Mduma, Mr. Holger Seebens and Dr. John Mburu for their support on technical matters regarding my research.

I also extend my appreciation to fellow Malawian students at ZEF, Hardwick Tchale, Blessing Chinsinga and Donald Makoka for being supportive throughout my stay at ZEF.

I am indebted to the respondents that were interviewed for the survey. Last but not least, I would like to thank my father, mother, brothers and sisters for their encouragement throughout the period of study.

Table of Contents

List of Tables

List of Figures

Executive Summary

Performance and Impact of Microfinance: Evidence from Joint Liability Lending Programs in Malawi

This study addresses performance and impact in group lending with joint liability in Malawi. It focuses on two aspects of performance: (i) Contractual compliance by beneficiaries and (ii) the effect of access to credit on the adoption of hybrid maize. The specific objectives of the study are (a) to determine factors influencing the incidence of moral hazard among credit groups (b) to examine the extent to which intra-group insurance occurs and to investigate its underlying determinants, and (c) to assess the impact of households' access to credit on the adoption of hybrid maize among households that vary in their credit constraints. The analysis on the first and second objective is guided by theoretical frameworks from Guinane and Ghatak (1999) and Besley and Coate (1995), respectively. The analysis on the third objective is based on the agricultural household model under credit market failure. Data used in the analysis is from a survey conducted by the International Food Policy Research Institute (IFPRI) in cooperation with the Rural Development Department of Bunda College, University of Malawi (RDD). The survey was carried out in Malawi in 1999/2000. In addition, a follow-up rapid appraisal was conducted in the same survey sites in 2004 to supplement on the information that had been collected during the IFPRI/RDD survey of 1999/2000.

The study shows that the likelihood of occurrence of moral hazard is lower in groups that were endogenously self-formed through peer selection. Peer monitoring through rules that encourage joint enterprise ownership reduces the incidence of moral hazard. The degree of pre-existing social ties captured by the number of villages from which group members come as well as the existence of peer pressure, particularly, before the due date of the loan reduces the likelihood of the incidence of moral hazard. Also consistent with theory, the study shows that matching problems resulting from the inclusion of new members as well as the number of loan cycles for which the group has been receiving loans induces risky behavior among borrowers. On the other hand, dynamic incentives captured in the willingness of group members to pay a full amount of a defaulter's loan in order to access further loans reduces the incidence of moral hazard, while the presence of members from past failed credit programs where loans were not vigorously collected induces moral hazard.

The analysis on intra-group insurance shows that although 89 percent of the borrowers understood and accepted that they were supposed to contribute to repay loans for defaulting members in the group, only 42 percent expressed willingness to offer that support. An analysis of factors influencing the willingness of members to provide mutual insurance revealed that factors of production as well as pre-existing social ties increased the likelihood that group members would be willing to support each other. Results further indicated that the likelihood of willingness by peers to provide mutual support varies with dynamic incentives. This encourages members to know and identify with one another, and thus building trust and interdependency. The presence of new members in the group, which potentially introduces a matching problem, works against mutual insurance. The cost of insurance, captured by the variation in loan size among group members, reduces the willingness of peers to contribute to repay defaulted loans of their peers.

The analysis on determinants of credit constraints and the impact of access to credit has interesting findings as well. The study shows that household head characteristics, types of crop grown, as well as the supply side factors such as the remoteness of the location in which the household is based, significantly affect the likelihood of a household being credit constrained. Participants in credit programs are less likely to report credit constraints, an indication that barriers to participation in credit markets continue to exist.

An investigation on the determinants of adoption shows that access to credit increases adoption among credit constrained households, while it has no effect among unconstrained households. Results also show that factors that affect adoption among credit constrained households are different from those that affect adoption among unconstrained households. Landholding size, for example, has opposite effects on adoption in the two regimes of households. Double-Hurdle estimates further reveal that factors that affect adoption decisions are different from those that affect the extent of adoption. A test for separation of consumption and production decisions using an on-farm labor demand model indicates that household demographic factors affect demand for labor in the constrained regime only, which justifies the sample separation that was done when assessing adoption decisions in the constrained and unconstrained regimes.

ZUSAMMENFASSUNG

Leistung und Wirkung von Mikrofinanz: Ergebnisse zu Kreditprogrammen mit Solidarhaftung in Malawi

Diese Studie betrachtet die Leistung und Wirkungen der Kreditvergabe mit Solidarhaftung in Malawi. Hierbei liegt der Fokus auf zwei Aspekten (i) Einhaltung der vertraglichen Vereinbarungen durch die Kreditnehmer sowie (ii) Wirkungen des Gruppenkredites auf die Adoption von Hybridmais.

Die spezifischen Ziele dieser Studie sind, (a) herauszufinden, welche Faktoren die Nichteinhaltung vertraglicher Konditionen (moral hazard) in Kreditgruppen beeinflussen, (b) das Ausmaß der informellen Versicherung zwischen Kreditnehmern innerhalb einer Gruppe und deren Bestimmungsgründe zu ermitteln und (c) die Wirkung des Kreditzuganges auf die Adoption von Hybridmais bei Haushalten mit variierenden Krediteinschränkungen zu untersuchen. Die Analyse des ersten und zweiten Zieles wird durch theoretische Bezugsrahmen von Guinane und Ghatak (1999) und Besley und Coate (1995) geleitet. Die Analyse des dritten Zieles basiert auf den landwirtschaftlichen Haushaltsmodellen unter Berücksichtigung des Kreditmarktversagens. Die in der Analyse genutzten Daten stammen aus Erhebungen des Internationalen Forschungsinstitutes für Ernährungspolitik (IFPRI) in Kooperation mit der Abteilung für ländliche Entwicklung des Bunda College, University of Malawi (RDD). Durchgeführt wurde diese Erhebung 1999/2000 in Malawi. Zusätzlich wurden sogenannte „rapid appraisal“ Studien in 2004 durchgeführt, und zwar an den gleichen Standorten wie die Erhebung des IFPRI/RDD.

Anhand der Studie wird gezeigt, dass die Wahrscheinlichkeit der Nichtrückzahlung des Kredits (moral hazard) in Gruppen sinkt, die sich durch Gruppenselektion selbst geformt haben. Das Monitoring durch Andere regelt hierbei die gemeinsame Unternehmensförderung und reduziert darüber hinaus das Auftreten einer Nichtrückzahlung des Kredites.

Der Grad von bereits vorhandenen sozialen Bindungen innerhalb der Herkunftsdörfer der Gruppenmitglieder und insbesondere der Druck der Gruppe vor dem Fälligkeitsdatum des Kredits reduziert die Wahrscheinlichkeit der Nichtrückzahlung des Kredites.Übereinstimmend mit der Theorie zeigt die Studie, dass Probleme durch Aufnahme neuer Mitglieder und Zahl von Kreditzyklen in der Gruppe zu Risikoverhalten bei den Kreditnehmern führen. Andererseits reduziert die Bereitschaft der Gruppenmitglieder, den bestehenden Kredit zurückzuzahlen, um kreditwürdig zu bleiben, die Häufigkeit einer möglichen Nichtrückzahlung des Kredites. Dagegen erhöhen Mitglieder aus früheren erfolglosen Kreditprogrammen, in denen Kredite nicht rigoros genug eingezogen wurden, das Risiko einer Nichtrückzahlung des Kredites. Was die informelle Versicherung zwischen Kreditnehmern innerhalb einer Gruppe betrifft, so zeigt die Studie, dass 89 Prozent der Kreditnehmer verstanden und akzeptiert haben, dass Sie sich an der Rückzahlung von Krediten säumiger Gruppenmitglieder beteiligen müssen, jedoch nur 42 Prozent Bereitschaft zeigten, dies auch zu tun. Eine Analyse der Einflussfaktoren zeigte, dass Produktionsfaktoren und vorhandene soziale Bindungen die Bereitschaft zur gegenseitigen Hilfe erhöhen. Die Ergebnisse zeigten weiterhin, dass die Bereitschaft zur gegenseitigen Unterstützung von den dynamischen Anreizen der Kreditvergabe abhängt. Die Mitglieder werden ermutigt, sich gegenseitig kennen zu lernen und sich miteinander zu identifizieren und so gegenseitiges Vertrauen und wechselseitige Abhängigkeit aufzubauen. Die Präsenz von neuen Mitgliedern in der Gruppe, die potentiell ein Problem mit sich bringt, schwächt die informelle Versicherung innerhalb der Gruppe. Die Kosten der Versicherung variieren je nach Kreditgröße unter den Gruppenmitgliedern und reduzieren die Bereitschaft, zu den Kreditversäumnissen anderer Mitglieder beizusteuern.

Die Analyse der Faktoren der Krediteinschränkungen und der Auswirkung des Zugangs zu Krediten zeigt interessante Ergebnisse. Die Studie zeigt, dass die Art der Haushalte, die Art der angebauten Pflanzen, sowie die Versorgungssfaktoren wie z.B. Abgelegenheit der Gegend, in der sich die Haushalte befinden, signifikant die Wahrscheinlichkeit der Krediteinschränkung eines Haushaltes beeinflussen. Teilnehmer eines Kreditprogramms sind weniger anfällig für Krediteinschränkung, ein Zeichen, dass immer noch Hindernisse für die Teilnahme an Kreditmärkten existieren.Hinsichtlich der Bestimmungsgründe der Adoption von Hybridmais zeigt die Studie, dass der Zugang zu Krediten die Adoption bei krediteingeschränkten Haushalten steigert, während dieser Aspekt keinen Einfluss auf nicht krediteingeschränkte Haushalte hat.

Die Ergebnisse zeigen weiterhin, dass die Faktoren, die die Adoption bei krediteingeschränkten Haushalten beeinflussen, andere sind als bei nicht eingeschränkten Haushalten.

Die Landgröße z.B. hat entgegengesetzte Auswirkungen auf die Adoption bei den zwei Haushaltstypen. Sogenannte Double-Hurdle Schätzungen zeigen, dass die Faktoren, die Adoptionsentscheidungen beeinflussen, andere sind als die, die das Ausmaß der Adoption beeinflussen. Eine Untersuchung zur Trennung von Konsum- und Produktionsentscheidungen mit Hilfe eines Modells zur Arbeitskraftnachfrage zeigt, dass demografische Faktoren der Haushalte die Nachfrage nach Arbeit nur in der kreditbeeinträchtigten Gruppe beeinflussen, was die Sample-Trennung rechtfertigt, die durchgeführt wurde bei der Untersuchung der krediteingeschränkten und nicht eingeschränkten Haushaltstypen.

List of Abbreviations

ADD	Agricultural Development Division
AHM	Agricultural Household Model
APIP	Agricultural Productivity Investment Programs
BRI	Bank Rakyat Indonesia
CUMO	Concern Universal Microfinance Operations
ECLOF	Ecumenical Church Loan Fund
FINCA	Foundation for International Community Assistance
GDP	Gross Domestic Product
IFAD	International Fund for Agricultural Development
IFPRI	International Food Policy Research Institute
MFI	Microfinance Institution
MMF	Malawi Mudzi Fund
MoAI	Ministry of Agriculture and Irrigation
MPRSP	Malawi Poverty Reduction Strategy Paper
MRFC	Malawi Rural Finance Company
MSB	Malawi Savings Bank
MSE	Micro and Small Enterprises
MUSCO	Malawi Union of Savings and Credit Cooperatives
NABW	National Association of Business Women
NGO	Non Governmental Organization
OIBM	Opportunity International Bank of Malawi
OLS	Ordinary Least Squares estimator
RDD	Rural Development Department
ROSCAs	Rotating Savings and Credit Associations
SACA	Smallholder Agricultural Credit Administration
SACCOs	Savings and Credit Cooperative Organizations

1 INTRODUCTION

1.1 Background of the Study

The majority of the one billion poor people live in developing countries where they lack access to financial services that are needed to uplift their welfare[1] (UNCDF, 2003). As noted by Kritikos and Vigenina (2005), the reasons for the continued exclusion of the poor from financial markets contain a risk and cost component. It is difficult to know their risk type and their willingness to repay the loan, both of which can be summarized as their creditworthiness. In addition, small individual loans are considered to be unprofitable in the traditional banking system such that most institutional lenders using conventional financial technologies consider the disbursement of micro and small credits as highly inefficient (Schaefer-Kehnert, 1983).

The provision of financial services such as savings, credit and insurance to low-income clients, also known as microfinance, has been widely publicized as a key ingredient to pro-poor economic development. Microfinance is currently considered as an important tool that can be used to achieve goal number one of the eight millennium development goals, which focuses on eradicating extreme poverty and hunger by the year 2015. In order to attract more attention to the provision of financial services to the poor, the United Nations declared 2005 as the International Year of Microcredit. The Year of Microcredit called upon the world to extend financial services to the poor and strengthen the powerful, but often untapped, entrepreneurial spirit existing in impoverished communities (ACCION, 2005).

In order to reduce transaction costs and information asymmetry problems associated with the disbursement of small uncollateralized loans to the poor, microfinance institutions have come up with lending innovations that enable them to lend to the poor and do so with a reasonable degree of financial self-sufficiency and achieve repayment rates that are reasonably high (Ghatak and Guinnane, 1999). An example of such innovations is the group lending with joint liability. Van Bastelaer (2000) defines Joint liability lending (JLL), as the provision of a private good (loan) in return for a public good (repayment). It involves the provision of loans to a group of individuals such that they are jointly liable to the repayment of the loan. A failure to repay the loan by one of the group members implies that the peers must contribute to repay the loan.

[1] Global demand for microfinance services is estimated to be 500 million households. Currently, only 4 percent of these households are reached by microfinance programs worldwide.

Group lending with joint liability has attracted a great deal of attention among microfinance practitioners for a number of reasons. First, through JLL, microfinance institutions are able to reduce high transactional costs by dealing with a group of borrowers in a single transaction. Second, through the information advantage that group members have about their peers and through intra-group insurance (risk sharing), problems of adverse selection are reduced. Third, as noted by Ghatak and Guinnane (1999), group lending emphasizes on peer monitoring which makes it easier to verify the state of the outcome (auditing) once one of the group members declares her/his inability to repay. In addition, JLL enables peers to enforce repayment using non-pecuniary measures when a group member is unwilling to repay. These perceived advantages of JLL are believed to be the main forces behind the success of microfinance institutions in reaching the poorest that are excluded by the conventional financial sector.

Recent success stories in microfinance are widely associated with the Grameen Bank in Bangladesh and the Indonesia's Bank Rakyat, both of which use JLL innovation. The Grameen Bank has used the technology to achieve high repayment rates while concentrating its lending on the poorest segment of the rural population of Bangladesh (Diagne *et al.*, 2000). Following this success, the technology is being replicated in several microfinance programs worldwide. Nevertheless, microfinance institutions remain skeptical about the performance of the mechanism because although group contracts have worked perfectly leading to repayment rates of 100 percent (like in the case of the Grameen Bank), Kritikos and Vigenina (2005) note that at times repayment rates dropped to 30 percent leading to a break down of the microfinance institution (MFI). Such negative examples have been observed in several countries in Asia, while Malawi is an example of countries from Africa.

The importance of a well functioning lending innovation such as JLL is multifaceted and can be best described in what Zeller and Meyer (2002) call the critical triangle of microfinance. The triangle is based on the assumption and the need that MFI must manage simultaneously the problems and institutional goals of:

1. achieving high outreach - thus reaching the poor both in terms of numbers and depth of poverty;
2. achieving financial sustainability - thus meeting operating and financial costs over the long term and
3. achieving high impact - thus having discernible effect upon clients' quality of life.

In Malawi, almost all MFIs have failed to achieve these goals such that they continue to suffer from problems of low outreach, limited impact and lack of financial sustainability. Most MFIs in Malawi operate non-profitably and this renders the execution of the Microfinance Regulatory framework unnecessary

(USAID, 2004a). The success of MFIs in addressing the three problems/goals, simultaneously, crucially depends on the institutional innovation employed. Although group lending with joint liability is a popular institutional innovation among MFIs in Malawi, its performance has not been plausible. For example, MFIs in Malawi continue to face high default rates mainly resulting from moral hazard, which negatively affects their sustainability, outreach, and consequently, their impact.

Following the success of JLL in some countries, an academic response has been the numerous attempts to theoretically explore reasons behind this success. Most of the theoretical propositions focus on the four problems that MFIs are assumed to face, namely adverse selection, moral hazard, costly monitoring and auditing, and limited enforcement (Ghatak and Guinnane, 1999). Most theorists believe that the incentives for peer-selection, peer-monitoring and peer pressure resulting from the joint liability clause are responsible for the high repayment rates of the Grameen Bank and other similar MFIs (Diagne et al., 2000). However, attempts to assess the performance and impact of such initiatives have produced mixed results. For example, in Malawi, Diagne and Zeller (2001) assess the impact of access to credit among small holder farmers and find that access to credit had no impact on farming efficiency unless farmers also had access to better technology and training.

An understanding of other components of JLL that have a bearing on the performance and impact has significant relevance to Malawi's overall development policy because group lending through joint liability is currently advocated as a key component in the Malawi Poverty Reduction Strategy (MPRS), (Government of Malawi, 2003a). The overall goal of the Malawi Poverty Reduction Strategy is to achieve sustainable poverty reduction through socio-economic and political empowerment of people. It moves away from seeing the poor as helpless victims of poverty, in need of handouts and as passive recipients of trickle-down growth. The poor are thus responsible for reducing their own poverty. Economic empowerment of the poor through economic stability and increased access to credit is seen as a panacea for encouraging participation in development activities by the poor. The MPRS stipulates the need to increase access to credit by the productive poor by organizing credit groups into Savings and Credit Cooperative Organizations (SACCOs) or Village Banks for purposes of mobilizing savings and providing credit to members. Nevertheless, the success of such initiatives will largely depend on the extent to which the design process meets the prerequisites for their proper functioning.

This study, therefore, examines the performance and impact of group lending with joint liability by assessing conditions under which such programs can mitigate moral hazard and induce intra-group insurance and lead to discernible positive impacts on beneficiaries.

1.2 Problem Statement

Although the national policy objective on microfinance is to develop a sustainable microfinance industry, microfinance institutions in Malawi continue to face difficulties in achieving both operational and financial self-sufficiency due to poor performance. The performance of a credit program can be evaluated in a number of ways. Zeller et al. (2001) point out that the assessment of performance of credit programs can be done with respect to two general areas as follows: First, by looking at the extent to which beneficiaries are able to take advantage of the services provided by the financial institutions and use them to enhance their own welfare. Second, looking at the extent to which beneficiaries comply with contractual obligations, such as repayment and risk sharing arrangements (in the case of joint liability groups). On the contractual side repayment rate is an important indicator of performance and it remains the most important determinant of the banks' lending costs. Zeller et al. (2001) note that, to institutions keen on achieving financial sustainability, default is bad and that the financial sustainability of an MFI rests on keeping the default rates below 5 percent.

As indicated in Figure 1.1, repayment rates for the Malawi Rural Finance Company which occupies more then 50 percent of the credit market share in Malawi, dropped from 95 percent in 1994 to 82 percent in 2002 (Lweya, 2006).

Figure 1.1 Repayment performance among MRFC loans (1994-2002)

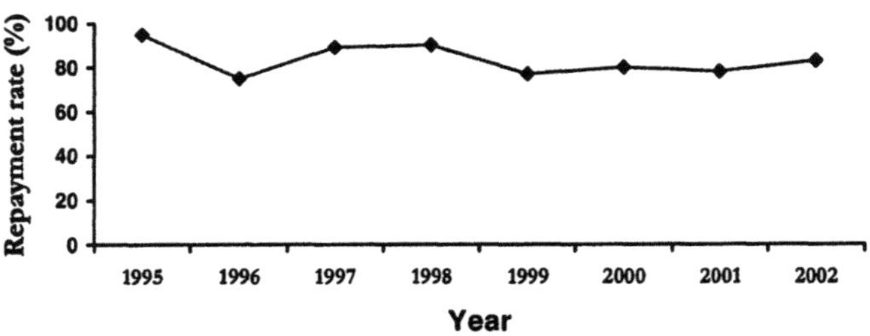

Source: Lweya KB (2006) PhD dissertation, University of Reading

There are a number of reasons for default to occur. Nevertheless, in Malawi a study by IFPRI on the design and sustainability issues in microfinance (Diagne *et al.*, 2000) revealed that more than 25 percent of loan defaults in credit groups from the Malawi Rural Finance Company (MRFC) were a result of the unwillingness to repay (moral hazard) and not the inability to repay. While a wide range of theoretical research on the link between joint liability lending, moral hazard and repayment performance has been documented, empirical research is uncommon, limited to Asian countries and sometimes gave mixed results. Above all, within the repayment literature, there is wide spread disagreement as to which part of the joint liability clause is more important in inducing repayment. De Aghion and Morduch (1998) and Diagne *et al.* (2000) contend that most studies have focused on the joint liability aspects of the Grameen Bank that emphasize on peer selection, peer monitoring and peer pressure and have ignored the other program features such as the direct monitoring by the lender, dynamic incentives and other social-cultural circumstances that can also affect repayment rates. Moral hazard models proposed by Stiglitz (1990) and Guinane and Ghatak (1999) have attempted to explain the role of interest rates and group dynamics in mitigating moral hazard in joint liability loans, respectively. However, only a limited number of empirical studies have been conducted so far to test the hypotheses of these theoretical models. Further, an important contribution to microfinance literature that this study seeks to make is that such theoretical propositions have ignored the importance of social structures within which JLL operates. The social and political structures can have a positive or negative effect on the success of joint liability lending.

Group lending with joint liability is built on the premise that when a member in a group fails to repay his or her loan, peers should repay the defaulted loan. As noted by Chowdhury (2005), this form of insurance provided by the group is one of the main reasons behind the success of joint liability lending schemes. Nevertheless, although microfinance practitioners have devoted great attention on 'mutual insurance' in group lending with joint liability lending, academic work on the same is rare. It is important to understand the way groups perform with regard to this form of risk sharing because, for the moment, MFIs are unwilling to absorb credit risks that lead to repayment failure which implies that borrowers will continue to be the main source of repayment insurance (Sadoulet, 2004). It is thus important to identify ways of enhancing the performance of such insurance initiatives among group members. Although JLL is built on the premise of mutual insurance, there are situations where it may not function as expected. In Malawi, a study by IFPRI revealed that although 89 percent of the borrowers from the Malawi Rural Finance Company's farm and non-farm loans understood that they were supposed to contribute to repay loans for defaulting members in the group, only 42 percent expressed full willingness to offer that mutual insurance (Diagne et al., 2000). The unwillingness of group members to repay the loans of defaulters in a joint liability arrangement defeats the very foundation upon which the joint liability clause is built. This study seeks to make a rare contribution to microfinance literature by investigating factors behind the unwillingness of group members to provide mutual insurance.

The third aspect of the problem relates to the fact that food security in Malawi is mainly defined in relation to the availability of maize, the main staple in the country. Although government policy on maize aims at increasing maize production through increased adoption of hybrid maize, its adoption remains low. It is estimated that only 30 percent of the total maize land is allocated to hybrid maize (Government of Malawi, 2004). Credit access has been advocated as a tool for enhancing hybrid maize adoption; however, its impact on maize adoption has not been fully investigated. Following such efforts, a number of impact studies have been conducted but their analysis was mainly qualitative. An exceptional study is one by Diagne and Zeller (2001) in which they observe that credit did not result into discernible welfare impacts.

The major shortfall in such studies is that they assessed impacts of access to credit without taking into consideration whether or not the household is credit constrained. Theoretically, credit access will only be effective for the credit "constrained" – thus, those with access to remunerative consumption, production and investment opportunities who are unable to pursue the opportunities for lack of financial resources because a lack of access to credit may not necessarily imply an unmet credit need (de Janvry *et al.*, 1997).

Besides, previous studies did not investigate the extent to which credit constraints lead to separabiliy of consumption and production decisions at household level. Households facing market failure make consumption and production decisions simultaneously and thus their production and consumption decisions are non-separable (Singh *et al.,* 1986). Considering separation in analyzing production decision models is important because the comparative statics for households facing a market failure are different from those without a market failure, such that models that do not take into account such differences will lead to inconsistent parameter estimates (Vakis et al., 2004). Knowledge of whether or not access to credit enables a household to make its production and consumption decisions separately is also crucial as it enables us to capture other potential constraining factors, such as complementally market failures that might make credit ineffective to beneficiary households. This is, therefore, a first attempt in Malawi to understand the affect of credit on households that differ on their credit constraint status.

1.3 Objectives

Building on economic theories of moral hazard, risk sharing and the Agricultural Household Model (AHM), the objective of this dissertation is to examine the performance and impact of group lending with joint liability. This focuses on assessing the extent to which borrowers are able to meet their contractual obligations as well as assessing the extent to which access to credit enables the beneficiaries to adopt hybrid maize cultivation. On the contractual side, the study aims at understanding the mechanism within which a borrowing group performs with regard to mitigating moral hazard, enhancing intra-group insurance and inducing repayment. An empirical investigation is conducted on credit groups from the Malawi Rural Finance Company in Malawi. The specific objectives are:

1. To examine the determinants of moral hazard in joint liability loans;
2. To assess the willingness of group members in credit groups to offer mutual insurance and examine determinants of the willingness to offer such insurance;
3. To analyze the impact of access to credit on the adoption of hybrid maize among households with different credit constraints status.

In accordance with the objectives, the study tests the following hypotheses:

1. The compliance to contractual obligations such as group loan repayment and Moral hazard is influenced by peer selection, peer monitoring, peer pressure, pre- existing social ties among group members and dynamic incentives. Thus, Moral hazard will be low in groups (1) formed through self selection, (2) have intensive peer monitoring (3) exercise sanctions and peer pressure (4) attach high value to access to loans from the same institution in future
2. Intra-group insurance will be high in groups (1) formed through self selection, (2) have intensive peer monitoring (3) exercise sanctions and peer pressure (4) attach high value to access to loans from the same institution in future and (5) with a low variation in the loan sizes between group members

3. While access to joint liability loans enhances the adoption of hybrid maize among credit-constrained households, it has a limited effect on unconstrained households.

1.4 Structure of the Dissertation

The thesis is structured into eight chapters. Chapter 2 describes Malawi's Microfinance sector, its environmental and socio-economic conditions. A review of literature on the performance and impact of group lending with joint liability is presented in Chapter 3. The chapter presents the historical perspective of microfinance, a review of theories and empirical studies. Through literature review the chapter identifies research gaps which this study is trying to fill. Chapter 4 describes the conceptual framework and the theoretical models used to address the three objectives of the study. The chapter adopts a conceptual framework proposed by Marr (2000) with some modification. In the same chapter, theoretical models of moral hazard and intra-group insurance are also presented. The two models address objectives of moral hazard and intra-group insurance, respectively. An Agricultural Household Model under credit market failure is presented to provide the theoretical basis for addressing the third objective on hybrid maize adoption.

Chapter 5 presents a discussion on determinants of moral hazard. The chapter empirically examines the significance of dynamic incentives, peer pressure, peer monitoring and social ties in mitigating moral hazard. In chapter 6, determinants of intra-group insurance are discussed. The chapter explores the extent to which peer monitoring risk pooling factors, the cost of insurance (captured by the variation in loan size), dynamic incentives and social ties induce members to help each other when they face repayment problems.

The analysis on the impact of credit on the adoption of hybrid maize is presented in chapter 7. The analysis in this chapter is based on an agricultural household model that links the adoption of hybrid maize with credit market failure. In addition, a test for separation in household production and consumption decisions is conducted using the on-farm labour demand model. Chapter 8 concludes the study by presenting a summary of main findings, addressing policy implications and providing suggestions for future research.

2 THE FINANCIAL SECTOR, MICROFINANCE IN MALAWI AND SURVEY DESIGN

2.1 Introduction

In this chapter, a brief review and characterization of the financial sector in Malawi is provided, and the microfinance sub-sector is discussed in detail. The environment for microfinance with respect to the country's macro economic performance, socioeconomic conditions, the legal and regulatory framework and the microfinance policy are described. The chapter concludes with a detailed description of activities of the Malawi Rural Finance Company, which is at the center of my empirical analysis. This information provides an understanding of the programs and the environment in which microfinance institutions operate before conducting a detailed econometric analysis on the performance and impact of group lending with joint liability.

2.2 Country Background Information

The Republic of Malawi is a land locked country lying south of the equator in South-eastern Africa. It is bordered by Tanzania to the north, Mozambique to the east and south, and Zambia to the west (see Figure 2.1). The country's territorial area is slightly over 118,000 square kilometers, of which 61 percent is arable land, 20 percent is taken up by the lakes and the remaining 19 percent is covered by mountains, forest reserves, human settlement and public infrastructure (Tchale, 2005). Lake Malawi, the third largest lake in Africa, covers 2.43 million hectares of Malawi's total area of 11.85 million hectares[2]. For administrative purposes the country is divided into three regions: the Northern, the Central and the Southern, which are further subdivided into 27 districts.

Figure 2.1: Map of Malawi showing the administrative regions and bordering countries

Source: Government of Malawi (2001) cited in Tchale (2005)

Malawi remains one of the poorest countries in the world with a GNP per capita of 145 US$ per year (National Statistics Office, 2004). The country has the highest rate of income inequality in Africa, with an estimated Gini-Coefficient of 0.62 compared to 0.48 recorded in the 1960s and early 1970s. The country's population is estimated to be 10.3 million, with an average annual growth rate of 2.1 percent which makes Malawi one of the most densely populated countries and with a fastest growing population in Southern Africa. The majority of the population (85%) lives in rural areas while its life expectancy at birth is 37 years. High HIV prevalence rates of 15 percent are partly to blame for the low life

[2] This draws from Swaminathan (2003) who cites the Encyclopedia Britannica, available online
at http://www.britannica.com/bcom/eb/article/0/0,5716,117899+1+109709,00.html and also the
National Statistical Office of Malawi database, available online at http://www.nso.malawi.net.

expectancy. The literacy rate is one of the lowest in the region estimated to be at 40 percent of the population (National Statistics Office, 2004)

2.3 The Financial Sector

The financial sector in Malawi is still small and very limited in its operations, with few levels of intermediation. The formal financial institutions are categorized into two, namely commercial banks and other financial institutions. Commercial banks are responsible for the provision of all types of savings services, lending and investment products. Other financial institutions are usually non-bank institutions with a limited scope of services. The financial sector in Malawi has eight commercial banks (providing savings, lending and other investment products), two leasing companies, one discount house, a building society, a finance company, four development institutions, one savings bank and several insurance companies and pension funds (United States Agency for International Development, 2004b). Burritt (2006) reports that, due to financial liberalization, private sector involvement in the financial sector, including the entry of new players, has increased. Two banks, National Bank of Malawi and Stanbic Bank, dominate the sector with 58 percent of the sector's assets, and 59 percent of its deposits. The first foreign shareholders entered the market in 1994 following banking sector reforms. Stanbic, formerly Commercial Bank of Malawi and formerly government controlled, is now 60 percent owned by Standard Bank of South Africa. Among the formal and regulated Financial Institutions, Opportunity International Bank (OIB) is the only commercial bank that specifically targets micro-saving and micro-credit clients.

In addition to the formal financial institutions, there are several semi-formal institutions that provide financial services to the communities. These include Non-governmental Organizations (NGOs), parastatals, and Savings and Credit Cooperatives (SACCOs). As a requirement, semi-formal financial institutions are mainly restricted to providing lending services and are not allowed to mobilize and intermediate savings. Almost all microfinance institutions belong to the semi-formal sector of financial institutions. The last category of financial services providers is an informal financial sector which caters mainly for the lower income clients. The sector comprises money lenders (Katapila), Rotating Savings and Credit Associations (ROSCAs) and networks of families and friends.

2.4 The Macro Economic Environment and the Agricultural Sector

Agriculture employs 85 percent of the labour force, accounts for about 36 percent of the Gross Domestic Product (GDP) and 90 percent of Malawi's export earnings (National Statistics Office, 2004). Tobacco accounts for more than 60 percent of the country's foreign exchange (United States Agency for International

Development, 2004b). The agricultural sector is subdivided into estates and small holder farmers. The latter accounts for 78 percent of the cultivated land and generates about 75 percent of Malawi's total agricultural output. From the foregoing discussion it can be seen that Malawi's agriculture is largely smallholder agriculture. More than 72 percent of the smallholder farms are less than 1 hectare, a size too small to achieve food self sufficiency at the household level with the current rudimentary farming methods. Crop production provides on average 73 percent of rural household income while 70 percent of all full time farmers are women who carry out 63 percent to 71 percent of all agricultural work (Diagne and Zeller, 2001).

Malawi has been instituting policy reforms with the goal of creating an enabling environment for a market oriented economy. Key policies on agriculture have focused on market liberalization, privatization and reversal of earlier policies that emphasized large scale agriculture and industrial development which resulted into large income disparities among the population. The current policies emphasize on small holder farmer improvement. Farmers are encouraged to change from subsistence forms of agriculture to a commercial form of agriculture. Efforts to improve small holder farmer productivity have focused on the liberalization of agricultural markets, including the removal of price controls and restrictions on cash crop production, such as tobacco and initiatives to improve farmer access to input markets. Emphasizing the significance of microfinance in the development of the agriculture sector, government is making efforts to increase farmer's access to credit with more emphasis on reaching the productive poor.

The economy has faced stagnation in the past five years with an average GDP growth of 1.3 percent per year. The World Bank recommended that a GDP growth of not less than 6 percent is needed for meaningful poverty reduction, particularly if growth must come from the sectors that poor Malawians are engaged in such as agriculture and manufacturing. The trend in GDP growth and inflation from 1998 to 2003 is presented in Figure 2.2.

Figure 2.2 shows that real GDP growth was highest in 1999, and lowest in 2001. The real GDP growth in 2001 and 2000 was partly affected by drought and declining world prices for tobacco. At the same time, due to political instability, the donors had not yet resumed their budgetary assistance to Malawi which led to increased domestic borrowing. Consequently, this led to an increase in the interest rates on domestic credit as government competed with the private sector for capital, driving up the demand (United States Agency for International Development, 2004a). With regard to the inflation rate, the country experienced a decline in inflation from 44.9 percent in 1999 to 9.2 percent in September 2003. This decline was as a result of tight monetary policies, combined with the distribution of free inputs and free maize by the government of Malawi. However, as noted by Burritt (2006), the inflation rose to 11.5 percent in 2004 due to high government spending before the May 2004 elections, and the depreciation of the Kwacha (Economist Intelligence Unit, 2004). The inflation rate further crept to 14 percent in 2005 due to food shortages in the country. Such instabilities in the inflation rates can be a major threat to the development of a sustainable microfinance industry in the country.

Figure 2.2 Malawi GDP growth and inflation rates

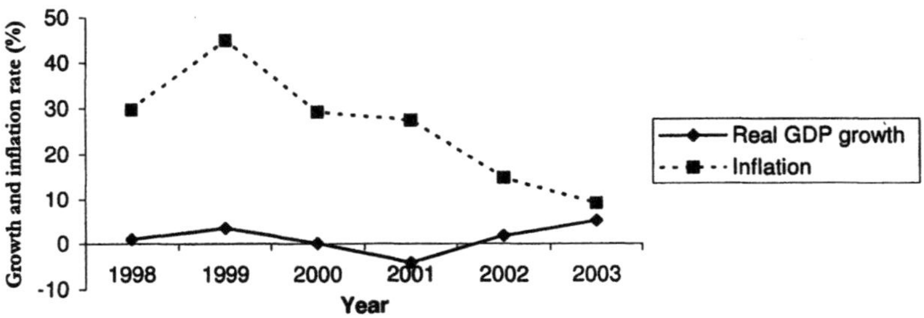

Source: United States Agency for International Development (2004a)

The domestic demand for credit in Malawi is generally high which leads to high returns on treasury bills compared to lending to the entrepreneurs. In 2003, for example, Burritt notes that MFIs found it profitable and less risky to purchase treasury bills than to lend to businesses due to the widening gap between interest charged on treasury bills and the reserve bank lending rates. There was a general decline in the profitability of enterprises resulting from increased interest rates.

A decline in the Malawi Kwacha exchange rate against the currency of major trading partners such as the Republic of South Africa has an impact on the micro, and small enterprises. Entrepreneurs that depend on imported goods will require larger loan sizes in order to purchase the same quantity of goods. However, it is difficult for MFIs to quickly adjust the supply of loans upwards for their clients when devaluation occurs. In addition, MFIs with small loan funds may be unable to increase maximum loan sizes if they do not set appropriate interest rates and control defaults so as to maintain their real value of the portfolio. Figure 2.3 shows the change in exchange rates against two trading partners (the Republic of South Africa and the United Kingdom) between 2002 and 2003.

Figure 2.3 Malawi Kwacha exchange rates (2002-2003)

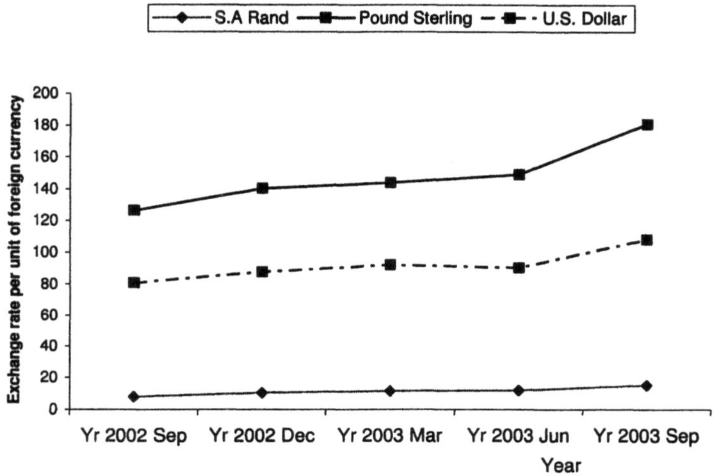

Source:USAID, (2004b)

As indicated in Figure 2.3, the value of the Kwacha against major trading partners declined by 50 percent against the South African Rand, by 30 percent against the Pound Sterling and by 36 percent against the US Dollar over the 2002-2003 period. Devaluations of this magnitude pose serious threats to the sustainability of microfinance in Malawi.

2.5 The Microfinance Policy

With effect from November 2002, the government approved the microfinance policy for Malawi and an Action Plan. Fairly generic in content the policy lays out the roles of various microfinance stakeholders and defines activities that need to be undertaken. The general goal of the policy is to promote the development of a sustainable microfinance industry which provides credit, savings opportunities and other financial services to the productive poor including women and persons with disabilities (Government of Malawi, 2002). In order to achieve the above stated goal, the policy aims to achieve four specific objectives as follows:

1. To create an enabling legal and regulatory environment as well as overall economic policies conducive to the development of microfinance. While recognizing that overall, the existing legal environment is not hostile to the development of microfinance in Malawi, Government, in collaboration with MFIs and other

stakeholders, wishes to further improve the legal environment through a review, revision, amendment and repeal of laws and regulations that are an impediment to the development of microfinance. In addition, the policy takes into account the variation in the kinds of institutions providing microfinance services, recognizes the need for a tailor made regulatory frame-work for specific kinds of MFIs. For example, microfinance institutions that mobilize savings require mandatory regulation through the Central bank.

2. To improve the capacity of implementing institutions and their clients and other key actors such as the Malawi Microfinance Network (MAMN), the Reserve Bank of Malawi and the Ministries of Commerce and Industry and Finance and Economic Planning. The lack of capacity has been identified as one of the constraints to the development of the microfinance industry in Malawi. The government recognizes the need to support the critical mass of Microfinance Institutions that provide financial services to the very poor on a sustainable basis. The policy objective with respect to capacity building aims at improving institutional viability of MFIs with a business orientation and enhancing human resources bases for the MFIs through sustainable training programs. The policy aims at using existing training facilities in formal financial institutions and centers of higher learning such as the University of Malawi to address the needs of local MFIs.

3. To promote the best practices in industry among MFIs, Government and the donor community. Best practices are those norms and operating modes derived from international experience by MFIs which have been able to achieve significant outreach to the poor while covering operating costs and moving towards full financial sustainability (Government of Malawi, 2002). Microfinance Institutions are encouraged to adopt cost recovery interest rates; introduce effective incentives to repay loans, and expand their outreach in order to reduce costs of their operations.
4. To increase the coordination among the various actors in the microfinance sector. The policy objective aims at developing the microfinance sector through an active involvement of stake holders such as the Ministry of finance and Economic planning, the Reserve Bank of Malawi and the Ministry of Agriculture and Irrigation.

2.6 The Legal and Regulatory Environment for Microfinance Institutions

Burritt (2006) defines frameworks as laws that govern organizations operating in the financial sector and permit them to provide financial services. In general, microfinance services can be provided by a wide range of institutional models under different legal frameworks. Examples of such frameworks include the Banking law, the Company law, the Cooperative law, and the NGO law. Other than the primary legislation which is made of laws and Acts passed in Parliament, a number of statutory guidelines and regulations guide the operations of MFIs in Malawi. As noted by Burritt (2006), regulations to which microfinance institutions adhere are prudential and non-prudential. A prudential regulation is designed to ensure the financial soundness of licensed institutions that collect public savings deposits, and to preserve the integrity of the financial system. Generally, only institutions that collect the public's savings are subject to prudential regulation. Non-prudential regulations include non-prudential reporting requirements, for example, the disclosure of interest rates or periodic performance reporting (Burritt, 2006). The Reserve Bank of Malawi oversees the implementation and supervision of banking regulations, while the Ministry of Industry and Commerce is responsible for administering commercial laws and cooperative law. Not-for-profits are governed by the Ministry of Women, Gender, and Youth.

As noted by Gallardo (2000) and Burrit (2006), currently Malawi does not have an operational Microfinance Regulatory Framework, however, MFIs and other stake holders are themselves pushing for an establishment of a regulatory framework which explicitly defines their role with the expectation that it will provide them more legitimacy. Institutions that provide microfinance services in Malawi operate under multiple legal forms. The following describes the primary legal frameworks under which microfinance suppliers currently operate:

NGO: Microfinance Institutions may operate as NGOs which may be engaged in multi-sector development activities with micro credit being one of the many activities implemented by the institution. Micro credit operations established under this act are usually started as donor or government projects, and fall under the supervision of the Ministry of Women, Gender and Youth.

Private company and Public company: A microfinance institution may operate as private company in which one or more persons form a private company limited by guarantee. Companies are limited by "guarantee" or "shares" and operate under the Companies Act. In companies limited by guarantee, where there are no shareholder owners, members' liability is limited by a nominal amount. PRIDE Malawi and FINCA Malawi are examples of Companies Ltd. by Guarantee while shareholding companies include the Opportunity International Bank of Malawi (OIBM), owned by the US-based NGO, Opportunity International, and government owned institutions including

MRFC and the Malawi Savings Bank. The National Bank of Malawi also operates in a limited way in the microfinance sector. To be a public company it requires that two or more persons form a company whose liability is limited by shares owned by the members. Institutions licensed under the Banking Act must be shareholding companies. The Ministry of Industry and Commerce has oversight responsibility for Companies. The Reserve Bank of Malawi provides regulatory and supervisory oversight over companies that have bank licenses.

Cooperatives: This requires that associations of ten members or more aged 18 years and above come together to form a common bond for mutual assistance. Such associations can be registered under the cooperative societies act (1946). The lending and deposit services of a cooperative society are to only its members. The Malawi Union of Savings and Credit Cooperatives (MUSCO) and SACCOs are examples of microfinance institutions registered under this act.

Parastatals: This is seen as a hybrid between a government agency and an NGO where the institution is wholly government- owned but structured under the Trustees Incorporation Act primarily to facilitate access to donor funds. With regard to the establishment and registration, parastatal institutions interested in providing financial services can be registered under the Trustees Act (1962), Companies Act (1986) or the Cooperate Society Act (1946).

2.7 Challenges and Obstacles to the Development of Sustainable Microfinance[3]

So far there are no significant policy barriers to entry of MFIs in Malawi. Nevertheless, Government remains a dominant player in the ownership structures and Boards of major financial institutions, including MRFC and Malawi Savings Bank (MSB). The strong role of government in lending operations has tended to reduce the overall efficiency and performance of institutions, has in some cases politicized lending decisions, and compromises overall sector performance. The government, however, has stated its intention to privatize and/or restructure parastatals. Indeed the analysis by Gallardo (2001) shows that there are no serious restrictions on the kinds of institutions that can offer credit services. However, as observed by Gallardo (1998), entry into the microfinance sector is not completely without hurdles. The most important initial hurdle relates to the overcoming of structural controls such as, the minimum capitalization requirements for entry, as well as geographical restrictions and limits on the range of activities and services of different types of financial institutions. Details regarding the significance of these problems are discussed below.

[3] This mainly draws from Gallardo (2000): Critical issues in developing sustainable microfinance in Malawi

Minimum capitalization: As noted by Burritt (2006), the regime for financial de-regulation in Malawi has brought about the removal of restrictions on the interest rates, capital movements and exchange controls. However, there has not been a relaxation of minimum capitalization levels for regulated and licensed financial institutions that could permit entry of MFIs into the formal financial sector, even though the present banking act gives RBM the discretion to grant exemptions from minimum amounts specified for capitalization of banks and non-bank financial institutions. Currently, the RBM uses as its internal guidelines on minimum required capitalization the amounts of US$1,500,000 in Kwacha equivalent for banks and US$750,000 in Kwacha equivalent for financial institutions (this requirement is not there for MFIs as the banking act largely focuses on commercial banks; possibly, US250, 000 for microfinance institutions). Indeed the most restrictive barrier to entry into the financial sector for MFIs is this minimum capitalization requirement. Following this observation Gallardo (2000) suggests that while there are no standard rules of thumb for the level of capitalization of MFIs that may be granted specialization status, albeit limited, the experience and practice of other countries could provide insights as to what may be feasible for the RBM to consider for Malawi's MFIs.

Restrictions on product design: There are stringent restrictions on product design. For example, only the full-service registered commercial banks are permitted to mobilize demand deposits as well as times and savings deposits from the general public, without restrictions as to the amount. Finance houses and merchant banks are not permitted to offer demand deposit services; the time (fixed) deposit products which they are currently allowed to offer must be MK10,000 or larger, and are of the 'wholesale' variety. More over, a finance house or a merchant bank is not permitted to mobilize the time (fixed) deposits directly from the public and, instead, must arrange with a commercial bank to underwrite its issue of time deposits. Indeed such restrictions may limit the growth and outreach of MFIs.

Exposure to risks: One of the challenges facing microfinance institutions in Malawi is the exposure to systemic risk (such as droughts and floods), lower density of population, higher transaction costs, weak physical infrastructure, and greater seasonality of activities. As noted by Burritt (2006), expanding the formal financial frontier to effectively serve the rural clientele who are the major beneficiaries requires significant innovation in product and financial technology development. Innovations are required that enable producers to deal with significant price and production risk, and financial service providers to deal with risks associated with clients willingness or capacity to repay. In Malawi, rural areas are characterized by the highest incidence and depth of poverty in the country, and therefore limited capacity to bear risk, for example taking on debt. Subsequently, demand for micro insurance, money transfer services and savings services, and loans for consumption smoothing may be more important than the demand for loans for production.

2.8 Demand for Microfinance Services in Malawi

Microfinance services are demanded by both households and the formal and informal sector enterprises. Households seek loans, savings, insurance, payment services and pension services. Despite the potential role of Microfinance services in mitigating risks and enhancing profitable investments at household level, access to sources of finance is limited in Malawi. According to the national GEMINI Micro and Small Enterprise baseline study (2000), about 19.8 percent of rural households and 10.5 percent of urban households reported acquiring a loan of some sort from either the informal or the formal sector. Given that more than 85 percent of the population and 80 percent of the MSE are in rural areas that are highly dependent on agricultural production, the agricultural sector represents the bulk of demand for microfinance services. This makes the demand for loans to be highly seasonal as demand is high between October and January when households seek inputs for their crop production.

The Malawi national GEMINI MSE Baseline Survey of 2000 that sampled over 22,000 rural and urban households and small businesses found that 747,000 micro and small enterprises exist in Malawi which employ 1.7 million people or 38 percent of the total labour force. Of the 747,000 MSEs, the survey estimated that 680,000 were micro-enterprises (ME). Applying a discounting factor of 50 percent, as a way of taking into account the fact that not all MSEs qualify for or wish to have a loan at any given time, United States International Agency for Development (2004) estimated demand for micro credit in Malawi at 340,000 potential clients. The survey also found out that only 6 percent of the MSEs surveyed received credit sometime during the five years prior to the survey. The GEMINI study actually underestimated the total number of MSEs since it did not account for enterprises where they could not sell 50 percent of the goods. This unaccounted segment would include smallholder households and other economically active enterprises that produce for consumption purposes and those whose annual sales did not achieve the 50 percent sales threshold. As regards the geographical distribution, just like the population of Malawi, the GEMIN survey (2000) reported that 83 percent of all MSEs are based in rural areas. The survey further found that the remaining 17 percent was concentrated in four urban centers of, Lilongwe, Blantyre, Mzuzu and Zomba. More recently Burritt (2006), using the standard of living approach estimated that at least 622,000 households are in need of microfinance services. Using the private sector approach, Burritt reports that at least 756 000 households are in need of credit services in Malawi. Although estimates by Burritt are not based on an in-depth market research (thus they are merely scenarios that give some indication of the size of the market), the results still provide an image of what the demand structure is like. Studies on demand for microfinance services have shown that the current supply of microfinance services falls short of the estimated demand. Households, particularly those in rural areas, demand a wider array of service offerings than is currently supplied by the market. These include savings services, insurance services, payment services and leasing opportunities.

2.9 Supply of Microfinance Services

Basic financial services to micro enterprises and low income households in Malawi are provided by a variety and range of private and publicly supported MFIs that include NGOs, Companies Limited by Guarantee, Savings and Credit Cooperatives and Commercial Banks including one bank specialized in microfinance. Burritt (2006) observes that the establishment of several forms of institutions promotes competition and enables service delivery to a wide range of market segments. Despite the multiplicity of these institutional forms, government-owned banks and donor funded, government backed programs dominate the microfinance market in Malawi providing an estimated 70 percent of cash credit and 80 percent of savings services (USAID 2004a). Since more than 85 percent of the working population lives in rural areas and derive their livelihood from agriculture, it is not surprising to note that Malawi's Microfinance sector is dominated by in-kind agricultural credit in form of fertilizer and seed. Table 2.1 indicates the leading microfinance institutions, their legal status and their market share. There are four publicly supported microfinance institutions that currently operate in Malawi.

Other than the Government controlled microfinance institutions, there are a number of private microfinance institutions offering services to the low income households. The key notable ones are, Opportunity International Bank of Malawi (OIBM), Malawi Union of Savings and Credit Cooperatives (MUSCCO), Pride Malawi and the Foundation for International Community Assistance (FINCA).

Apart from the government supported and privately owned institutions, there are a number of NGOs that are getting involved in the provision of microfinance services as part of their broader development programs targeting the poor and marginalized segments of Malawi's population. The more prominent ones include: Concern Universal Microfinance Operations (CUMO), The National Association of Business Women (NABW) and The Ecumenical Church Loan Fund (ECLOF).

There are also numerous other small credit programs run by various national and international NGOs, which are often implemented in collaboration with a Malawi government institution (Chirwa *et al.*, 1996). However, of all these credit programs, only MRFC and MUSCCO can claim to have national coverage. All the other programs operate in a few districts and, in conjunction with other noncredit developmental programs (Chirwa, 2002). Although the issue of credit supply in rural areas is well addressed, there is a market absence of institutions that can collect savings and on-lend savings to borrowers in rural areas. The Malawi Rural Finance Company which has permission from the Reserve Bank of Malawi to collect savings deposits is not permitted to lend them. More than 70 percent of the savings collected by MRFC are compulsory deposits which serve as mandatory cash collaterals for loans, rather than savings products that microfinance clients can withdraw at will to manage cyclic cash flows (Burritt, 2006). The absence of institutions that can efficiently intermediate savings in rural areas is a big gap in Malawi's microfinance market.

Table 2.1 Microfinance providers in Malawi

		Savers		Loans		Market share
MFI	Legal status	Number of clients	Amount of savings	Number of clients	Amount of loan	
MSB	GoM Company /Bank	200,000	500,000, 000	0	0	0
MRFC	GoM Company	77,461	30335565900	77,461	1,129,609	51
DEMAT	GoM Trust			4,300	5,555,099	0.21
SEDOM	GoM Trust			-	-	
ADMARC	GoM Company			-	46,350,330	1.79
OIBM	Bank	20,000	313,195,581	3,152	143793,309	7
MUSCCO	Cooperative	51,000	535,547,462	51,000	469,986,231	21
PRIDE	Company	9,698	44,797,515	9,698	168,903,305	8
FINCA	Company	17971	101,436,240	17,971	248,878,009	11
CUMO	NGO	6000	1651218	6,000	30,000,000	1
NABW	NGO	0	0	2,202	1,359,643	0.05
ECLOF	NGO	2,394	3,964,550	2,394	18,963,039	1
Others (APIP)	Misc.			-	345,314,470	13.32

Source: United States Agency for International Development (2004b) Deepening Malawi's Microfinance Sector Project (DMS)

2.10 Evolution of Group Lending with Joint Liability in Malawi

Chirwa (2002) notes that credit outside the formal and informal financial system in Malawi predates the colonial era. In 1958, the Nyasaland African Loans Board was established to offer cash or in-kind credit (seeds and fertilizer) to Malawian farmers. In 1964, the Central Loans Board with a secretariat in Ministry of Finance superseded the Nayasaland African Loans Board. The launching of four Agricultural Development Projects in 1968 and the National Rural Development Programme in 1978 provided a conduit for extending credit to the rural communities through the provision of agricultural input loans. Within the framework of Agricultural Development Projects, the Small holder Agricultural Credit Administration (SACA) was established to facilitate the provision of credit to the rural communities. Indeed through SACA Malawi is known as one of the countries with a long experience in group lending technology, dating back to 1973, three years before the Grameen Bank was established. Before its collapse in 1992, SACA was one of the most successful examples of government-supported credit program with high repayment rates averaging more than 97 percent. The repayment rates in 1991/92 and 1992/93 seasons were down to 22 percent and 15.5 percent, respectively. While the drought in 1991/92 season had contributed to the difficulties in repayment, the political changes that were taking place during the transition period to multi party democracy are partly to blame for the collapse of SACA.

Nevertheless, although the previous credit programs in Malawi exhibited features in today's joint liability lending, Buckley (1996) notes that the program mainly targeted farmers that were well-off, typically with land holdings capable of producing a surplus above subsistence needs(>1 hectare). Chirwa (2002) notes that the realization of the neglect of the 'core poor' motivated the establishment of the Malawi Mudzi Fund (MMF) in 1989 as a pilot project in Machinga and Mangochi district. The MMF was a replica of the Grameen Bank of Bangladesh and it became operational in 1990. Financial services were offered to groups of 5 women with five groups forming a Mudzi Center. The operations of the MMF continued until 1994, when its activities were incorporated into the Malawi Rural Finance Company (MRFC) as a Mudzi Rural Fiancial Services Project (MRFSP). MRFC was created by the government of Malawi with funding from the World Bank to take over operations of SACA in 1994. MRFC adheres to commercial lending practices and charges commercial interest rates of between 40 and 50 percent. By 2004 MRFC had a clientele base of more than 8,000 credit groups. Although by 2005 there were several other private and non-governmental organizations offering microfinance services to rural Malawians, only MRFC can claim to have a nation wide coverage, while the rest operate in specific locations.

2.11 The Malawi Rural Finance Company

MRFC is owned by Government, registered under the Companies Act 1984 as a private limited liability company. The Malawi Rural Finance Company succeeded the failed Smallholder Agricultural Credit Administration (SACA) in 1993 with financial and Technical Assistance from the World Bank which provided a US$25 million credit line under the Rural Financial Services Project. The International Fund for Agriculture (IFAD) also provided a US$12 million credit line under the Mudzi Financial Services Project. MRFC began operations in October 1994 retaining much of the SACA's infrastructure that consisted of rural extension service offices of the Ministry of Agriculture and Irrigation (MoAI). Headquartered in Lilongwe, MRFC operates in all regions and districts of the country through 8 branches, 27 supervisory satellite offices and 163 local MoAI field offices (see Figure 2.4). Not including the in-kind loans disbursed through government led programs United States Agency for International Development (2004a) reports that MRFC provides 60 percent of microfinance loans in Malawi. While the majority of its portfolio is seasonal loans to agricultural producers, the number of business loans and corresponding portfolio has risen steadily in recent years in MRFC's attempt to diversify its portfolio (Burritt, 2006).

Figure 2.4 Malawi Rural Finance Company Network

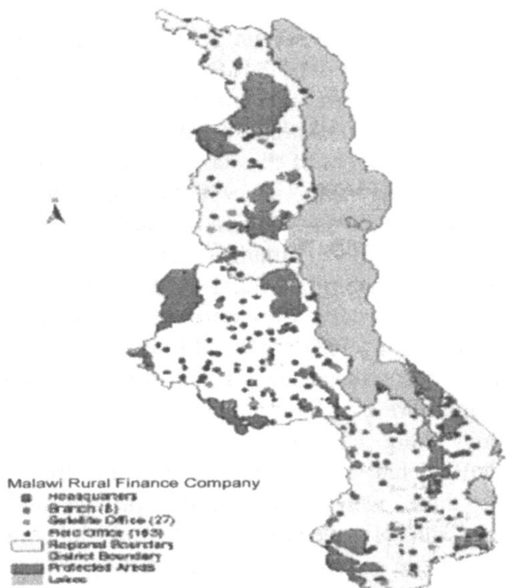

Source: United States Agency for International Development (2004b)

2.11.1 MRFC financial products

The company's principal activity is to provide financial services in the rural areas. These services include deposit taking and lending activities. MRFC provides seasonal agricultural loans, medium-term agricultural loans, small business loans and personal loans to employees of various organizations. MRFC is also permitted to mobilize savings but it is not allowed to intermediate savings under its current legal status. More than seventy percent of the loans provided by MRFC are agricultural loans. With regard to the lending strategies, MRFC employs a variety of methods ranging from group lending, to individual lending. Apart from the conventional MRFC credit program, MRFC also occasionally participates in both the Agricultural Productivity Investment Program (APIP) and the Mudzi Credit Project. MRFC requires cash collateral and land on all loans except the Mudzi Small Business Loans Scheme. Smallholder farmers taking seasonal loans are required to make initial compulsory deposited of an equivalent amount of 15 percent of the loan's value. Commercial loans require 20 percent cash deposit plus an additional collateral equal to 130 percent of the amount borrowed.

With regard to their interest policy, MRFC charges competitive market determined interest rates on its loans. A three-tier variable interest rate structure is offered. Prime customers pay the lowest rate; repeat customers pay a rate that is 2 percent higher than prime customers while first time customers pay 3 percent above the prime customer rate. In view of the lack of bankable collateral by most of prospective customers, MRFC organizes resource poor customers in solidarity groups in an attempt to create a "social collateral" so that loans can be given even to those who do not have any collateral to offer.

2.11.2 Outreach and savings

The agricultural loans in MRFC account for about 80 percent of the total loans disbursed annually. Although MRFC is legally able to mobilize public deposits, it has thus far not been very successful at it. As indicated in Table 2.2, although the number of deposits increased, the average deposits per account in five years did not significantly change in nominal terms.

Table 2.2 MRFC Savings Mobilization 1998-2002

Amount in MK	Fiscal Year Ended 30th September 2002				
	1998	1999	2000	2001	2002
Customer deposits	71,928	102,920	135,055	186,787	189,486
N. deposit accounts	51,843	70,292	103,697	130,588	135,588
Avg. Deposit per account	1,387	1,464	1,302	1,430	1,398

Source: Restructuring and privatization of MSB and MRFC: Draft Final Situation Assessment cited in United States Agency for International Development (2004b)

Looking at the composition of MRFC client deposits, nearly 70 percent of savings was mandatory collection of cash collateral. Voluntary savings and contract savings accounted for 21 percent and 10 percent, respectively Privatization Working Committee (PWC), 2003). Among the several reasons given for the low MRFC's savings mobilization is that the cash collateral mobilized by MRFC is deposited in a group account for solidarity loans and there is little incentive on the part of individuals to save in excess of what is required. Excess savings would be used as intra-group insurance to repay the loan of a co-member who defaults. Another reason given is that since MRFC focuses on seasonal loans with long grace periods its savings products are neither well designed nor aggressively marketed by loan officers who lose contact with the client during off-season period.

2.12 Survey Design

The data set used in this study is from Malawi, collected by IFPRI on a study titled 'Design and Sustainability Issues of Rural Credit and Savings Programs for the Poor in Malawi", conducted in 1999 through to 2000. The data set is available from the International Food Policy Research Institute (IFPRI), based in Washington D.C. The data set is from a group and household rural finance survey of 99 credit groups all of which are beneficiaries of the Malawi Rural Finance Company. The survey was conducted by IFPRI in collaboration with the Rural Development Department of Bunda College of Agriculture, University of Malawi.

The primary purpose of the survey was to provide information which would help policy makers and rural banking financial institutions that meet the needs of poor rural households. Besides the "joint liability" issue, other program-design and sustainability issues identified by the 1995 IFPRI/Bunda study on " the determinants of access to and participation in existing formal and informal credit and saving programs" were investigated (Diagne et al., 2000). The MRFC credit groups selected for the survey come from 4 of the 27 satellites offices of MRFC. The four satellite offices are located in 4 different districts of Malawi (see Figure 2.5 for the location of the study sites). The groups were selected using a stratified random sampling guided by a sampling frame obtained from MRFC's Management information System. The four sites cover the three regions of Malawi (Central, South and North). Because of logistical constraints, the sample frame of the groups in each satellite office was restricted to 2 field offices only 4. The survey covered microfinance groups from three different joint liability programs operated by MRFC: MRFC seasonal agricultural loans, Mudzi seasonal agricultural loans and Mudzi non-farm business loans.

[4] The average number of field offices per satellite office is 5.

There are significant differences in the design, orientation and target population of the programs. There are also significant differences in the design and operation between the groups in the seasonal agricultural programs depending on the type of crop for which the loans are intended (tobacco, maize, cotton and rice). Using the 1997 repayment status, groups were classified into 3 categories: fully–paid groups, partially-paid groups and nothing paid groups. A stratified random sampling procedure was then used to randomly select the sample groups from the three selected strata. A group was classified as 'fully paid' if the 1996/97 was fully paid before due date. It was classified as a 'partially paid' group if only part of the 1996/97 group loan had been paid by the due date. And a group was classified as 'nothing paid' if no member had paid anything by the due date of the survey.

Figure 2.5 Map of Malawi showing locations of the RDD/IFPRI survey districts

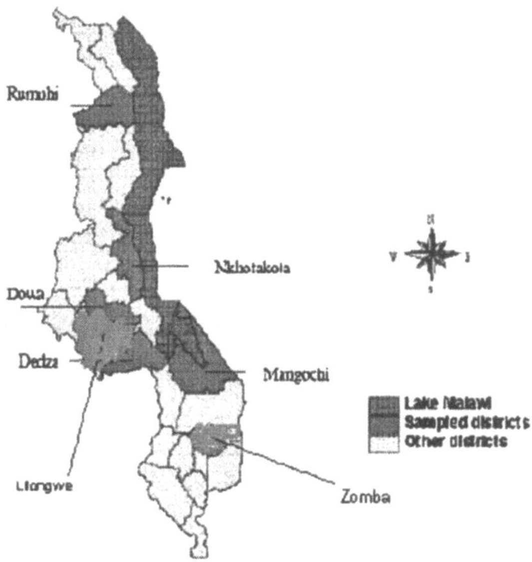

Source: Diagne and Zeller (2001)- Impacts of access to credit in Malawi.

The field work consisted of three rounds. The first two rounds took place in June and November 1998, respectively, while the third round was carried out in August 1999. The data used for my analysis comes from the second round of the survey. For the second round data a group leader and three randomly selected members were interviewed for each group. One non-participant and one past participant randomly selected but living in the same village were also interviewed for the two rounds combined. A detailed structured questionnaire covering the formation, composition and repayment history of the group since its creation was administered to each respondent. The questionnaire specifically included questions aimed at quantifying the degree of information asymmetry within each group and the extent to which peer selection, peer monitoring and peer pressure had been taking place. Also collected using the questionnaire was the extent to which the joint-liability has been enforced in each loan cycle. The quantified information gathered from the structured questionnaire was complemented by qualitative information from transcripts of anecdotal stories reported by the respondents and from focus-group discussions involving 36 additional credit groups surveyed during the third round.

The analysis on the impact of access to credit on the adoption of hybrid maize draws from a survey of households conducted by the International Food Policy Research Institute (IFPRI), and the Department of Rural Development at Bunda College of Agriculture in 1996 (for details see Diagne and Zeller, 2001). The survey was conducted in three rounds, however this study used data from the first round of the survey. The objective of the IFPRI study was to investigate the effects of access to credit on household welfare. The survey covered 404 households selected via stratified random sampling method, from the three regions and from 5 districts of Rumphi, Nkhotakota, Dowa and Dedza and Mangochi. The survey questionnaire consists of seven modules. Only 3 modules were of relevance to this study, namely, household demographics, crop and livestock production and credit and savings. This data is also available on request from the International Food Policy Research Institute (IFPRI).

3 LITERATURE REVIEW ON THE PERFORMANCE AND IMPACT OF MICROFINANCE

3.1 Introduction

The chapter presents a review of theories and empirical studies related to the performance and impact of joint liability lending schemes. The chapter is geared towards the identification of existing research gaps, which this study will be trying to fill. The review is focused on the three specific objectives of the study. In the second section I present a historical review of microfinance innovations, and present examples of successful microfinance institutions and their characteristics. In section three I present a discussion on the economics of lending with joint liability.

In sections four and five I review empirical studies that focus on determinants of moral hazard and mutual insurance in group based credit, respectively. Section six reviews studies that focus on household level impacts of microfinance. The review under this section is confined to studies that investigate the differential impact of access to formal credit on technology adoption and poverty. The final section highlights problems with joint liability lending and highlights specific areas of research to which this study makes a significant contribution.

3.2 Microfinance Evolution a Global Perspective and Examples of Successful Microfinance Institutions

In the past four decades, microfinance has evolved significantly resulting from the creativity of microfinance practitioners. As noted by Kritikos and Vigenina (2005), the proponents of the microfinance paradigm have shown that the problems of risk and cost could be addressed by introducing new micro-lending technologies that involve peer groups that are seen as a substitute for the conventional collateral and which also reduce the cost of screening monitoring and enforcing loan contracts. In most countries where such technologies have been implemented, the results have been good; although in certain instances mixed results have been observed. Group lending or solidarity approach to credit delivery is an example of such innovations. The technology is based on the assumption that the poor represent a much lower credit risk than the formal financial sector generally assumes and that under specific circumstances, they can be trusted to repay small uncollateralized loans using a lending technology that relies on traditional and personal interactions among borrowers (van Bastelaer, 2000).

Although group lending is considered a recent innovation, and that its recent popularity, certainly, is connected with the success of the Grameen Bank, Prescott (1997) points out that group lending existed long before the establishment of the Grameen Bank. Prescott points to existence of the Irish Loan Funds in the early 1700s through the early 1800s which used a form of group lending. The Funds were usually located in rural areas, took deposits and made small uncollateralized loans to finance a small investment project such as an animal project. The loans resembled the present-day group loans in that all borrowers were required to obtain two consigners for each loan and both consigners were liable for repayment. Prescott notes that while each fund was independent, the funds were regulated by a Central loan fund Board.

Woolcock (1998) and Guinnane (1993) describe the conditions that led to the first deliberate attempt to establish financial institutions with the poor in developing economies on the basis of their social, rather than material, resources. They refer to the People Banks, also known as the credit cooperatives that Friedrich Raiffeissen created in mid-nineteenth century in Germany. These cooperatives provided credit based on the policy of unlimited liability to people in rural areas where people new each other well. The Germany credit cooperatives are considered as forerunners of lending schemes that rely on joint liability. The cooperatives financed loans through local deposits. Potential borrowers applied for loans specifying the use for which the loan was intended and could receive the loan only upon identifying a co-signer to act as security. The loans could be acquired for several uses including, fertilizer, machinery, livestock for agriculturalists, raw materials for artisans and stock for shopkeepers, while consumption loans were avoided by policy (Ghatak and Guinnane, 1999). The popularity of the Germany cooperatives is mainly attributed to their ability to obtain high repayments from people that had no collateral acceptable to the commercial lenders.

The Grameen Bank is the most popular Institution in as far as modern group lending technology is concerned. The bank was founded by Muhammad Yunus, an Economics professor at the University of Chittagong, in Bangladesh in 1976 as a research project. By 1994, the Bank had served half of all villages in Bangladesh, with a total membership of more than two million, of which 95 percent were women (van Bastelaer, 2000). The bank currently lends to more than two million people in about 36,000 villages in Bangladesh, most of whom are the landless women. The borrowers organize themselves into self selected groups of five people usually from the same village. Before the actual receipt of loans, group members go through a series of trainings offered by loan officers from the Grameen Bank. The bank exercises sequential group lending in which only two or three of the group members get a loan at time. The remaining group members only receive the loans upon successful repayments of the other members that got the loan. These groups are combined into larger entities called Centers. The Centers are responsible for the management of two important funds, namely the compulsory savings deposits coming from the 5 percent fee charged on initial loans, and the emergency fund coming from compulsory surcharges on borrower interest. The emergency fund is used to provide insurance coverage for events such as natural disasters or a borrower's death or default (Ghatak and Guinane, 1999). In general, both the credit cooperatives and the Grameen Bank exhibit forms of joint liability in that all embers are liable for other member's default

Burritt (2006) reports of Accion Communitaria del Peru (ACP) as another example of successful microfinance institutions. ACCION began operations as a non-profit NGO focusing on community development. In the early 1980s, ACP focused its activities on the provisioning of credit to micro entrepreneurs but later transformed into a specialized microfinance bank with few restrictions on product offerings in the 1990s as the first licensed and regulated bank dedicated to microfinance in Peru. Its name was changed to MiBanco, and today it continues to be promoting the economic development of Peru's low-income majority population through the provisioning of financial services (Burritt, 2003).

Following transformation, MiBanco began offering savings services. MiBanco has also significantly diversified its product offerings in both urban and rural areas to include working capital loans, housing loans, credit lines, passbook savings, term deposits, remittances, fixed asset loans, and foreign exchange services. MiBanco uses a range of lending technologies including both traditional asset-based lending as well as non-traditional guarantees. MiBanco also participates in a Women's World Banking network, Global Network for Banking Innovation in Microfinance. Burrit observes that by the end of 2002, MiBanco had 99,121 active clients, accessing both credit and savings services. More than 50 percent of its clients are women. Loan sizes range from $100 to $100,000, and loan terms range from 3 months to five years. About 19 percent of MiBanco's loans are group loans and 81 percent are individual loans. 71 percent of individual loans are not guaranteed.

Another example of successful microfinance institutions also cited in Burritt (2006) is the Bank Rakyat Indonesia (BRI), a state-owned commercial bank that began as an agricultural development bank. While it now maintains a commercial focus, it is still largely focused on rural banking services, particularly to the agricultural markets. The bank was established in the early 1970s to channel credit to farmers through a program intended to promote national rice production. By the 1980s lending volumes were very low and default rates were greater than 50 percent. The government decided to convert it into a rural banking network that would offer a wide range of financial services to low-income clients. After decades of focusing on cheap, subsidized credit, BRI recognized the huge demand for savings services among clients and developed appropriate services to meet that demand. With the success of this product and indications that BRI could be financially viable, BRI launched savings products called SIMPEDES (rural savings). Savings deposits skyrocketed as money kept in people's homes and non-financial assets converted to money were deposited in the Bank. The survival of BRI during the Indonesian financial crisis is largely attributed to its diversified services that included savings mobilization.

3.3 Theoretical Economics of Joint Liability Lending (JLL)

Economics of information and of contracts has been the basis for explaining the performance of JLL. Plunket (1904) cited in Guinnane (1994) calls the discovery of group lending with join liability the "apparent miracle of giving solvency to a community composed of almost entirely insolvent members". Most joint liability lending economic models are an effort to formalize the idea that a well structured joint liability institution can deal effectively with the four major problems facing the lenders by utilizing the local information and the social capital that exists among them. Ghatak and Guinnane (1999) summarize these problems as follows: (a) the difficulty to ascertain what kind of a risk the potential borrower is (adverse selection), (b) to make sure that the borrower will utilize the loan properly once made available so that he/she will be able to repay (moral hazard), (c) to learn how her project really did in case he/she declares his/her inability to repay (auditing cost) and (d) to find methods to force the borrower to repay the loan if he/she is reluctant to do so (enforcement). The joint liability lending institutions are assumed to be out-performing the convention lending institutions in some social context for two reasons. First, members of a community may know more about one another in terms of actions and states than an outside institution such as the bank (Ghatak and Guinnane, 1999). This assumes that there is no information asymmetry between members of a community or group. In this way adverse selection, moral hazard and auditing problems are lessened. In reality, however, this may not be true because there are a number of cases where group members may not know each other, particularly in societies with sparse population densities as well as in urban areas.

Second, as observed by Ghatak (1999a), a major source of market failure in credit markets is that a bank can not apply financial sanctions against poor people who default on the loan. Joint liability lending institutions on the other hand are able to use poor people's neighbors to impose pecuniary sanctions on defaulting members at a low cost. In so doing auditing costs and limited enforcement problems faced by conventional banks are administered in the non-conventional system through joint liability lending. The joint liability lending institutions give the poor incentives to collect information from their group members and use the information to apply non-financial sanctions to non paying members.

3.4 Moral Hazard: A Review of Related Literature

Moral hazard in lending refers to situations where lenders cannot observe either the effort made or action taken by the borrower or the realization of the project returns (de Aghion and Moduch, 2005). A very limited number of empirical studies have been conducted on determinants of moral hazard in JLL schemes. Among the few attempts are studies by Wydick (1999) and Hermes *et al.* (2005). Wydick assesses the incidence of moral hazard among credit groups in Guatemala and provides evidence that joint liability works because of social cohesion and better information flow. Nevertheless, the study fails to assess the extent to which other key variables of group dynamics such as, dynamic incentives, sanctions and matching problems influence the incidence of moral hazard. Hermes *et al.* (2005) study the incidence of moral hazard among credit groups from Eritrea and observe that social ties and peer monitoring are key factors influencing the likelihood of moral hazard among borrowers. Again their study does not explore the significance of matching problems and sanctions in influencing the incidence of moral hazard.

The role of screening in mitigating adverse selection and hence moral hazard is discussed by Ghatak (1999b). Ghatak argues that despite information asymmetry, joint liability lending allows for pareto superior equilibrium in credit markets if group formation is conducted appropriately. Ghatak shows how groups formed through self selection will result into members with homogenous quality. Ghatak shows that through the assortative matching process, groups end up with less risk borrowers, directly reducing moral hazard, which leads to a lower equilibrium interest rate leading to a pareto superior outcome relative to individual lending.

The significance of peer monitoring in improving repayments in group credit is highlighted by a number of authors. Stiglitz (1990), for example, observes that the major problem facing MFIs is ensuring that borrowers exercise prudence in the use of the funds so that the likelihood of repayments is enhanced. Stiglitz notes that a partial solution to this problem is peer monitoring: giving neighbors or group members the responsibility to monitor each other. The incentive for peer monitoring comes from the fact that peers are supposed to pay loans for any defaulting group members. It is for this reason that peer- monitoring is largely seen as responsible for the successful financial performance of the Grameen Bank of Bangladesh and of similar group lending programs elsewhere. Nevertheless, most literature including Varian (1990) has assumed that group members can monitor actions costlessly and fully side contract on the choice of actions. Following this observation, Banerjee , Besley and Guinnane(1994) conclude that when monitoring is costly, group members enforce side contracts by punishing deviations from pre-agreed actions with social sanctions. In an attempt to show that monitoring is also prone to moral hazard, Aniket (2004) analyses group lending in a multi-agent double moral hazard setup. Aniket shows that with costly monitoring and under simultaneous lending, borrowers would not monitor the peers unless given explicit incentives to monitor. Thus borrowers have to be promised rents ex-ante to avoid collusion. Aniket further argues that even with costless monitoring the problem of collusion is more pronounced in simultaneous group lending than under sequential group lending.

As an attempt to further understand the design of credit contracts with peer monitoring , de Aghion (1999) analyses how the distribution of risk within the peer group , the group size and the different monitoring structures in the presence of peer monitoring costs may account for the contrasting performance of group lending with joint liability. De Aghion addresses the question 'Are successes or failure in group lending in any way related to the distribution of risk among participating borrowers? Or to the size of the peer group? Or to the structure of monitoring? De Aghion finds that collective agreement with joint responsibility can potentially induce peer monitoring and reduce the incidence of strategic default. The study further shows that relative benefits from peer monitoring are maximized when risks are positively correlated across borrowers and also when the size of the group is neither too small (due to cost sharing and commitment effect) nor too large (due to a free riding effect). Thus although risk diversification as measured by a lower correlation of output might be good for repayment, it is not good for monitoring.

In general larger group sizes are found to be good for MFI for insurance purposes, however, large groups are more prone to experiencing free-riding on monitoring among borrowers. De Aghion identifies four effects that group size can have on the performance of the group as follows:

(a)- A free riding effect: A large group size discourages individual monitoring effort. Indeed with a large number of members in a group, there is an increase in the probability that at least one borrower will be fortunate and will therefore be able to repay for a borrower who defaults strategically. This reduces the incentive for individuals to monitor their peers.

(b)- Joint responsibility effect: There is a strong presumption that the joint responsibility effect encourages more intense monitoring as the number of borrowers increases since each extra member in the group monitors every other member. Although this is a duplication of monitoring efforts, it is to the advantage of the overall group repayment outcome.

(c)- Cost sharing effect: This increases the peer monitoring effort. As the group size increases, the cost of monitoring another borrower becomes smaller given that such a cost is shared among increasingly large numbers of peers.

(d)- Commitment effect: It is assumed that as the size of the group increases each borrower becomes increasingly fearful about strategic default by her peers since she would have to repay for a large number of defaulting borrowers.

de Aghion observes that although most MFI have restricted attention on the standard mutual structure of monitoring , other structures such as the rotating pyramid structure[5] and the circular structure are potentially more efficient because mutual monitoring leads to a duplication of effort.

Studying the incentive rationale for the use of group lending as a method of financing liquidity-constrained entrepreneurs, Che (2002) observes that the joint liability lowers the liquidity risk of default but creates a free-riding problem. Che points out that in the static setting, the free-riding problem dominates the liquidity risk effect, thus making group lending unattractive. However, when the projects are repeated over time, the joint liability feature provides the group members with a credible means of exercising peer monitoring and sanctioning, which can make the group lending attractive, relative to individual lending.

In contrast to the emphasis on peer monitoring, Fuglesgang *et al.* (1993) argue that the monitoring by lending institutions is all that matters most when it comes to improving repayment rates. They observe that even micro lenders that are famous for the joint liability methodology such as the Grameen of Bangladesh do in fact also rely heavily upon highly motivated and locally recruited loan staff officers as monitors and organizers. Following this

---

[5] A structure in which at every period a different borrower at the top of the pyramid monitors her peers at the bottom of the pyramid.

observation, Conning (2000) questions whether such delegated monitors might not be just as good at monitoring, and perhaps better at enforcing loan repayment than peer monitors, in which case joint liability clauses may be superfluous or may be serving other purposes.

The role of peer pressure is discussed by Diagne (1998). Diagne proposes a peer pressure model in which borrowers are incompletely informed about their partners willingness to apply or tolerate social sanctions and shows how peer pressure can be used to mitigate default in situations where potential defaulters are intolerant of sanctions. An extension of the model by Diagne (1998) and Paxton (1996) further proposes the importance of dynamic incentives and incentive match in inducing safe behaviour among borrowers. Despite such theoretical propositions on the importance of dynamic incentives, and matching problems, empirical literature is silent on their role on moral hazard.

The role of sanctions in enhancing the willingness of individuals to repay their loans is also discussed in Besley and Coate (1995). They show how moderately successful group members may wilfully decide not to repay their loans because of the burden of having to repay the unsuccessful members' loan. They note however, that in the presence of strong social ties among group members, wilful default is minimized because potential defaulters are afraid of facing sanctions from both the bank and the community.

Ahlin and Townsend (2003) make first attempts to modify existing models on repayment and moral hazard by testing some unexamined dimensions of the models. One such test is the introduction of productivity differences across groups. Based on the assumption that the production function can be decomposed multiplicatively into a piece related to the risk factor and a piece related to productive inputs, such as loaned capital and human capital, they assign the derivative of the utility difference with respect to human capital. In their empirical analysis they find that productivity represented by the average level of education positively influences repayment. However the average land holding size (another productivity variable considered in the model) had no effect on repayment performance. A theoretical framework on moral hazard and its extensions is presented in chapter 4.

3.5 Intra-group Insurance: Review of Related Research

While perceived advantages of group lending through mutual insurance appear to be obvious, empirical research has lagged behind. Indeed as observed by Varian (1990), joint liability lending can be advantageous for lenders if group members can insure one another across states of nature that are unobservable to the lender. Nevertheless, group members need incentives to mutually insure each other against idiosyncratic risks by repaying loans for members with genuine failure. In an attempt to investigate incentives required to promote intra-group insurance, Wydick (1999) examines the role of social cohesion in stimulating intra-group insurance among credit groups from Guatemala and observes that peer monitoring is a key determinant of intra-group insurance.

In contrast to most literature on intra-group insurance in joint liability schemes, Rai and Sjodtröm (2000) argue that joint liability is not enough to efficiently induce borrowers to help each other. If borrowers share information about productivity shocks that the bank does not possess, then efficiency requires that borrowers send reports to the bank. They note that in practice such cross-reporting occurs at village meetings, where loan repayments are collected by Grameen (Rahman, 1999). The implication of their argument is that, where there is no cross reporting it is more likely that members with good payoffs will renege their insurance promises as there is little incentive for them to help repay their peer's loan.

The role of dynamic incentives has been well documented in theoretical literature. Dynamic incentives are important in group contracts because they are the main mechanism available to the lender to enforce repayment through the threat of terminating a credit relationship. In concurrence with this notion *de* Meza and Webb (2000) note that the set of incentives implicit in group contracts relies on the value of long–term relationship between funds-constrained borrowers and imperfectly informed lenders. As the relationship matures, the relaxation of the funds-constraint on the borrower's side may threaten the long term stability of the program as the incentive to repay tends to weaken. In a similar context, Diagne (1998) notes that the value of future access to loans, (dynamic incentives) is an essential element in understanding joint liability. Diagne notes that it generates interdependency among group members and in turn interdependency generates peer pressure. The knowledge that each member belongs to a group where they are supposed to insure each other in order to access loans in future creates an incentive for monitoring and auditing within group members. The significance of dynamic incentives is also acknowledged by Sadoulet (2003). Sadoulet notes that by denying access to future loans to all group members of a defaulting group, joint liability helps in making the insurance promise credible within credit groups and thus reneging on insurance promises is minimized. This is because if a partner fails to fulfill an insurance promise ex-post, the borrower too will loose access to future loans. In this way the MFI sanctions borrowers who renege on their insurance promises.

Questioning the sustainability of intra-group insurance, Wydick (2001) observes that intra-group insurance is sustainable as along as the loss of future access to credit is sufficiently costly. While dynamic incentives are linked to the generation of interdependency among members, the extent to which it induces the willingness of group members to help each other in loan repayment is undetermined. Nevertheless, Zeller (1998) observes that insurance contracts between members can cover idiosyncratic risks, such as illness or individual crop failure. Wener (1995) cited in Zeller (1998) observes that 75 percent of the

sample groups in Costa Rica had members defaulting on their loan, but more than half of these groups managed to fully repay the loan to the financial institution by using group savings or by forcing the consigner of the loan to repay for the defaulter. Zeller concludes that the threat of lost access to future loans may induce members to set up implicit insurance contracts.
The other side of literature has attempted to explore the shortcomings of overemphasizing on intra-group insurance as a means to improving loan repayments. In this regard, Varian (1990) notes that the major problem as it relates to mutual insurance lies in its weak insurance capacity. This may occur in groups that are homogenous in terms of wealth such that their risk sharing ability is constrained. In addition, mutual insurance is only possible when group members face idiosyncratic shocks and may be ineffective for covariate shocks. However, even for idiosyncratic shocks, group members can only ensure each other below a certain minimum level of default, otherwise joint liability may lead to the domino effect (one group member defaults and the rest follow) once members realize that the group will default, and therefore, its future access to loans likely to be terminated. Most theoretical studies still argue that mutual insurance is beneficial under any scenario. For example, Varian (1990) and Rashid and Townsend (1992) explore the significance of mutual insurance among group members in the presence of idiosyncratic shocks, and if borrower returns are not highly correlated and observe that mutual insurance is beneficial to group members.
Although the importance of peer selection in enhancing repayment has been acknowledged in most literature, there are disagreements as regards the extent to which it can be used to enhance intra-group insurance. Questioning the significance of peer selection at group formation, Sadoulet and Carpenter (2001), argue that group formation through self selection may lead to both homogenous and heterogeneous groups with respect to risk depending on the circumstances. They observe that when joint liability leads to heterogeneous groups, riskier members pay a premium in good states of nature to safer borrowers. In the same context Kugler and Oppes (2005) observe that by allowing transfers between members, heterogeneous formation of the group is Pareto improvement over homogenous formation, however it is not obvious that peer selection leads .heterogeneous groups. Indeed Kritikos and Vigenina (2005) show that self-selection sometimes leads to heterogeneous group formation. From the discussion above it is apparent that literature is not conclusive as regards the component of the joint liability mechanism that is important in explaining the willingness of group members to offer mutual insurance. In the theoretical chapter, I present a theoretical framework describing the circumstances under which intra-group insurance is feasible.

3.6 The Impact of Access to Credit on Adoption: A Review of Related Literature

A number of adoption studies report that technology adoption is linked to farmer resource endowment in terms of human, physical and financial capital, risk preferences, location factors and the characteristics of the technology itself. Among the key endowment factors is the farm size. It generally hypothesized that larger farms tend to adopt new technologies faster than smaller farms. Just, Zilberman and Rauser (1986) point that considering the uncertainty and the fixed transaction and information cost associated with innovations, there may be a critical lower limit on farm size that prevents smaller farms from adopting. As the costs increase, the critical size also increases. Innovations with large transactional costs are therefore less likely to be adopted by smaller farmers. Ferder *et al.* (1985) however point out that it is difficult to isolate the impact of farm size on technology adoption from others in the sense that farm size may, for example, be related to other factors such as credit access, wealth and risk preferences. More over, access to credit is directly related to farm size. In Malawi, for example, where farm size is sometimes used as criteria for credit eligibility it may be difficult to isolate credit effects from farm size effects.

De Janvry *et al.* (1999) report that households can reduce exposure to consumption risk through risk management (interventions which are ex-ante relative to income realizations) and through risk coping (ex-post relative to income), and there is hence a trade off between the two. Since risk management has an opportunity cost on expected income, improved access to risk coping instruments such as credit may allow households to take higher risks in production and achieve higher expected incomes (Binswanger and Rosenzweig, 1993; Morduch, 1992). Access to risk coping instruments such as flexible credit, by the poor has been used, as a way of raising expected incomes.

Using IFPRI data from Malawi, Zeller *et al.* (1998) investigates factors that affect the extent of adoption of maize and tobacco. They observe that adoption of agricultural innovations is mainly influenced by human capital, labour availability, farm size and access to commodity markets. The study notes that, although yields for local maize were lower by 49 percent compared to hybrid maize, the local maize varieties were grown by half of the households. The main reason was that hybrid maize exhibited higher risks than local maize. The study points out that risk exposure and capacity to bear risk and credit constraints are key factors that influence adoption. The implications from this study are that households with lower risk bearing ability are likely to prefer local maize to hybrid maize.

In general, the major gap in studies that have assessed the impact of access to credit is that they did not take into account whether all not households included in the analysis faced binding credit constraints. Theoretically, credit access will only be effective to credit constrained households. This study is therefore a rare attempt to assess the impact of access to credit on the adoption of hybrid maize among households that differ in their credit constraints.

3.7 Innovative Aspects of this Study

This section seeks to summarize the research gaps, and to highlight those research issues that are addressed in this dissertation thesis. Although the advantages of group lending over individual lending are becoming common knowledge, there are a number of issues that remain unresolved. Literature shows that while theories explaining the success of joint liability lending are largely based on experiences of the Grameen Bank, the applicability of the technology is limited to certain environments and that there are still problems as regards the optimum conditions that are necessary for the proper functioning of the joint liability mechanism. Below I review some of the problem areas.

For example, group size can have conflicting effects on the performance of joint liability lending. Ghatak (1999a) notes that if project returns are uncorrelated, an increase in group size is good as it increases the risk pooling capacity of the group. However when groups get larger, there may be free riding in the provision of some activities which have the character of public goods such as monitoring and auditing. In most cases the disadvantages experienced with larger groups outweigh the associated advantages. This is supported by a number of empirical studies. Mosley and Dehal (1985) cited in Ghatak and Guinane (1999), for example observe that in case of the Nepalese credit programs, there is little mutual trust among groups that are larger than twenty persons. However, there is still lack of consensus as regards the optimal group size.

With regards to the group formation process most microfinance practitioners devote attention to the way in which groups are formed. They emphasize the role of screening during group formation and suggest conditions under which screening is done optimally. Most contend that groups that were formed through self-selection perform better than those that are formed by program officials. This is directly associated with the degree of pre-existing social ties among group members. However, efforts to replicate the same principle of selection have proved difficult under some circumstances. For example in Malawi most of the credit groups are either formed by the credit officers or the traditional leaders. Further, Balkin (1993) notes that in the Chacago Full Circle fund in the USA, whose clients were urban based, it was difficult to create groups through self selection because potential members did not initially know each other. In such circumstances some form of adaptation has to be made to ensure that members are brought together in a linked lending system. The problem stated above is directly associated to the problem of social ties in group based credit. Social ties are important in joint liability lending as they strengthen the functioning of group solidarity. However, this may not be applicable in developed countries or in urban areas where the social and cultural environment is very different from the countries such as Bangladesh where the joint liability lending technology was first pioneered. Wydick (1999) shows that for lending programs from Guatemala groups in which members' businesses were close together had higher repayment rates. However, Mondal and Tune (1993) finds that the Good Faith Fund of Arkansas failed to fully replicate the Grameen Bank model because of significant social and cultural differences. They note that Arkansas has much lower population density and has significant racial and religious heterogeneity compared to Banglandesh where the Grameen bank operates. This makes it difficult to execute self-formation and solidarity among groups.

Indeed most theoretical models presume that a set of parameter values are satisfied, however, the mechanism will not work everywhere. For example, both group lending and individual lending are aided by dynamic incentives, but only to the extent that borrowers care about future credit availability and view the lender as preferable to alternatives. The reliance on social ties among potential group members as a prerequisite for an effective functioning of joint liability lending scheme implies that the lack of social ties and the unwillingness to impose sanctions will lead to the failure of the mechanism even if dynamic incentives are in place. Further, such theoretical propositions have ignored the importance of social and cultural structures, such as the role of political and traditional leaders in the performance of joint liability lending. This study will attempt to explore the significance of such factors.

As noted by Ghatak and Guinane (1999), theoretical models of enforcement through joint liability schemes rely on the dynamic incentives inherent in the lenders' threat of cut off from future loans for all members of a defaulting group. In most cases, however, lenders are facing difficulties of carrying out this threat when poor borrowers default. In Malawi, for example an IFPRI study found that in 18 percent of the groups that did not fully repay the 1998 loans, they also received the 1999 loans despite their default status (Diagne et al., 2001). The study also found out that in about 25 percent of the defaulted groups, defaulters were still members of the groups, an indication that sanctions were not always implemented. The inability to implement the threat of termination of credit access has been cited by Ghatak and Guinane (1999) as one of the reasons why the Irish credit cooperatives failed. The Malawi Mudzi Fund (MMF) borrowers from Malawi are yet another example of this. Borrowers under the MMF were aware that it was a government program which made some to think that they would not be held to strict standards of repayment. The same happened in Malawi in 1992 for the SACA loans when government announced that farmers that had failed to repay their loan due to drought would be allowed to get loans in the next season. Unfortunately, there were no rules as regards how genuine defaulters were to be identified and this led to default rates of more than 75% in that year, although part of it was blamed on the drought. This study also seeks to explore the extent to which sanctions occur and their effect on the performance of group lending with joint liability.

Although peer pressure and peer monitoring have been theoretically proposed as positive and important factors in enhancing the functioning of the joint liability mechanism, they can sometimes have no effect on the functioning of the group. For example, Diagne *et al* (2000) in their study on credit groups from Malawi, note that peer pressure had negative impacts on repayment. In addition they note that peer monitoring was rare and when it happened it never enhanced repayment.

Some credit schemes have limits on the number of loans that they have to offer to an individual. Ghatak and Guinane (1999) note that under such circumstances borrowers may withhold payments especially when they are getting what they believe will be their last loan from the program. The same situation could occur among programs that are seen to be non-permanent in nature and when borrowers suspect that the program might not exist in the future to provide loans, then they may withhold their money. The Agricultural Productivity Investment Program (APIP) for Malawi is a good example in this regard. APIP is an EU funded program which offers agricultural input loans to small holder farmers in Malawi. Due to its non permanent nature, the program has suffered default rates of more than 50 percent while other programs such as the MRFC programs enjoy repayment rates of more than 80 percent.

The emergence of new credit programs on the credit market is appositive development as it creates competition among the providers. However, there are instances where competition would work against repayment. Buckley (1996) gives an example of Malawi where two credit programs, SACA and Malawi Mudzi fund operated side by side. Buckley observes that many borrowers who were participants in Mudzi fund had been dropped from earlier participation in the SACA program for default. To the extent that the two programs continued to exist side by side and they undermined each other. Buckley notes that threat of sanctions on defaulters is ineffective if borrowers can simply move to another program once they have defaulted in one. Indeed this should be considered as a real threat to the sustainability of microfinance in the developing countries where a lot more credit institutions are being created. While competition among credit providers is good, such competition could undermine the very basis of joint liability scheme, particularly if the competition is among institutions that rely on dynamic incentives. In addition there is a general observation by some theorists that although dynamic incentives are an important aspect in the Grameen Bank, to some extent, these incentives do not require group lending at all. This study will attempt to clarify some of the dilemmas addressed in this chapter in the empirical analysis.

3.8 Conclusion

In conclusion, this chapter highlighted a number of issues related to performance and impact of joint liability lending and its implications on the sustainability of microfinance. The chapter provided a brief review of the global perspective of microfinance, the economics of group lending with joint liability, a review of empirical studies and concluded with a presentation on dilemmas in joint liability lending and innovative aspect of this research. It is apparent that while a number of theoretical models have been proposed on determinants of moral hazard and intra-group insurance, empirical tests are rare. The review also shows that although studies on the impact of credit have been done elsewhere, very few have taken into account whether or not a household is credit constrained. Further, the review showed that theoretical models that explain the performance of JLL have ignored the effect of social and cultural structures within which group lending occurs. Therefore, this research is an attempt to fill this gap which will be a direct input to microfinance institutions in Malawi that thrive to achieve great outreach and impact in a sustainable manner.

4 THEORETICAL FRAMEWORK

4.1 Introduction

This chapter develops the basic conceptual framework and theoretical models upon which the analytical methodologies used to address the three objectives are based. The analytical framework is based on relational pathway capturing group contract compliance and household's impact of credit. A detailed description of theories of moral hazard and risk sharing are presented as well as the frameworks for analyzing contract compliance in joint liability lending programs. With regard to household impact of credit on the adoption of hybrid maize, I present a theoretical framework that is based on an Agricultural Household Model (AHM) under credit market failure.

4.2 A general Conceptual Framework

Below, I present a general conceptual framework for analyzing the relationship between participation in group based credit programs, performance and impact.
Zeller *et al* (2001) describe that the evaluation of the performance of a credit program can be done in two general areas: (1) the performance of clients in complying with the contractual arrangements and (2) the extent to which beneficiaries are able to take advantage of the services provided by the financial institutions and use them to enhance their own welfare. On the contractual side, performance indicators may include, among others, repayment performance, the extent to which beneficiaries avoid moral hazard, the amount of group savings and the regularity of group meetings held in each loan cycle. The impact of credit access has traditionally focused on changes in household welfare indicators such

as asset growth, consumption smoothing, nutrition, food security and productivity.

The focus in this study is on two forms of contract compliance, namely, mitigation of moral hazard and compliance to the promise of intra-group insurance. The analysis on the impact of access to credit on households focuses on the extent to which credit access enhances the adoption of hybrid maize. The interaction process of the performance and impact of group based lending is described using a conceptual framework presented by Marr (2000). The framework allows for a detailed discussion of the dynamics of joint liability lending, the problems encountered in credit markets and theoretical perceptions of how group lending addresses such problems. The point of emphasis in this framework is the linkage between group dynamics, compliance to contractual obligations such as repayment, and moral hazard and its implications on household welfare.

As indicated in Figure 4.1, the framework presents an understanding of the impact process that is dynamic and continuous in nature. It shows how MFI policies affect group dynamics and how group dynamics can influence repayment and through that process lead to desirable household welfare impacts. The framework shows how individual behavior, with regards to attitudes towards risk, changes as a result of group dynamics and how this then leads ultimately to changes in livelihoods strategies. Such changes may induce households to take up riskier but higher return investments that in turn will lead to welfare improvements.

Most studies on performance and impact of group credit tend to focus literally on factors that affect repayment and the impact of credit on individual borrowers from a lender's view point without looking at the potential effects of group dynamics. The interaction process between members of the group is usually assumed to be neutral. However, this process can bring significant benefit and costs to group members such that it would affect their investment behavior and the way they overcome problems of risk, vulnerability, voiceless ness, powerlessness and isolation (Marr, 2000). Therefore, the framework highlights the underlying causes of the impacts tracking how change in borrower's behavior and strategies determine ultimate impacts. In addition through this framework it is possible to capture the association between credit impacts and contractual compliance which helps in understanding how the resulting effects of group dynamics feed back into the microfinance institution. Marr (2002) notes that using the feedback process, an MFI is able to modify its policies and practices to meet needs of clients as well as its institutional needs.

The framework starts with the MFI setting policies from which terms and conditions of financial contracts are drawn. The microfinance institution facilitates group formation through a self selection process which facilitates positive assortative matching. The MFI policy is seen as addressing four key problems, namely, adverse selection, moral hazard, auditing and limited enforcement. In addition, most MFIs, due to donor requirement will have policies that aim at achieving the three pillars of the triangle of microfinance (Zeller and Sharma 2001), namely expanding the outreach, achieving maximum impacts, and ensuring that the services are delivered in a manner that promotes sustainability of the MFI. These donor driven policies in turn have a direct impact on targeting (client selection) as well as the type and functioning of groups. From the MFI, the framework focuses on the process of group formation. Within the group formation process there are some key features that have a direct bearing on how members interact with themselves and also how they relate with MFI officers. Such interactions have implications on the way duties of screening; monitoring, enforcement and support, which are crucial in addressing the four problems, are performed at group level. The interactions within the group and with MFI officers lead to changes in behavior among members with respect to preferences and attitudes towards risk, cooperation and rent seeking behavior. The behavioral change among members in turn has a direct effect on household decisions regarding livelihood and investment strategies.

Figure 4.1 The analytical framework for assessing the impact of credit on poverty

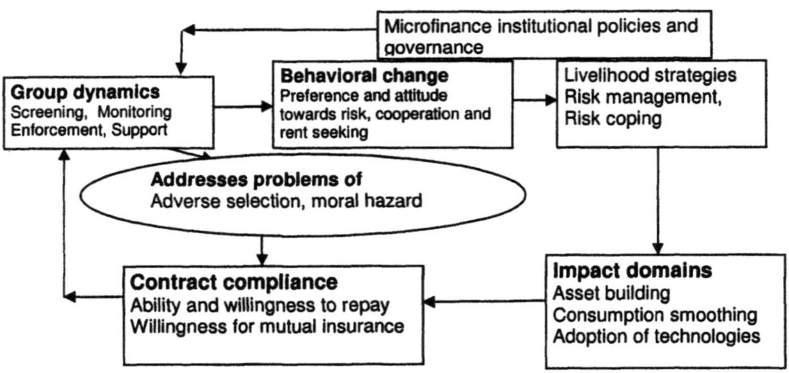

Source: Adopted with some modification from Marr (2002)

Access to credit changes investment behavior in a number of ways. First access to credit alleviates the capital constraints on households enabling them to acquire inputs for investments that they would otherwise not acquire. Diagne *et al.* (1997) observes that access to credit also reduces the opportunity costs of capital-intensive assets relative to family labour, thus encouraging labor-saving technologies and raising labor productivity. Credit access increases household risk-bearing ability and alters its risk-coping strategy. Through intra-group insurance which also increases one's risk bearing abilities, a household may take up investments with higher risks and higher returns.

Households, however, continue to re-assess decisions taken and where necessary they make adjustments in their coping and risk management strategies. Through this process microfinance is seen to result in a diverse range of impacts domains. For purposes of this study, the framework focuses on impact domains at households and enterprise level. The focus of this study is the role of microfinance on the household's farm-income generating activities, with specific reference to the adoption of hybrid maize. With regards to contractual compliance this study focuses on the willingness to repay (thus avoiding moral hazard) and the willingness of group members to support each other when one of the members faces a repayment problem (intra-group insurance). Intra-group insurance is particularly of interest because it forms the basis of joint liability loans. When a member's project returns are lower than the value of loan to be repaid, other group members will repay the defaulter's loan.

Depending on the willingness and ability of members to comply with contractual agreements, the sustainability of the MFI is affected and this in turn motivates the MFI to modify its policies and practices. The most commonly used policies in addressing such problem include modifications in joint liability obligations, collateral substitutes, and monitoring systems, all of which have implications on group dynamics and the resulting impacts at individual level.

4.3 The Dynamics of Joint Liability Lending

Matin (1997) describes joint liability as situation in which two or more parties are liable for repayment of a debt or obligation and a creditor can be compensated from them either individually or jointly. It is an arrangement whereby a group of borrowers guarantee each other's loans. The technique has proved effective in many different countries and settings worldwide. Following its initial success in Asia, most group loan contracts in developing countries have a joint liability clause. It is widely believed that joint liability lending is a potential break through strategy in economic development as it enables the poor, for example without land title or collateral to access group loans that they would otherwise never access individually. The premise of group lending with joint liability is that if one borrower cannot pay a loan, then other members of the joint liability group will do so (Ahlin and Townsend, 2003).

Figure 4.2 shows a relational presentation of loan transactions and stages in the joint liability lending model starting from identification of borrowers through to repayment. Each stage in the figure is associated with a problem that the joint liability clause is assumed to address, and a hypothetical or theoretical solution. Following the loan receipt are the stages of monitoring, return realization, repayment or non-repayment. The process ends with penalties of non-refinancing in case of default.

Figure 4.2 A dynamic presentation of problems and solutions in a multistage joint liability loan

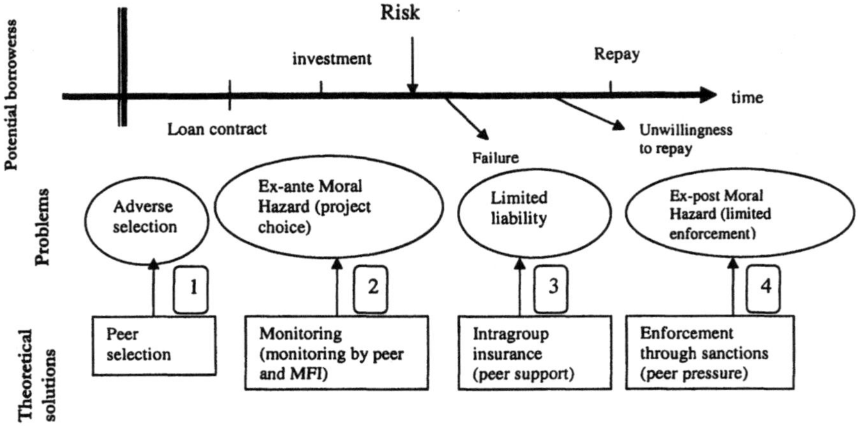

Source: Adopted with some modification from Sadoulet (2004)

At the beginning of the period you have a pool of potential borrowers trying to access credit. However, borrowing is conditioned upon group affiliation. According to Ghatak (1999a), realizing that a borrowing group will sign a joint liability contract with the lender, each borrower, through peer selection tries to match with members of similar risk. As proposed by Ghatak (1999a), the self-selection process reduces the incidence of adverse selection. There are conflicting arguments regards the extent to which self selection leads to homogenous matching. Some empirical studies, such as one by Zeller (1998) have argued that homogenous matching weakens the capacity for intra-group insurance and that usually group members select their peers in a way that they diversify their risk coping mechanisms.

Following the selection stage is the investment period. At this stage, the lender is faced with an *ex ante* moral hazard problem. This occurs when a borrower either decides to invest in a risky project or misuses the funds or when the borrower does not apply enough effort to manage the investment, which may lead to low returns. In theory peer monitoring can be used to mitigate this problem. However, complementary monitoring by the officers from microfinance institutions (MFIs) can also significantly reduce the incidence ex-ante moral hazard. Since monitoring by MFI officers is assumed to be more costly than peer-monitoring, joint liability lending emphasizes on monitoring by peers.

The third stage involves investment outcomes. The investment may fail due to a number of reasons, some of which are beyond the control of the borrowers such as idiosyncratic shocks. The problem now is that there exists limited liability. Under joint liability lending members that do not have repayment problems can assist in paying the defaulters' loan (intra-group insurance). The final problem is related to ex-post moral hazard. This is a second dimension of the general moral hazard issue in lending contracts. It occurs when the levels of effort have been carried out and the returns of the investment have been realized, when a borrower finds it optimal to diverge the funds for repayment of the loan to other purposes. In joint liability loans, implementing peer pressure and social sanctions can solve the problem of ex-post moral hazard.

4.4 Theoretical Framework for Moral Hazard

There are two forms of moral hazard, namely *ex-ante* and *ex post*. *Ex- ante* moral hazard occurs at the investment stage. After loan disbursement some borrowers may take a risky action of not investing the loan in a safe project or by misusing the loan. *Ex-post* moral hazard occurs when borrowers with a successful project and enough payoff to make repayment, willfully decide not to make that payment because they want to maximize their private benefits. Both forms of moral hazard may lead to default and they are the focus of this study. In this section I start by presenting a standard framework for moral hazard and later outline a proposed framework under joint liability.

4.4.1 The standard model for moral hazard

Following Salanie (2000), the standard moral hazard model assumes that the principal cannot directly observe the effort level of the agent. Once a contract has been signed the agent must choose between *n* possible actions $a_i,..........,a_n$ .These actions produce one among *m* outcomes which I may denote $x_1,................,x_m$. Assume further that when the agent chooses action a_i, the principal observes the outcome x_j with a probability p_{ij} that is positive. The agent receives a wage w_j when the principal observes the outcome x_j. The income for the principal is $(x_j - w_j)$. The specification for the Agent's von Neumann-Morgenstern utility function can be written as $u(w)-a$, where u is increasing and concave. Assuming neutrality for the principal as in most of the literature, his von Neumann-Morgenstern utility function is written as
$x-w$. When the Principal offers a contract w_j the agent's utility maximization problem can be written as :

$$\underset{i=1,....,n)}{Max}\left(\sum_{j=1}^{m} p_{ij}u(w_j)-a_i\right) \qquad (4.4.1)$$

If the Agent chooses a_i then the (n-1) incentive constraints is

$$\sum_{j=1}^{m} p_{ij}u(w_j)-a_i \geq \sum_{j=1}^{m} p_{kj}u(w_j)-a_k \qquad (IC_k) \qquad (4.4.2)$$

where k=1, …..n and $k \neq i$.
The agents' utility maximization problem is also subject to the following (individual rationality constraint) participation constraint:

$$\sum_{j=1}^{m} p_{ij}u(w_j)-a_i \geq \underline{\mu} \qquad (IR) \qquad (4.4.3)$$

where $\underline{\mu}$ is the utility derived from taking an outside option.

4.4.2 Moral hazard in credit markets

Building on the basic principles stated in the standard model specified above, Guinane and Ghatak (1999) propose a moral hazard model for credit markets which can be presented in two stages. First, the model is presented under individual lending and then later a scenario under group lending is presented. The model shows that joint liability lending can be used to mitigate the moral hazard problem among group members. The model starts by assuming a single borrowers, loan (individual liability) under the assumption that borrowers are risk neutral. Output takes two values, high Y^H and low Y^L. Normalizing the low output values to 0, the output is high with probability p and 0 otherwise. Assuming that each project requires 1 unit of capital, then the repayment to the lender plus interest equals $\rho > 1$. Borrowers will only be willing to borrow if the utility from borrowing (which results from the payoffs) is no smaller than some utility $\underline{\mu}$ that represents the utility the agent can obtain by taking on an outside option. This participation constraint, which also implies that the projects are socially profitable, can be expressed as follows:

$$pY^H - \rho \geq \underline{\mu} \qquad (4.4.4)$$

Borrowers choose actions, which can be thought of as a level of effort $p \in [0,1]$, for which they incur a disutility cost of $\frac{1}{2}\gamma p^2$ (where $\gamma > 0$). Following this specification a social surplus and the equilibrium p which is subject to moral hazard can be computed. Under individual lending the following equilibrium value of p will be chosen[6]

$$p = \frac{Y^H + \sqrt{(Y^H)^2 - 4\rho\gamma}}{2\gamma} \qquad (4.4.5)$$

[6] For a detailed description , see Ghatak and Guinnane (1999)

Under joint liability scenario it is assumed that when a borrower's project fails the partner is liable for the amount q. This is an incentive for each member to care about the safety of the project chosen by the peers and it is acknowledged as a justification for peer monitoring. If one of the members chooses an action p' then the payoff function of a borrower who chooses action p is

$$\max_{(p)} pY^H - rp - qp(1-p') - \frac{1}{2}\gamma p^2. \qquad (4.4.6)$$

Assume that the borrower chooses action p to maximize his individual payoff, taking his partner's action p' as given. Then her best response function is given by:

$$p = \frac{Y^H - r - q}{\gamma} + \frac{q}{\gamma}p'. \qquad (4.4.7)$$

At the equilibrium the p under joint liability just like under individual liability has two values while the denominator of the joint liability expression is lower than that of the individual liability. The model shows how the equilibrium value of p and hence repayment rate is higher under joint liability compared to individual lending.

The model outlined above assumes that members can monitor each others actions perfectly at no cost, as well as they enforce any agreements regarding their choice of p. However, in reality, peer monitoring can be costly. In addition, joint liability lending allows for the imposition of sanctions on group members that renege on their repayment promises. Ghatak and Guinnane (1999), further, propose extensions to the model by including the cost of monitoring and considerations for the effect of sanctions in choosing the level of p[7]. Diagne (1998) further makes extensions to the model by including the impact of peer pressure and dynamic incentives in inducing repayment.

A theory of adverse selection and assortative matching proposed by Ghatak (1999a) is also relevant for explaining moral hazard. *Adverse selection* also called *anti-selection* is a term widely used in economics and insurance. On the most abstract level, it refers to a market process in which bad results occur due to information asymmetries between buyers and sellers: In such cases the "bad" products or customers are more likely to be selected than the good customers. Information asymmetry also called asymmetrical information occurs when one party to a transaction has more or better information than the other party.

Akerlof (1970), in a seminal paper 'the market of lemons' used the asymmetric information term to describe how markets can go into non existence due to *adverse selection*. A notable contribution on the role of the adverse selection problem on the performance of credit markets is one by Ghatak

[7] For a detailed description , see Ghatak and Guinnane (1999)

(1999b). Ghatak emphasizes the implications of adverse selection on repayment performance. The assumption is that the principal does not know the quality of the borrowers and therefore he does not differentiate between risky and safe borrowers. All borrowers get loans at a common interest rate with safe borrowers cross-subsidizing the high-risk borrowers. With an outside option safe borrowers drop out of the pool leaving a set of riskier borrowers. Ghatak shows that when individuals are given a chance to self-select into groups, there is an incentive for each member at group formation to know characteristics of each potential member so that they can match with similar risk type. The self-selection process leads to the emergence of a pool of safe borrowers, which in turn results, into the provision of loans at lower interest rates. Nevertheless, empirical work by Zeller (1998) and Hermes (2005) shows that self-selection process does not always lead to the formation of groups composed of members of similar risk types. In fact these studies show that groups end up with heterogeneous types of members type and that the heterogeneity is good for repayment, particularly, if the borrowers' returns are negatively correlated.

Ahlin and Townsend (2003) make extensions to the moral hazard model by testing several unexamined dimensions. For example, in the model by Stiglitz (1990), they allow for borrowers in a joint liability group to play non-cooperatively. In addition to introducing productivity differences across groups, they also allow for project returns to be correlated. They parameterize the degree of correlation, take a derivative and determine that correlation in returns actually increases the likelihood of repayment while productivity reduces moral hazard due to an increase in payoffs for safe projects. The key hypothesis to be tested is that moral hazard will be low in groups that (1) are formed through self selection, (2) have intensive peer monitoring, (3) exercise sanctions and peer pressure (4) attach high value to access to loans from the same institution in future

4.5 Theoretical Framework for Risk Sharing (Intra-group Insurance)

There are several occasions where group members will need support from other members in order to repay their loan. After loan disbursement some borrowers may take a risky action of not investing the loan in a safe project or misuse the loan, known as *ex ante* moral hazard. This leads to repayment problems which will eventually require the contributions from other members to settle the loan in the event that the member who misused the loan is un able to pay himself. Even after investing the money in a good project, there is a risk that a good project could fail. Once the project fails, the borrower is bound to face repayment problems that require the support his peers. Insurance is also important where a borrower with a successful project decides to willfully default (*ex post moral hazard*) because they want to maximize their private benefits. Intra-group insurance enables the lending institution to recover its money in the event of both, moral hazard, or idiosyncratic shocks.

The theoretical framework presented below, initially proposed by Besley and Coate (1995) and later cited in Kugler and Opess (2005), illustrates how intra-group insurance can be used to harness market failure among poor households that have no collateral. The framework starts with a discussion on individual borrowing as a benchmark and then later discusses the case of joint liability.

4.5.1 Individual lending

The starting point is a risk neutral borrower requiring one unit of capital lasting one period and that yields θ units of income. The project return is unknown at the beginning of the period, however, it is assumed that it is distributed on $[\underline{\theta}, \bar{\theta}]$ according to the continuous distribution function F(θ) and satisfying $F(\underline{\theta}) = 0$. At the end of the period the borrower has to repay the principal plus interest of an amount r>*1*. When the borrower defaults he incurs a penalty $p(\theta)$ which is assumed to be a continuous and increasing function. The penalty function represents a loss to the borrower due to seizure of profits from the project by the lender and it increases with project returns. The borrower chooses the repayment option only if the cost of repayment is less than or equal to the penalty in the case of default ($r \leq p(\theta)$). I relate the penalty function and the cost of repayment to the project return by specifying a critical project return at which a borrower is indifferent between repayment and default. Thus the critical project return is specified as $\theta = \phi(r)$, where $\phi(.) \equiv p^{-1}(.)$ is defined as the inverse of the penalty function, $p(.)$. Considering that the penalty function is increasing in project return, it means that the loan can only be repaid if the project return is greater than the critical project return. The probability of repayment and individual borrowing is therefore given by the following expression;

$$\Pi_I(r) = 1 - F(\phi(r)), \text{with } F(\underline{\theta}) = 0 \qquad (4.5.1)$$

The underlying assumption is that $\phi(1) \geq 0$ such that it is not possible to make repayment for every project return.

4.5.2 Joint liability borrowing

Taking the two borrower joint liability scenario, the two acquire a loan of two units of capital at the beginning of the period, each running an independent project. At the end of the period they earn returns θ_1 and θ_2 for individuals 1 and 2, respectively. Assume further, that they are jointly liable to repay a total loan principal plus interest rate of $2r$ at the end of the period. Loan delinquency is assumed to attract penalties of $p(\theta_1)$ and $p(\theta_2)$. The repayment game is explained in two stages. In the first stage of the repayment game, both borrowers decide whether or not to contribute to their share, r. If they both contribute, the loan is repaid and their payoffs are $(\theta_1 - r, \theta_2 - r)$. However, if they fail to contribute, the loan is not repaid and the following penalties are imposed on them by the lender: $(\theta_1 - p(\theta_1), \theta_2 - p(\theta_2))$. If one of the borrowers decides not to contribute at the second stage of the repayment game, the other borrower has to decide whether or not to repay the whole loan alone. Assuming borrower two decides not to contribute and the loan is repaid by borrower 1, the following pay off will result: $(\theta_1 - 2r, \theta_2)$. If they both decide not to repay, the following payoff results; $(\theta_1 - p(\theta_1), \theta_2 - p(\theta_2))$.

The former option in which borrower 1 pays his loan plus the loan of borrower 2, is advantageous to borrower 2 because he does not have to face sanctions from the lender.

A joint liability payment is only possible under two scenarios as follows. First if the return from one of the group members is equal to or greater than the critical project returns for the two borrowers combined, thus $\theta_i > \phi(2r)$ *for either i=1 or 2*. Second, the joint liability payment is also possible when $\phi(r) < \theta_i \leq \phi(2r)$ for both borrowers. Otherwise, whenever the critical value of either of the individuals is greater than the project return for only one individual, ($\phi(r) > \theta_i$ *for either i=1 or 2)* mutual insurance will not be possible, and group default is likely to occur. The repayment under group lending can thus be expressed as follows:

$$\Pi_G(r) =^{r} 1 - \{F(\phi(2r)\}^{2o} + [F(\phi(2r) - F\phi(r)]^2 \qquad (4.5.2)$$

Comparing the repayment rate under joint liability lending with individual lending gives us the following equation:

$$\begin{aligned}\Pi_G(r) - \Pi_I(r) &=^{r} 1 - \{F(\phi(2r)\}^{2^o} + [F(\phi(2r)) - F(\phi(r))]^2 - [1 - F(\phi(r))] \qquad (4.5.3)\\ &= F(\phi(r))[1 - F(\phi(2r))] - [F(\phi(2r)) - F(\phi(r))]F(\phi(r))\end{aligned}$$

The above equation is expression of the trade-off faced by lenders who would like to adopt group lending to improve repayment rates. Of more relevance in my analysis is the first term which represents the effect of intra-group insurance. The term is the probability that one borrower will have a return above $\phi(2r)$, when the other has a return below $\phi(r)$. Under individual lending, a return below $\phi(r)$ would lead to default. Under joint liability lending, however, a borrower with a return above $\phi(2r)$ will not only repay his own loan but also the loan for the other borrower with a lower return. This form of insurance is a key factor in joint liability lending. The second term represents the negative spill over from individual default under joint liability. It is the probability that one borrower has a return between $\phi(2r)$ and $\phi(r)$ while the other has a return below $\phi(r)$. While under individual lending, the borrower with a return above $\phi(r)$ would repay, under joint liability, he/she may decide to default because the cost of repaying both loans exceeds the penalty of default. This is a form of strategic default that all joint liability lending institution would like to avoid.

From the forgoing discussion, mutual insurance can be said to be directly related to borrower returns (θ_i) and the cost of repayment (r), both of which determine the critical value. The two are of interest in this study because they vary substantially with loan and group characteristics. Nevertheless, this is only one side of the story as the framework emphasizes on the issue of project returns. In reality, there are situations where individuals may renege their insurance promises wilfully. This is particularly likely to occur in credit groups from Malawi, where cross-reporting of returns of successful peers to the lending institution doesn't take place. Under such circumstances, it is likely that more than project returns, other factors that have been highlighted related to group dynamics will influence the willingness of members to offer intra-group insurance.

In order to assess the probability of mutual insurance in group lending, I relate group specific characteristics which proxy, correlation of borrower returns as a measure of risk sharing ability, productivity, and variables that reflect the cost of insurance, with the *willingness* of group members to offer mutual insurance. In addition to these variables I also include the following variables: peer monitoring, peer pressure, dynamic incentives, and variables capturing incentive match or matching problems in loan demand and supply. The key hypothesis to be tested is that intra-group insurance is influenced by peer selection, peer monitoring, pre- existing social ties among group members and dynamic incentives.

4.6 The Impact of Credit on Adoption and the Agricultural Household Theory

Static household models that stress the role of pervasive risks, limited information, and imperfect markets on household's behavior have been widely used. Singh et al. (1986) note that predictions derived from these models differ markedly from those under a standard household model where separability between production and consumption decisions is assumed. Under separability, allocation of resources in production can be decided independently of consumption decisions. However, separability breaks down when there is a market failure such that production and consumption decisions need to be taken jointly. In agricultural production, expenditure and income profiles are markedly seasonal and thus the liquidity constraints in financing production and consumption can be particularly acute (de Janvry et al., 1999). This prompts households to adjust their income generating strategies and their expenditure patterns to bring the distance between the two profiles within the range of available credit.

Thus in this study I assume a static household model that links adoption of improved technologies with a growing season liquidity constraint. It is assumed that a household chooses between growing a local maize variety (*lm*) that is not subject to the growing season liquidity constraint and hybrid maize (*hm*) which is subject to the growing season liquidity constraint.

The household is assumed to be maximizing the following utility function:

$$\underset{c_{hm}c_{lm},c_m,c_l}{Max} U(c_{hm}, c_{lm}, c_m, c_l; z^h) \qquad (4.6.1)$$

where:

U is the utility function to be maximized,

c_{hm}, c_{lm}, c_m and c_l are quantities consumed of hybrid maize, local maize, manufactured good, and leisure, respectively.
z^h is a set of household characteristics that influence consumption

Subject to:

$$p_{xhm}q_{xhm} + p_m c_m + p_{hm}c_{hm} + p_{lm}c_{lm} = p_{hm}q_{hm} + p_{lm}q_{lm} + w(l_s) + K \qquad (4.6.2)$$

Liquidity constraint

$g(q_{hm}, q_{lm}, l_{lm}, l_{hm}, q_{xhm},; z^q) = 0$ production function

$l_s + l_{lm} + l_{hm} + c_l = E,$ time constraint

where:
q_{hm}, q_{lm} are quantities of hybrid maize and local maize produced , respectively
l_{lm}, l_{hm} and l_s are quantities of labor used in the production of local maize, hybrid maize, and labor sold out by the household, respectively
q_{xhm} is the quantity of extra inputs required for the production of hybrid maize, such as improved seed, pesticides, etc,
Z^q is a set of fixed factors in production and farm household specific characteristics that influence production,
p_{xhm} and w are input prices for inputs specific to hybrid maize and the wage rate on the labor market, respectively,
p_{hm} and p_{lm} are farm gate prices for hybrid maize and local maize.
p_m is the price for the manufactured good,
E is the total time endowment,
K is the liquidity from past savings, credit, and pre-harvest transfers.

In peasant economies with rare opportunities for off farm income, maximizing the consumption function is closely associated with maximizing farm profits which are then used to finance the consumption decisions. In this case it means maximizing profits from the production of hybrid maize and local maize. The maximization problem above yields the following Lagrangean function:

$$\begin{aligned} L &= U(c_{hm}, c_{lm}, c_m, c_l; z^h) \\ &+ \lambda_1 \{ p_{hm} q_{hm} + p_{lm} q_{lm} + w(l_s) + K - p_{xhm} q_{xhm} - p_m c_m - p_{hm} c_{hm} - p_{lm} c_{lm} \} \\ &\quad + \lambda_2 (g(q_{hm}, q_{lm}, l_{lm}, l_{hm}, q_{xhm}, ; z^q) + \lambda_3 (E - l_s - l_{lm} - l_{hm} - c_l) \end{aligned} \tag{4.6.3}$$

Assuming an interior solution, the maximization problem yields the following first order conditions:

$$\frac{\partial L}{\partial c_{hm}} = U_{hm} - \lambda_1 p_{hm} = 0 \tag{4.6.4}$$

$$\frac{\partial L}{\partial c_{lm}} = U_{lm} - \lambda_1 p_{lm} = 0 \tag{4.6.5}$$

$$\frac{\partial L}{\partial c_m} = U_m - \lambda_1 p_m = 0 \tag{4.6.6}$$

$$\frac{\partial L}{\partial c_l} = U_{cl} - \lambda_3 = 0 \tag{4.6.7}$$

$$\frac{\partial L}{\partial q_{xhm}} = -\lambda_1 p_{xhm} + \lambda_2 \frac{\partial g}{\partial q_{xhm}} = 0, \ \lambda_1 \succ 0 \tag{4.6.8}$$

$$\frac{\partial L}{\partial l_{hm}} = \lambda_2 \frac{\partial g}{\partial l_{hm}} - \lambda_3 = 0 \tag{4.6.9}$$

$$\frac{\partial L}{\partial l_{lm}} = \lambda_2 \frac{\partial g}{\partial l_{lm}} - \lambda_3 = 0 \tag{4.6.10}$$

λ_1 is a multiplier associated with the credit constraint. The multiplier represents an additional amount of inputs for the production of hybrid maize (q_{xhm}) that a farmer will purchase for each additional unit of cash or credit. This is valid only when the farmer fails to acquire optimum inputs required due to lack of cash. Thus it is only relevant to credit or liquidity constrained households. For unconstrained households the multiplier does not have an effect on their production decision. There are therefore two scenarios depending on whether the credit constraint is binding or not. First, I consider a case where there is no binding constraint on the amount which the household can borrow. Thus the credit constraint is not binding and therefore, $\lambda_1 = 0$. Under this scenario, the first order conditions for the optimum input requirements are given as follows

The optimum quantity of input q_{xhm} is given by:

$$\frac{\partial L}{\partial q_{xhm}} = \lambda_2 \frac{\partial g}{\partial q_{qxm}}, \ \lambda_1 = 0 \qquad (4.6.11)$$

$$q^u{}_{xhm} = \ q^u{}_{xhm}(p_{hm}, p_{lm}, p_{xhm}, z^q, E) \qquad (4.6.12)$$

The superscript u refers to the unconstrained case.

In the second scenario we have a household that can not borrow as much as it wants. The household is said to face a credit constraint $(\lambda_1 > 0)$. The first order Kuhn Tucker conditions under such a scenario are still based on the same objective function except that in this case the amount of credit K, is treated as one of the parameters that is exogenously determined by the lender. The first order condition for the interior solution is:

$$\frac{\partial L}{\partial q_{xhm}} = -\lambda_1 p_{xhm} + \lambda_2 \frac{\partial g}{\partial q_{xhm}} = 0, \lambda_1 \succ 0 \qquad (4.6.13)$$

since the constraint is binding I must solve the optimum quantities of q_{xhm} and λ_1 as follows:

$$q^c{}_{xhm} = \ q^c{}_{xhm}(p_{hm}, p_{lm}, p_{xhm}, z^q, E, K) \qquad (4.6.14)$$

The superscript c refers to the constrained case. *De* Janvry *et al.* (1992) used a similar theoretical framework to assess the effect of structural adjustment policies on the peasantry in Morocco. Vakis (2002) used an extension of the model to assess the effect of diversification on technology adoption among farming communities from Peru. The model is quite relevant to Malawi because in Malawi farmers pass through two seasons annually, thus the rainy season which is characterized by intense production activities and high capital requirements and the dry season when farmers have excess liquidity and less production activities. When farmers face liquidity constraints during the growing season, they will try to borrow from available sources to enable them invest in agricultural activities that give them high returns. However, when framers realize that they do not have access to any external sources of capital, they will avoid any attempts to invest in high return investments that may be capital intensive.

In the model presented above, the difference between the constrained and unconstrained regimes is that in the constrained case farmers are unable to buy optimal quantities of hybrid maize input q_{xhm}. The amount of credit, therefore, becomes an important determinant of the farmer's ability to adopt hybrid maize. The amount of hybrid maize input demanded, therefore, does not only depend on the price of maize and other inputs but also on the amount of credit (K) available to the household. The hypothesis to be empirically tested here is that, while access to credit (K) does not influence the adoption decision for the liquidity unconstrained farmers, it does so for the constrained.

4.7 Conclusion

The objective of this chapter was to highlight the basic conceptual framework and theoretical models upon which the analysis in this dissertation is based. Three separate frameworks were presented each for a specific objective being addressed. The application of these frameworks is not however restricted to the objectives being addressed in this dissertation. The risk sharing framework and the moral hazard framework, for example have been widely used in assessing repayment performance in a number of group lending programs. The agricultural household model presented in this chapter can also be used to assess other policy impacts such as programs that influence the smallholder farmers' time preference, poverty alleviation through the provision of seasonal agricultural credit aimed at reducing seasonal cash constraints and consumption smoothing, as well as policies that aim at reducing the cost of both inorganic and organic inputs, such as direct input subsidies (Tchale, 2005). Each of the models presented seeks to test specific hypotheses that will be tested in the empirical chapters.

The moral hazard model has been adopted in the empirical chapters to test the extent to which self selection, peer monitoring, sanctions, peer pressure and dynamic incentives can be used to reduce the incidence of moral hazard. The model on intra-group insurance seeks to test the hypothesis that intra-group insurance is likely to be strong in groups with strong social ties, with small variation in loan size among group members, where there is a low correlation in output and where group members attach high value to access to loans from the same microfinance institution.

The analysis on household impact seeks to show that liquidity constraints may considerably reduce the capacity of constrained households to seize opportunities of increasing production in response to higher prices or improved technologies with high returns. As noted by *de* Janvry *et al.* (1999), the ability of farmers to benefit from higher prices and higher return technologies offered by some policy changes depends on the relaxation of the liquidity constraint, confirming the fundamental importance of credit component to accompany policies of this nature if they are to induce supply response. The empirical chapter is, therefore, aimed at testing the hypothesis that access to credit will influence adoption among credit constrained households, but it will have no effect among unconstrained households.

5 DETERMINANTS OF MORAL HAZARD IN JOINT LIABILITY LENDING PROGRAMS IN MALAWI

5.1 Introduction

Imperfect information causes at least four problems in credit markets, namely, adverse selection, moral hazard, lack of insurance and lack of enforcement. It is now common knowledge that, moral hazard, coupled with the lack of collateral by the poor is the key reason why credit markets fail for them. The problem of moral hazard may arise when individuals engage in risk sharing under conditions such that their privately taken actions affect the probability distribution of the outcome. It occurs in a principal-agent relationship when actions taken by an agent are not pareto-optimal (Holmstrom, 1979).

Joint Liability Lending (JLL) is celebrated as a contractual innovation that has achieved the apparent miracle of enabling previously marginalized borrowers to lift themselves up by their own bootstraps by creating 'social collateral' to replace the missing physical collateral that excluded them from access to more traditional forms of finance (Conning 2000). Nevertheless, the problem with joint liability lending programs is that the poor are given access to credit without collateral, and in the event of default, they can not be punished beyond a mere denial of future access to credit. This form of *limited liability* can induce borrowers to take risky decisions.

In Malawi moral hazard is common occurrence among credit groups. Diagne *et al.* (2000) note that the main reason for default in credit groups from the Malawi Rural Finance Company (MRFC) is the unwillingness to repay (moral hazard) and not the inability to repay. The unwillingness to repay accounted for 25 percent of all defaults in MRFC credit groups. The high incidence of moral hazard has a negative impact on the sustainability of microfinance in Malawi. Despite the magnitude of moral hazard and its potential negative consequences on the microfinance industry in Malawi, no study has been conducted to assess the driving forces behind its high incidence. Thus, the objective of this chapter is to examine the extent to which moral hazard occurs in credit groups and analyze determinants of the likelihood of its occurrence. It is an attempt to contribute to moral hazard literature by testing the extent to which peer selection, peer monitoring, social ties, peer pressure, dynamic incentives and matching problems influence the incidence of moral hazard. I adopt a theoretical framework presented earlier which was proposed by Ghatak and Guinane (1999) with some extensions proposed by Diagne (1998), Paxton (1996) and de Aghion (1999). I use data from Malawi, collected by the International Food Policy Research Institute (IFPRI) in 1999. The data comes from 99 credit groups, all of which are beneficiaries of the Malawi Rural Finance Company's (MRFC) farm and non-farm loans.

The next section presents a review of moral hazard in microfinance in Malawi. The third section presents the specification of the empirical moral hazard model. Section 4 presents the data and the variables used in the analysis of moral hazard. In section 5 I present and discuss results, while section 6 concludes.

5.2 Moral Hazard and Repayment Capacity among Microfinance Clients in Malawi

As noted by Burritt (2006) despite what appears to be a large potential market, real or "effective" demand for loans may be constrained by both the capacity and willingness of borrowers to repay. More importantly, demand is constrained by the limited range of products that correspond to the risk profile and production patterns of potential borrowers. Burritt notes 5 factors that influence both the capacity and willingness of microfinance clients in Malawi to repay the loan as follows:

The capacity is affected by the macroeconomic instability that creates uncertainty about prices for inputs and what is produced, particularly for commodities like tobacco, tea, and sugar. The Malawi economy is highly unstable, largely resulting from currency devaluations as well as unstable weather conditions, both of which lead to losses among borrowers.

High real interest rates, as well as high transaction costs in rural areas work against the ability and willingness to repay. Most microfinance institutions are required to offer loans at market rates. However given the macroeconomic environment it is almost impossible for entrepreneurs to realize profits from their investments that would enable them repay their loan, while expanding their businesses.

There is an absence of appropriate financial services that meet the risk management needs of borrowers and institutions. In most cases microfinance institutions are restricted to the provision of credit services; while borrowers may need other services such as insurance and savings services than help them smooth their consumption.

There is a predominant use of business profits to meet households' immediate needs as a coping strategy rather than to reinvest in businesses as a profit-maximizing strategy.

There is a relatively low level of revenue generation, or turnover. Most microfinance clients have small businesses whose turn over is usually low. In addition a GEMINI study (2000) revealed that most entrepreneurs complained of lack of effective demand for their microfinance products.

Considering that Malawi's economy is dominated by smallholder agricultural production, the capacity of farmers to repay principal and interest is highly sensitive to farmers' yields and the prices of both agricultural inputs and outputs. Evans and Ford (2003) show that low repayment rates historically have been linked to the decline in the profitability of maize due to devaluation of the kwacha and the rise in the prices of agricultural inputs.

Many small producers complain that revenue and profits are also limited by poor access to markets. Borrowers may be eliminated from the credit market when their returns are inadequate to make both interest and principal payments. In an IFPRI study, Diagne and Zeller (2001) note that during the 1993-1996 production seasons households that took loans realized lower net crop incomes than non-borrowers due to costly in-kind fertilizer products, low yields, and the cost of credit. In an attempt to reduce the effect of production and yield risks faced by producers and microfinance institutions, government has previously implemented policies that allowed producers and institutions to manage such risks such as setting minimum price guarantees by state-owned marketing boards, but as noted by Bryla *et al.* (2001) such attempts have proven difficult to sustain, costly and inefficient. In a study by Diagne *et al.* (2000) it was revealed that the rigidity in repayment policies exercised by some microfinance programs is partly to blame for the defaults. Borrowers complained that repayment schedules, did not match their own cash flows, making it difficult for them to meet their payment obligations.

As noted earlier, the willingness to repay largely depends on the incentives offered by the contract that borrowers sign with the lending institutions. Among the key incentives is the assurance for further credit access conditional upon repayment from the same institutions. As noted by Gonzalez-Vega (2005), institutional vulnerability and credit rationing due to undercapitalized operations in developing countries like Malawi, may affect borrower's perception of the sustainability of services and subsequently their willingness to repay. Willingness to repay may also be affected by the lack of legislature in the judiciary system that makes it difficult for microfinance service providers to enforce repayment obligations. The emergence of several microfinance initiatives sometimes with conflicting or political objectives has largely contributed to the confusion on the parts of borrowers about whether they are receiving loans or grants or whether they have obligations to repay. A study on the causes of loan default in the MRFC Tikolore program in Ntchisi, (Evans, 1997) revealed that political motives were the major cause of loan default in the district. Farmers were unwilling to repay their loans because they were told the loans were supposed to be grants. Microfinance institutions in Malawi, therefore, are in a continuous process to explore innovations that may enable them to accurately assess both willingness and capacity to repay although the key constraint is the high amounts of non-profit loans offered by non-government organizations usually at very low interest rates which sometimes send conflicting messages to clients that live in the same communities.

In addition to efforts by the Microfinance institutions, the Government of Malawi through the Malawi poverty Reduction Strategy (MPRS) recognizes the problem of high default rates among the low-income credit clientele as one of the constraints to the development of a sustainable microfinance industry in Malawi. To address the problem, the MPRS proposes the introduction of tougher and more efficient legal sanctions to ensure that borrowers make an effort to repay the debts. The creation of credit reference bureaus is proposed as a key step towards arresting the default problems. The MPRS also acknowledges the need for the strengthening of enforcement legislation so that the legal process of dealing with defaulters is speeded up. The government proposes the promotion of the formation farmer clubs and co-operatives in order to reduce problems of identity and collateral. Significant funding and effort is also proposed for the formation of grass-root organizations such as farmer groups and associations in Malawi in an effort to reduce transaction costs of delivering financial services and as a way of reducing transactional costs of assessing the willingness and capacity of individuals to repay their loans.

5.3 Empirical Model

In this study, the incidence of moral hazard in a group was captured by asking the group leader whether or not some group members had misused borrowed funds and whether or not some members had wilfully decided not to repay after getting enough returns from their investments on which the loaned funds had been used. Groups, in which some members had misused loaned funds or where some members defaulted wilfully, were considered to have experienced moral hazard.

Guided by the theoretical framework presented earlier, variables that are associated with the incidence of moral hazard are identified from the data set. The empirical strategy focuses on testing whether or not particular covariates, vector $X = (X_1 .... X_n)$ are associated with the incidence of moral hazard. The probability of moral hazard in a specific group *g* as a function of covariates can be written as

$$P(H^g = 1 \mid X^g) \qquad (5.1)$$

The moral hazard model $P(H^g = 1 \mid X^g)$ can thus be written as a function $P(\beta' X^g)$, where β is an $M\chi 1$ vector of parameters and X^g is an $M\chi 1$ vector containing group g´s values for the M covariates. The likelihood of a group reporting the incidence of moral hazard is assumed to be determined by a latent variable y* which can be expressed as follows in a regression relationship:

$$y_i^* = \beta'_i \mathrm{X}_i + \mu_i \qquad (5.2)$$

where X is a vector of characteristics, which, it is hypothesized that they affect the likelihood of the occurrence of moral hazard, β'_i is a vector of coefficients for variables associated with moral hazard. In practice y* is unobservable. What we observe is a dummy variable defined as

$$y = 1 \qquad \text{if } \; y_i^* > 0 \qquad (5.3)$$
$$y = 0 \qquad \text{otherwise}$$

From the relations 5.2 and 5.3 we get

$$\Pr ob(y_i = 1) = \Pr ob(u_i > -\beta' X_i) \qquad (5.4)$$
$$= 1 - F(-\beta' X_i)$$

In this case the observed values of *y* are just realizations of a binomial process with probabilities given by (5.4) (Maddala, 1997). Hence the likelihood function is

$$L = \prod_{y_i=0} F(-\beta' X_i) \prod_{y_i=1} [1 - F(-\beta' X_i)]. \qquad (5.5)$$

The functional form of *F* in (5.5) will depend on the assumptions made about μ_i in (5.2).

In this study I assume that μ_i are $IN(0, \delta^2)$. Because of this assumption of a cumulative normal distribution of the error terms, the estimation of determinants of moral hazard is done using the Probit model. The moral hazard model was specified as follows:

$$\text{Prob}(y = 1 \mid x) = \alpha + \sum_{i=1}^{Pr=2} \beta_{1i} x_{1i} + \sum_{i=1}^{Scr=4} \beta_{2i} x_{2i} + \sum_{i=1}^{pm=3} \beta_{3i} x_{3i} + \sum_{i=1}^{st=6} \beta_{4i} x_{4i} \sum_{i=1}^{pp=2} \beta_{5i} x_{5i} + \sum_{i=1}^{Dinc=2} \beta_{6i} x_{6i} +$$
$$+ \sum_{i=1}^{Im=3} \beta_{7i} x_{7i} + \sum_{i=1}^{Ctr=8} \beta_{8i} x_{8i} + \mu_i \qquad (5.6)$$

Where:

x_1´s are a set of variables (Pr=2) that measure group production factors
x_2´s are a set of variables (Scr=4) that measure the quality of screening
x_3´s are a set of variables (pm=3) that measure the quality of peer monitoring
x_4´s are a set of variables (St=5) that measure the strength of social ties in the group
x_5´s are a set of variables (pp=2) that measure the quality of peer pressure
x_6´s are a set of variables (Dinc=2) that measure the quality of dynamic incentives
x_7´s are a set of variables (Im=3) that proxy the degree of incentive match
x_8´s are a set of variables (Ctr=8) that are control variables

5.4 Data

The study is based on data collected by the International Food Policy Research Institute (IFPRI) in 1999 from 99 MRFC credit groups located in 4 of the 27 satellite offices of MRFC. I was involved in the IFPRI survey as a research assistant. My role was to supervise data collection, data entry and data cleaning. In addition, I was involved in writing a preliminary report of the survey which included a documentation of anecdotal stories from 36 credit groups. A detailed structured questionnaire covering the formation, composition and repayment history of the group was administered to each respondent. The questionnaire specifically included questions aimed at quantifying the degree of information asymmetry within each group and the extent to which peer selection, peer monitoring and peer pressure had been taking place. Also collected using the questionnaire was the extent to moral hazard occurred in credit groups. A brief discussion of descriptive statistics is presented below.

5.4.1 Formation structure and conduct of the groups

The sample consisted of both farm and non-farm credit groups. As indicated in Figure 5.1, the majority were tobacco credit groups (47%), followed by the non-farm business groups (28%). Maize and cotton groups accounted for 17 percent and 8 percent of the sample, respectively. These four types of credit groups belong to three different joint liability programs operated by MRFC: MRFC seasonal agricultural loans, Mudzi seasonal agricultural loans, and Mudzi non-farm businesses. There are significant differences in the design, orientation, and target population of the programs. There are also significant differences in the design and operation between the groups in the seasonal agricultural programs depending on the type of crop for which the loans are intended (tobacco, maize, cotton and rice (Diagne *et al.*, 2000).

Based on information from group leaders, results in Table 5.1 indicate that only 25 percent of the groups were formed by ordinary village residents on their own (through peer selection). The agricultural extension workers (Field Assistants) and the Credit Assistants formed 44 percent and 16 percent of the groups, respectively8. The importance of the FA's in the formation of the groups is consistent with the policy followed by MRFC with respect to group formation.

[8] Diagne *et al.* (2000), emphasize that Agricultural Extension workers, also known as Field Assistants in Malawi, play a very important role in the formation of MRFC credit groups. For planning and administration purposes, Malawi is divided into Extension Planning Areas (EPAs) headed by an Agricultural Development Officer (ADO). MRFC field credit offices (which are the first contact points of borrowers) are located in the EPA offices and handle both the farm and non-farm groups. In all EPAs both the Credit Assistant and the Field Assistant work under the direct supervision of the ADO although the first is a paid employee of MRFC, while the Field Assistant and the ADO are employees of the Ministry of Agriculture.

The policy consists of letting the agricultural extension workers, who are under the ministry of Agriculture and are called Field Assistants (FA) in Malawi, identify and propose to its Credit Assistants (CA) the groups wanting to borrow from MRFC. The CAs then perform the screening and undertake the group training activities. It is generally assumed from the perspective of MRFC that groups identified and proposed by the FAs have been endogenously formed through a peer selection process. It is, however, not clear as to the extent to which such groups whose formation was initiated by FAs and CAs can be considered to be endogenously self formed. Anecdotal stories during the field survey, however, indicated that FAs exerted a lot of influence on who to be included in the groups. In a number of cases FAs included friends and relatives in the credit groups which led to group default in some cases. It appeared, however, that the CAs were usually more objective when selecting members in a group than the FAs as stories of default due to biased selection were rarely reported in groups formed by CAs. Village chiefs formed about 11 percent of the credit groups. In some cases chiefs were also reported to be involved in the same malpractices of including relatives and friends during group formation. In addition although chiefs only formed 11 percent of the groups, their influence is also felt in groups that were formed by the FAs or CAs because as indicated in Table 5.1, in about 24 percent of the groups, village chiefs had called the FAs/CAS to the village to come and form the groups. Ordinary villagers were reported to have called the FAs/CAs in only 17 percent of the groups.

Figure 5.1 Types of credit groups (in percentage):

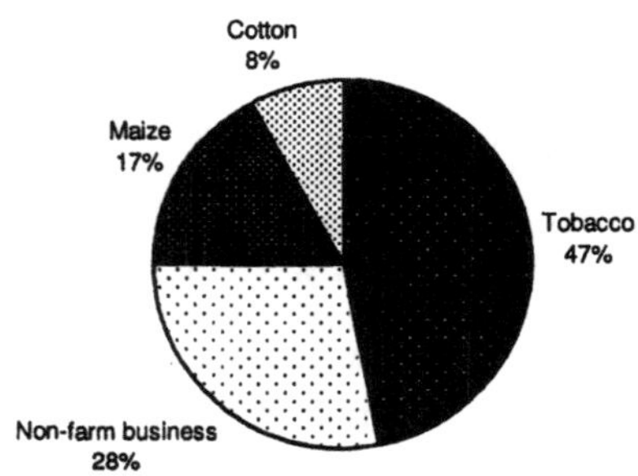

Source: Own calculation from RDD/IFPRI 1999 Rural Finance Survey

Due to the nature of their main job, FAs appear to have more influence in initiating the formation of tobacco groups (58%) compared to maize groups (25%), cotton groups (25%) and business groups (39%). In contrast, the CAs are more influential in the formation of non-farm business groups (25%) compared to tobacco (11%), cotton (15%) and maize (19%).

Table 5.1 Group formation by type of group

Characteristic	Tobacco (n=46)	Maize (n=16)	Cotton/Rice (n=8)	Non-farm business (n=28)	Total (n=99)
Who initiated the group					
Village chief (%)	9	6	25	14	11
Ordinary village residents(%)	22	44	38	14	25
MRFC credit assistant (%)	11	19	13	25	16
Field Assistant (extension) (%)	58	25	25	39	44
Other	0	6	25	7	3
Who called the FA/CA					
Nobody	58	47	71	61	58
Village Chief	25	37	11	15	24
Ordinary villagers	13	14	18	24	17
Age of the group (years)	4	5	8	3	4
Evidence of screening (%)	43	51	31	42	43
Average number rejected	4	4	3	4	4
Previously affiliates of other NGOs	20	13	25	57	30

Source: Own calculation from RDD/IFPRI 1999 Rural Finance Survey

The issue of screening was addressed by asking group leaders if some individuals that had wanted to join the group had their applications turned down. Results indicate that about 43 percent of the groups showed some evidence of screening, as indicated by the positive number of membership applications rejected when the group was being formed. On average about 4 members per group were rejected. Screening is more evident in maize groups (51%) than in tobacco (43%), non-farm business (42%) and cotton (31%). The evidence of high levels of screening among maize groups may be attributed to the fact that maize groups lack a built-in mechanism for self selection because maize is a main staple food in Malawi and has to be grown by almost all farmers. On the other hand the capital and labor intensive nature of tobacco allows for the self selection process to start earlier. About 30 percent of the groups had been previously affiliated to other credit institutions before joining MRFC.Thus despite the screening process members from past failed credit programs where loans may not have been rigorously collected, leading to default were part of the existing MRFC groups. A matter of fact according to Diagne *et al.* (2000) about 80 percent of the groups surveyed included past members of SACA or another NGO. Overall about 41 percent of group members were either past SACA members or members from another NGO. The nature in which group formation takes place is evidence of how difficult it can be to exclude risky borrowers from groups since village chiefs or other local authorities can impose themselves to the groups either directly or indirectly through their relatives and friends. Potentially good borrowers are usually left with no choice except joining a group that is full of risky borrowers for purposes of receiving credit.

5.4.2 Group composition and social ties

Questions on group composition mainly focused on homogeneity of groups in terms of wealth, social status gender and kinship. Results in Table 5.2 indicate that 62 percent of the groups contained members that were slightly heterogeneous in terms of wealth while only 21 percent indicated that the group members were very heterogeneous. The remaining 17 percent indicated that group members were homogenous. With regards to gender composition, 55 percent of the groups were mixed with about 66 percent women composition.

Table 5.2 Group composition and social ties

	Tobacco (n=46)	Maize (n=16)	Cotton (n=8)	Non-farm business (n=28)	Total (n=99)
Group wealth distribution					
About the same (%)	13	27	59	11	17
Slightly different (%)	65	60	25	65	62
Very different (%)	23	13	16	24	21
Group with mixed gender (%)	62	77	91	25	55
Percent women in a group (%)	50	56	26	100	66
Groups with members from Village authority (%)	93	86	76	89	90
% of member from the village Authority's family (%)	25	21	15	13	20
Groups with family members from CA or FA family (%)	10	2	12	8	8
Number of villages from which members come	3	2	3	2	3
Groups with members from PAST SACA or another NGO (%)	80	95	73	65	78
% members from PAST SACA or another NGO	38	73	43	26	41
Evidence of sanctions (members excluded for default)	38	23	8	22	29
Groups with new members admitted (%)	18	51	26	22	26

Source: Own calculation from RDD/IFPRI 1999 Rural Finance Survey

As regards the social status, 90 percent of the groups included members from families of their respective village authorities (village chiefs or other traditional authorities). About 8% included members from families of FAs or CAs. Groups are generally composed of members from more than one village. In about 21 percent of the groups where members came from more than one village the average number of villages from which members came was 3. About 78 percent of the groups contained members from previous credit programs. In general PASTSACA members accounted for 41 percent of the group members. A good proportion of groups exercise sanctioning (members are excluded for default) as witnessed by 29 percent of the groups in which members were excluded for default. As a result of the exclusion of defaulting members, groups allow new members to join. As indicated in Table 5.2, 26 percent of the groups admitted new members in their groups during the respective loan cycle.

5.4.3 Peer monitoring and peer pressure

Peer monitoring is an important aspect of joint liability lending. In the IFPRI study peer monitoring was assessed by examining the extent to which members have access to information and by assessing the extent to which group members are willing to engage in peer monitoring activities to enforce proper loan use and report misuse of loans. The extent of peer monitoring was also assessed by observing rules followed by groups. One such rule that directly relates to monitoring is a rule on joint enterprise ownership. Groups were asked whether they had any rules that encouraged joint ownership of enterprises.

Table 5.3 shows the extent of group members' general knowledge of the composition of groups. As can be seen, 14 percent of the members did not have any general knowledge of the sizes and demographic composition of their respective groups. Also about 15 percent lacked knowledge about the sizes and terms of their group loans. Lack of knowledge on the general characteristics of the group is taken as an indication that members are not actively involved in monitoring. The results also reveal that even among members that claimed to know something about the characteristics in question there was a wide variation in their responses regarding group characteristics indicating that information flow among members belonging to the same group was limited to some extent. The average number of group meetings attended by the CA in each group per year was 14. This translates into slightly more than a visit per year per month. Field Assistants were said to be more influential in their monitoring activities because of the nature of their work. The average number of meetings held by members without the presence of the CA was 21 per year while the average number of non-meeting follow-up visits to the chairpersons and defaulting members by the CA was 11 per year.

Peer pressure was defined to take place when members complained to the village authorities or took (threatened to take) punitive action against defaulters. As indicated in Table 5.3, peer pressure was applied in 39 percent of all groups before or after the due date. Although peer pressure was applied in 57 percent of the groups where loans were partially paid before due date, it was only successful in inducing some defaulters to repay in 37 percent of the groups. This shows how less frequent peer pressure takes in joint liability groups from Malawi and how more likely it is to fail than succeed in inducing defaulters to repay their loans.

Table 5.3 Extent of peer monitoring and peer pressure

Characteristic	Tobacco (n=46)	Maize (n=16)	Cotton (n=8)	Non-farm business (n=28)	Total (n=99)
Peer Monitoring					
Proportion with no general knowledge of composition (%)	8	34	32	13	14
Proportion with no knowledge of total	11	25	29	16	15
Group loan size and terms of the loan					
Number of meting by CA per year	14	13	16	16	14
Number of meetings without CA	20	19	28	22	21
Number of non-meeting visits by CA	11	11	11	10	11
Rules encourage joint enterprise Ownership	66	53	50	43	56
Peer pressure					
Groups where peer pressure was applied after or before due date(%)	35	54	39	37	39
Peer pressure before due date (fully paid groups) (%)	17	29	11	18	19
Peer pressure before due date (not fully paid groups) (%)	55	87	45	47	57
Peer pressure applied successfully (%)	23	80	45	36	37

Source: Own calculation from RDD/IFPRI 1999 Rural Finance Survey

5.4.4 Group repayment outcomes and moral hazard

Table 5.4 shows ex-post group repayment outcomes. In general 23 percent of the total loan was defaulted. Delinquency rates were lowest among tobacco groups (14%) mainly due to the fact that MRFC makes direct loan deductions from tobacco sales at the point of sale. The delinquency rates were highest among cotton (42%), and non-farm business groups (31%). With regards to group repayment status, results indicate that 51 percent of the groups were partially paid while 49 percent were fully paid groups. There are no significant differences in group repayment status across the four types of groups.

Table 5.4 Ex-post group repayment outcomes and incidence of moral hazard

Characteristics	Tobacco (n=46)	Maize (n=16)	Cotton (n=8)	Non-farm business (n=28)	(n=99)
Delinquency rates (%) of total loan value	14	27	42	31	23
Group repayment status by due date (%)					
Fully paid group	51	50	0	53	49
Partially paid group	49	50	100	47	51
Reasons for default (%)					
Willful default (able but unwilling)	25	36	17	21	25
Failure caused by natural disasters	20	36	25	7	18
Failure cause by mismanagement	8	8	39	24	16
Not enough profit	20	14	24	36	24
Theft	4	0	0	1	2
Family problems	5	0	2	4	4
Illness	2	0	0	3	2
Death of borrower	4	0	1	1	2
Others	13	6	2	2	7

Source: Own calculation from RDD/IFPRI 1999 Rural Finance Survey

As regards the reasons for default, twenty five percent defaulted wilfully. Wilful default occurs when individuals have enough return to repay the loan but are unwilling to pay which is a form of *ex-post* moral hazard. Loan default due to miss-management (*ex-ante* moral hazard) was reported in 16 percent of the groups. This gives a total of 41 percent of the loan defaults caused by moral hazard. The incidence of moral hazard is highest among maize groups (36%) implying that they probably lack some mechanism of enforcing screening and repayment. Other major causes of default include low profits (24%) and failure caused by natural disasters (18%). The high incidence of moral hazard is used as a justification in this study to assess factors that can be used to explain such high incidences.

5.4.5 Description of variables in the model

Dependent variable

The dependent variable is dichotomous taking the value of one if the group reported the incidence of moral hazard and it is zero otherwise. The incidence of moral hazard in each credit group was captured by asking the chairperson of each group about whether some members had defaulted wilfully, or whether they had misused loan funds that were meant for an investment. Normally, group leaders know the behaviour of all members in the group and thus I expect the information they provide to be reliable. Following this question, it was possible to observe both *ex post* and *ex ante* moral hazard. From the 99 credit groups, 42 groups reported some incidence of moral hazard. It should be pointed out, however, that not all moral hazard leads to group default as members may contribute to pay the defaulters' loan.

Explanatory variables

From the theoretical framework discussed earlier, the empirical specification is based on 8 categories of explanatory variables whose full descriptions and a priori expectations of their effect on moral hazard are defined below. The explanatory variables in the model include screening, peer monitoring variables, variables that capture the extent of social ties, peer pressure and sanctions. In addition to these variables I use this study to test the significance of extra variables, which have been reported in literature as having a potential for inducing or mitigating moral hazard behaviour among borrowers. Such additional variables are in the following categories: production related factors, dynamic incentives and variables that capture matching problems. Descriptive statistics of the explanatory variables are presented in Table 5.5.

Table 5.5 Descriptive statistics of regression variables and their expected effects

Variables	Description	Mean	Exp sign
Dependent variable			
HAZARD(1=yes) 0=otherwise	Whether some members willfully defaulted or misused the loan	0.42	
Independent variables			
Production factors			
AVGLAND	Average land holding of group members in hectares	3.17	-
EDUCATION	Average years of formal education of group members	4.72	-
Screening			

Table 5.6 (continued)

SCREEN	Whether some individuals who wanted to join the group rejected	0.439	-
FASCREEN	Group was formed by the Agricultural extension worker (1=yes, 0=no)	0.46	-
PEERSELECT	Whether group was initiated by peers (1=yes, 0=no)	0.241	-
VHSCREEN	Group was formed by the Village headman (1=yes, 0=no)	0.12	-+
Peer monitoring			
JOINTENTERP	Members have joint enterprises (1=have joint enterprises)	0.6	-
GCOMPNAI	Percentage of group members not knowing group composition	0.066	+
GLONCNAI	Percentage of member not knowing loan characteristics		+
Social ties			
COWEALTHOMO	An index of wealth heterogeneity (1=Group is homogenous)	0.14	-
VILLAGENUMBE	Number of villages from which members come	2.76	+
PMFAMVG	At least one member is from the family of a village headman (1=yes)	0.82	-+
POLITCLAN	Number of members from the clan of a politician	0.61	-+
CHAIRFAMILY	Number of members from the family of club chair person	1.50	-+
Peer pressure			
PRESUDUEDATE	Whether group exerted pressure before due date (1=yes)	0.14	-
LEFEXCMG	Number of members that were excluded from group (sanctions)	0.27	-
Dynamic Incentive			
CONTRIBPAY	Whether would be willing to pay full cost of defaulters loan (1=yes, 0=no)	0.46	-
PAYPENATY	Would only be willing to pay ten percent penalty	0.37	+
PAST SACA	At least one member was from past failed credit programs (1=yes, 0=no)	0.78	+
Incentive Match			
NEWMMBAVG	Number of new members in the group	1.41	+
LONCYCLE	The loan cycle for which loan was received (1-5)	2.74	+
Control Variables			
GPSIZE	Number of members at the start of the season in a credit group	16.84	-+
CREDLIMIT	Average credit limit in a group per individual	4642	+
MAIZE	Dummy for maize credit group (1=maize,0=others	0.19	-+
COTTON	Dummy for cotton credit group (1=cotton,0=otherwise)	0.04	-+
NON-FARM	Dummy for non-farm credit group (1=non-farm 0=otherwise)	0.30	-+

Source: Own calculation from RDD/IFPRI 1999 Rural Finance Survey

a) Production related factors

Following Ahlin and Townsend (2003) I include factors of production in the model. The intuition is that higher production increases the payoff of safe projects relative to risky projects subsequently leading to the softening of the moral hazard problem. For this study I use two variables to capture factors of production, namely, the land holding of group members in acres, (AVGLAND) and the average years of education of the group members (EDUCATION). I expect a negative sign for all the production related variables. Thus, I expect moral hazard incidence to decline with the increase in the level of production factors. This is because highly productive groups are more likely to get payoffs that are higher than the critical values to repay both their loan and that of any defaulting members.

In concurrence with this line of thinking, Holmstrom (1979) in his paper on moral hazard and observability shows that default penalties decrease with the increase in payoffs such that the incentive for moral hazard also decreases with a decline in penalty. Besides, it is more likely that some members in less productive groups, will not get enough returns (above the critical value for repayment to occur) to repay their loan, which will induce other members who have enough returns to avoid paying their loan too (strategic default).

b) Screening

The following variables were considered as proxies for the extent of screening: SCREEN is a variable which measures whether or not there are some non-members that were rejected by the group when they wanted to join the group. In addition there are three variables that capture the extent to which self selection is taking place during the group formation process. The variable PEERSELECT is used to capture whether or not a group was self-formed by the members. Ghatak (1999b) shows how adverse selection problems can be solved through group lending schemes that provide incentives for similar types to group together through self-selection. Peer selection is thus seen as key to improving repayment. I expect that the likelihood of incidence of moral hazard will be low among groups that are self-formed.

However, the implementation group lending with joint liability can be affected by a number of institutional and social cultural values in the communities. While the ideal situation requires group formation through the self-selection process, it may not be possible under certain conditions. In this survey, for example, less than a third of the groups were formed by ordinary village residents (self-selection or peer selection), while the rest were formed either by the village chiefs or by the agricultural officers and credit assistants. In this regard I include two extra variables to capture the extent of screening as follows: FASCREEN and VHSCREEN capturing the formation of groups by the extension workers and the village chief, respectively. All screening variables are dummies. I expect peer selection to have a negative impact on the incidence of moral hazard. However the impact of the two other screening variables is undetermined as it depends on the quality of screening and the influence that leaders have on the group.

c) Peer monitoring

Following Stiglitz (1990), Conning (1999) and de Aghion(1999) I test the significance of peer monitoring variables in the moral hazard model. I construct peer monitoring indicators following Diagne (1998) who notes that in order for peer monitoring to be an effective substitute to the lender's own monitoring activities, group members must: 1) have better access to relevant information and 2) be willing to engage in peer monitoring activities to enforce proper loan use or report any incidence of moral hazard. The survey used two methods to obtain evidence of the two components.

First, I capture the proportion of members responding "I don't know to specific questions on group composition and loan characteristic variables. The percentage of members from each group indicating that they lack knowledge of the group and loan characteristics is taken as an a measure of poor access to relevant information and the quality of information flow within groups, respectively.

As described above the variable GCOMPDNI measures the percent of group members not knowing group composition, while GLONCDNI measures the proportion of group members that don't know the characteristics of the loan. With regards to loan characteristics the variable captured the knowledge of sizes, duration and interest rates. Both variables are assumed to be good indicators of monitoring. I expect the likelihood of moral hazard to increase with the proportion of individuals in a group reporting that they don't know their group composition and loan characteristics.

Second, the survey captured the extent of monitoring by asking members whether they owned joint enterprise at group level (PMJOINTENT). This is a dummy variable and it is equal 1 when it is reported that at least some members have joint enterprises within the group, and 0, otherwise. I expect that the incidence of moral hazard will be lower in groups that have joint enterprises due the effect of peer monitoring

d) Social ties and social capital

Coleman (1993) observes that social capital functions as a source of social control. In concurrence with this notion Olomola (2000) notes that through social homogeneity, rule enforcement, and trust can be reinforced, both of which will enhance social capital. Olomola observes that the capacity to enforce rules (social control) in groups where members are socially homogenous is higher than in groups with membership heterogeneity. The proposition, leads to a presumption that groups that are homogenous in terms of wealth, social status or kinship should have lower default rates than heterogeneous groups. Floro and Yotopolos (1991) show how the success of group lending can be attributed to its ability to harness social ties between borrowers to improve loan repayment. This is based on the presumption that people that are close in terms of social ties know each other better and are more likely to be averse to harming each other through default. It is for this reason that most joint liability lending institutions will encourage homogenous group formation in terms of social status and wealth. Nonetheless, other studies such as one by Zeller (1998) find that to the contrary, social homogeneity leads to repayment problems among credit groups from Madagascar. In this study I use five variables to capture the magnitude of social ties within a borrowing group. VILLAGENUMBER measures the number of villages from which group members come. The larger the number of villages relative to the group sizes the smaller the social ties. This variable can also be a measure of the ease of monitoring. Groups composed of members from the same village are likely to know each other better and much easier to monitor than members coming from many villages. This variable is expected to have a positive sign.

PMFAMVG measures the presence of some members that come from the clan or family of a village headman in a group. The village chiefs have considerable influence on the operations of seasonal loans because of the MRFC requirements for their signatures before the fertilizer loan packages are delivered to club officials. The presence, therefore, of a village chief in the group or indeed his/her relative will have significant effects on the quality of interactions within the group. Considering the potential influence of the village chief on the behavior of group members, I expect that moral hazard will be low if the chief is honest and high if the chief is dishonest as other members would want to default when they see that the chief has defaulted. However I don't capture the extent of honest by the village chief. As such the expected sign for this variable is undetermined.

POLITCLAN measures the presence in a group of members that are from the clan of a politician. Political leaders in Malawi have a significant impact on the way loan are perceived by the borrowers and this can have a significant impact on moral hazard behavior. The collapse in 1994 of a government administered credit program, the Smallholder Agricultural Credit Administration (SACA) was mainly attributed to the political influence. Politicians were blamed for sending conflicting messages to the borrowers during their political campaigns, such that most borrowers believed that the loans were donations from government. I, therefore, expect some political influence on groups that have social ties with politicians, although I don't have a predetermined expectation as the type of influence will depend on the honesty of the politician in consideration.

CHAIRFAMILY represents the number of group members that belong to the family of a group chair person. Considering the strength of influence that the chairperson has on group members I expect that such influence could have implications on moral hazard. Nevertheless, the expected effect on moral hazard is undetermined because it depends on the character and values of the chairperson.

e) Peer pressure and sanctions

The existence of peer pressure was captured by asking group leaders whether members in a group ever exerted pressure on their peers before and after the due date of the loan repayment. Active peer pressure was said to exist when members complained to the village authorities or threatened to take punitive action against defaulters. The way the question was phrased implies that peer pressure may only be captured in groups that had default problems. A theoretical paper by Diagne (1998) predicts that peer pressure should be relevant only in groups that are heterogeneous in the incentive compatibility of the dynamic incentive constraints of its members. This only occurs in groups that are heterogeneous in risk. However, in order to reduce that bias I only focus on peer pressure before the due date of the loan (PRESUDUEDATE). I expect peer pressure to have a negative impact of the incidence of moral hazard in the group.

In addition, the presence of sanctions in the group was captured as an extra variable called LEFEXCMG. This variable captures the number of members that were excluded from the group in the previous loan cycle as a result of loan default or non-cooperative behavior. I assume that this provides a picture on the extent to which sanctions are implemented among groups. I expect that the likelihood of moral hazard will decline with the evidence of sanctions in the group.

f) Dynamic incentives and further access to credit

Dynamic incentives are based on stated preferences and willingness to pay as opposed to the actual behavior. I expect the dynamic incentive constraints resulting from joint liability to create incentives for peer selection, peer monitoring and peer pressure. The value of future access to credit can best be captured by discounting benefits from future access to credit and comparing with benefits from not repaying. However, in the IFPRI survey, a revealed preference approach was used by asking the following question:

If you are in a group where some members have defaulted but you have fully repaid your loan, and you were asked, in addition to loosing you 15 percent required deposit, to choose among the following three options, which one will you choose?

1. Contribute to repay in full the loans of defaulters, and be part of a new group where the defaulters are excluded
2. Pay another 10% penalty and be part of a new group where the defaulters are excluded
3. Accept a lower loan size next time and be part of a new group where the defaulters are excluded

The first option is directly related to the full joint liability principle (no loans to non defaulters until all loans are paid). The two other options were aimed at exploring alternative liability options (limited liability) which would maintain the same incentives for peer monitoring and peer pressure, both of which have direct relevance to the mitigation of moral hazard. Diagne *et al.* (2000) note that the key difference between the three options is that in the first one the penalty is dependent on the total amount of defaulted loans while it is not in the two other ones. The rationale behind these two alternative options is that they should lead to fewer strategic defaults compared to the first option. Therefore, the first option should lead to higher penalties among non-defaulters in a group where there are more defaulters. Groups choosing the first option are likely to attach higher value of the future access to credit. The second option is assumed to be more costly than the third option, as such those choosing the second option are assumed to attach a much higher value to future access to credit than those choosing the third option in which they would be willing to accept a lower value of the loan.

I expect that the choice of either of the options is a good indicator of the importance or value that the group attaches to future access to credit. The inclusion of these variables in my model also helps me to explore the potential of limited liability contracts (as substitutes to full joint liability) in mitigating moral hazard. The two options are entered as dummy variables. CONTRIB is equal 1 when the first option is chosen and PAY is equal 1 when the second option is chosen.

An extra variable is included to capture dynamic incentives and the value of future access to credit. PASTACA captures the presence of at least one member in a group, who was from the past failed credit program where people defaulted and therefore the program was discontinued. The presence of such members in a group should increase the probability of moral hazard in the group as they may not attach the same value to credit access from the current institution following their past experience in a failed program. It is generally accepted that if clients have experienced former failed programs in which loans were never rigorously collected, there might be little incentive for them to comply to contracts in the new credit program (Buckley, 1996).

g) Mismatching

In order to capture incentive match in a group I introduce two variables in the model. First I include a measure of the age of the group (LONCYCLE). Theoretically, the age of a credit group is negatively associated with repayment. Paxton (1996) notes that as the age of the group increases group members acquiring different skills in their areas of entrepreneurship, such that they start developing divergent credit requirements. The matching problems arise when the demand and supply for credit among group members can no longer match, which could lead to default by some members whose supply of credit is not incentive compatible. In most cases group lending starts with high repayment rates. However, this declines with time. Therefore, I expect the likelihood of moral hazard to increase with loan cycle.

Second, I include a variable that captures the presence of new members in a group (NEWMMBAVG) at the beginning of the loan cycle. Screening among groups is continuous as group members continue to exclude bad risk borrowers and replace them with safe ones. However, this could also lead to a matching problem sighted by Paxton (1996). The matching problem arises when credit terms and conditions are no longer appropriate for each member as credit is repeated again. Though not necessarily in the same context as mentioned by Paxton, the presence of new members in a group potentially introduces the same problem since they enter the group after their colleagues have already developed several entrepreneurship skills that also change their credit requirements. I expect that the presence of a matching problem in a group will increase the likelihood of moral hazard.

h) Control variables

In addition, I included in the model control variables that are program dummies for the maize group (MAIZE), cotton group (COTTON), and non-farm income generating activity group (NONFARM). Group size (GPSIZE) is the number of members in a group. Following *de* Aghion (1999) the effect of group size on loan repayment can be multifaceted with opposing effects. As indicated in the literature review I expect that group size will affect moral hazard behavior in 4 ways as follows: 1) the free-riding effect, 2) the joint responsibility effect, 3) cost sharing effect and the commitment effect. Thus the expected sign for group size on moral hazard is undetermined. I also include the value of the maximum amount of credit a group can access at any time, known as the credit limit (CREDLIMIT), as a control variable. Its impact on moral hazard is ambiguous. Finally, location variables for Lilongwe, Zomba and Nkhotakota are also included to control for location specific characteristics.

5.5 Empirical Results and Discussion

The maximum likelihood probit estimates of the above moral hazard equation are presented in Table 5.6. In line with a priori expectations, results indicate that groups formed through peer selection have a lower incidence of moral hazard. This implies that peer selection enables groups to screen a risky borrower which is in concurrence with Ghatak's theory of adverse selection. Ghatak (1999a) observes that self selection process leads to the emergence of a pool of safe borrowers which can lead to a reduction in the likelihood of moral hazard. Both peer monitoring variables are significant and their signs conform to the a priori expectations. First the proportion of group members reporting that they do not know the composition of the group has a positive and significant coefficient. This signifies the non-occurrence of monitoring in some groups, which increases the likelihood of moral hazard. The presence of individuals with joint enterprises has a reducing effect on the incidence of moral hazard. This conforms to a priori expectations that moral hazard is less likely in groups with joint enterprises because members are more likely to monitor each other's investment decisions and the levels of output.

Only one of the variables measuring levels of social ties, the number of villages from which group members come is significant, with an a priori expected sign. As indicated in Figure 5.2 the probability of moral hazard increases with the number of village from which members of the group come. Groups composed of members from many villages are more likely to experience moral hazard problems than those composed of members from the same village. MRFC groups in this study were, on average, composed of members from 3 villages. The presumption is that members from the same village are likely to exhibit strong pre-existing social ties and, therefore, less likely to harm each other through default.

Nevertheless, as a spatial variable the number of villages can also be an indicator of the cost of monitoring. This, therefore, could suggest that groups with members from villages that are further apart face difficulties in peer monitoring resulting into a higher probability of moral hazard.

The presence of peer pressure has a significant and negative impact on the incidence of moral hazard. This is in conformity with my a priori expectation. This finding also conforms to the finding by Wydick (1999), in which he observes that the willingness to apply peer pressure has a significant effect on reducing moral hazard within borrowing groups from Guatemala. The presence of social sanctions returned a conflicting sign but it is insignificant.

The dynamic incentives captured by the willingness to pay a full value of defaulted loans, which is also a measure of the willingness to accept full joint liability is negative and significant. The implication is that the full joint liability clause is a key mechanism through which the incidence of moral hazard can be minimized.

Figure 5.2 Predicted probability of moral hazard by number of villages

Source: Own calculation from RDD/IFPRI 1999 Rural Finance Survey

The variable capturing the preference for limited liability where individuals are only required to pay 10 percent penalty is insignificant. The findings are consistent with a priori expectations in that full joint liability strengthens togetherness in the group which makes it less likely that individuals would want to harm each other through default.

The presence of members from past failed programs in a group has a significant and positive coefficient. This conforms to a priori expectations that members that have ever participated in previously failed credit programs where loans were not rigorously collected have a tendency to take risky actions that have a negative impact on repayment. In the same context, Buckley (1996) discusses the abandonment of offers in joint liability lending programs. Buckley notes that a problem arises with JLLIs in that the institution sometimes keeps the group but abandons the joint liability which is the pillar of group lending. Buckley likens the situation to the abandonment of joint liability in Smallholder Agricultural Credit Administration (SACA) in Malawi. He notes that at first SACA lent to individuals under joint liability and the repayment was good. However, in 1992 SACA adopted a policy of allowing any individual that had repaid his or her *own* loan to access further credit even if one or more of the borrowers in his/her group was in default. This led to a severe drop in repayment rates.

Both variables capturing mismatching problems conform to a priori expectations by returning positive and significant coefficients. First, the presence of new members in a group is likely to introduce a matching problem as the loan demand for new members may not match those of old members due to differences in the levels of business skills. This in turn makes it difficult for the lending institutions to meet the loan demand for such a diverse group of individuals leading to an erosion of incentives for repayment among some members whose loan supply does not create the incentive to repay.

Table 5.7 Determinants of Moral hazard- Maximum likelihood Probit estimates

Variable		Coeff.	Z-statistic	$\frac{dy}{dx}$ [9]
Production factors	PRODARABLE	-0.215	-1.54	-0.038
	PRODLEVELSCH	-0.201	-1.31	0.036
Screening	SCREEN	-0.042	-0.11	0.009
	SCRFA	-0.319	-0.63	-0.083
	PEERSELECT	-0.838*	-1.66	-0.428
	SCRVGHEAD	-0.311	-0.5	-0.018
Peer monitoring	PMJOINTENT	-0.608*	-1.87	-0.294
	GCOMPDNI	3.266*	1.77	0.203
	GLONCDNI	-1.828	-1.07	0.034
Social ties	VILLAGENUM~R	0.377***	3.39	0.056
	PMFAMVG	-0.251	-0.58	-0.129
	CHAIRFAMILY	-0.046	-0.77	0.001
Peer pressure	PRESUDUEDATE	-1.025**	-2.02	-0.329
	LEFEXCMG	0.279	1.3	-0.037
Dynamic incentives	CONTRIBPAY	-1.311**	-2.36	-0.415
	PAYPENATY	-0.265	-0.5	0.011
	PASTSACA	1.200**	2.25	0.383
Matching problem (incentive match)				
	NEWMMBAVG	0.306***	3.23	0.309
	LCYCLE	0.478**	2.51	0.116
Control	GPSIZE	0.025	0.68	0.005
	MAXIDLMG	0.001**	2.0	0.001
	MAIZE	-0.694	-1.08	-0.351
	COTTON	-0.654	-1	-0.174
	NONFARM	0.211	0.44	-0.037
	LILONGWE	1.553**	2.06	0.538
	ZOMBA	1.927***	2.77	0.648
	NKHOTA	2.385*	1.81	0.663
Constant		-1.436	-1.28	
Total observations		99		
Observation with dependent =0		58		
% Correctly predicted		72.73		
Wald chi2(23)		44.72		
Prob > chi2		0.009		
Pseudo R2		0.3315		
Log pseudo-likelihood		45.64		

Source: Own calculation from RDD/IFPRI 1999 Rural Finance Survey

Note: * P<0.10; ** P<0.05; *** P<0.01 ,

[9] The marginal effects measure the changes in a regressor on the conditional probability that $y = 1$. The marginal effect of regressor x_i is expressed as follows: $\frac{d\Pr(y=1 \mid x)}{dx_i} = \phi(\beta' x_i)\beta_j$, where β_j is the sign of the marginal effect

Second, the variable that measures the age of a group has a positive effect on moral hazard. Again this is related to the matching problem in loan cycles proposed by Paxton (1996). In the first meeting every one agrees to the terms and conditions of the loan. However, as members continue to receive loans from a lending institution; they develop skills at different levels. This leads to a diversity in their loan requirements which in turn makes it difficult for the lender to match the demand and supply of credit among group members. As more members become unsatisfied, the incentive for repayment declines leading to moral hazard. In the study area more than 50% of the groups were formed more than 4 years before the date of survey (seep appendix 6.1)

Figure 5.3 Predicted probability of moral hazard by number of new members

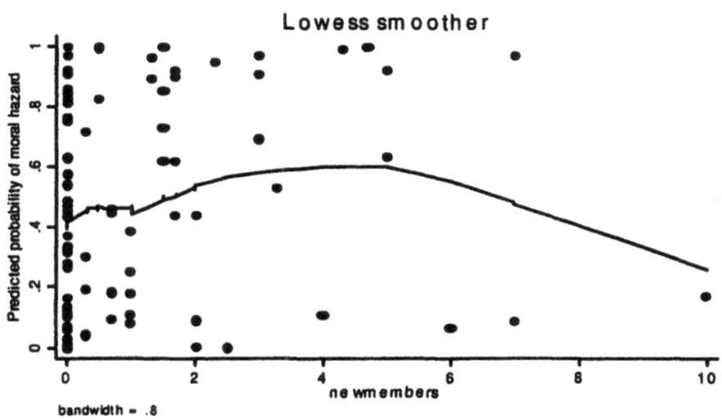

Source: Own calculation from RDD/IFPRI 1999 Rural Finance Survey

The maximum loan size available to the group increases the likelihood of moral hazard. As indicated in Figure 5.4, groups with access to larger sizes of loan had a higher probability of reporting moral hazard than those with lower loan sizes. This is consistent with a theoretical proposition by Stiglitz (1990) in which it is observed that the expected utility of risky projects increases faster in loaned funds than that of a safe project.

The increase in the size of the loan increases the relative attractiveness of risky projects leading to moral hazard. Moral hazard was also high in Zomba, Lilongwe and Nkhotakota, but it was lower in Rumphi district. The differences in the likelihood of moral hazard between districts can mainly be attributed to the cultural differences among people living in these districts as well as the differences in the access to markets. Rumphi district is in the northern region where access to markets and other sources of capital is very limited, such that households accessing credit would take it as a golden opportunity to maintain a long term relationship with the lending institution.

Figure 5.4 Predicted probability of moral hazard by size of loan

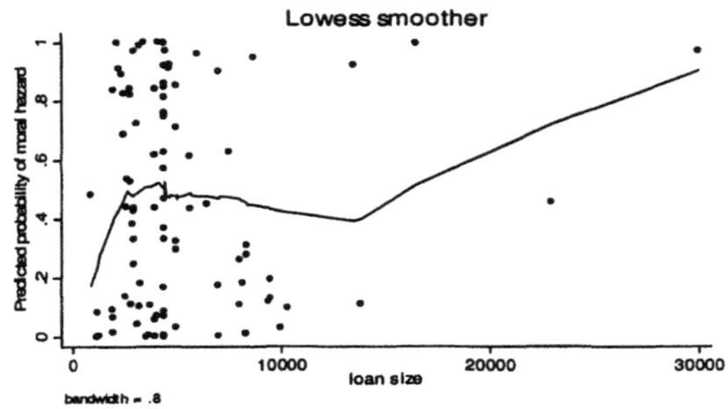

Source: Own calculation from RDD/IFPRI 1999 Rural Finance Survey

The three other districts have access to other markets due to their proximity to urban centers and, therefore, less likely to attach higher value to MRFC loans. Other control variables such as group size and program dummies were insignificant. In addition, production related variables had no significant effect on the incidence of moral hazard, although they returned expected signs.

5.6 Conclusions and Policy Implications

Joint Liability Lending (JLL) is celebrated as an innovation that has made previously insolvent individuals solvent by creating 'social collateral' to replace the missing physical collateral that excluded them from access to more traditional forms of finance. Nevertheless, the problem with joint liability lending programs is that the poor are given access to credit without collateral, and in the event of default, they can not be punished beyond a mere denial of future access to credit. This form of limited liability can induce borrowers to take risky actions. While theorists have attempted to propose conditions under which joint liability contracts can be self-enforcing to the extent that moral hazard would be minimized, the performance of joint liability lending programs has produced mixed results.

Motivated by the absence of empirical studies on determinants of moral hazard, this chapter assessed the extent to which moral hazard occurs in credit groups and has analyzed factors that influence its occurrence. It is hoped that the results will inform policy regarding necessary prerequisites to the success in group lending in mitigating moral hazard. Guided by theoretical propositions of Ghatak and Guinane (1999), Diagne (1998) Paxton (1996) and Ahlin and

Townsend (2003) the study tested the hypotheses that peer selection, peer monitoring, social ties, peer pressure and dynamic incentives reduce the incidence of moral hazard.

Results indicate that in Malawi, despite the widely documented high potential of joint liability lending in mitigating moral hazard, the mechanism is still prone to moral hazard. About 40 percent of the credit groups reported that they experienced either a misuse of funds or a mismanagement of an investment by some of their group members. The analysis further shows that the likelihood of occurrence of moral hazard is lower in groups that were endogenously formed through self-selection. Peer monitoring through rules that encourage joint enterprise ownership reduces the incidence of moral hazard.

The degree of pre-existing social ties captured by the number of villages from which group members come as well as the existence of peer pressure, particularly, before the due date of the loan reduce the likelihood of the incidence of moral hazard. These findings offer support to theoretical propositions by Ghatak and Guinane (1999) and Diagne (1998) and are in concurrence with the hypotheses of this study.

Indicating the significance of the matching problem, results further show that a higher number of new members in a group and an increase in the number of loan cycles leads to a rise in the incidence of moral hazard. The analysis on the effect of dynamic incentives on moral hazard also produced interesting results. The number of group members from past failed credit programs increases the likelihood of moral hazard. Groups that attached higher value to access to credit from MRFC were less likely to experience moral hazard problems.

A number of policy implications can be drawn from the results. First, the significance of peer selection should be of great interest to group based microfinance institutions such as MRFC. In order for group lending to be effective in mitigating moral hazard, MRFC must encourage the formation of groups through self-selection. The self-selection process will facilitate screening of potentially bad borrowers hence reducing moral hazard. The negative effect of borrowers from previously failed credit programs has an important policy implication as well. In Malawi the emergence of several microfinance institutions, some with conflicting objectives, has created alternatives for bad borrowers such that defaulters in one credit program would borrow from another credit program without facing any sanctions. This seriously reduces the value that such members may attach to accessing credit from a particular institution, particularly, when they know that they can still borrow from other institutions. In order to address this problem, the government of Malawi must introduce a policy that supports the establishment of credit reference bureaus from which past records for potential borrowers can be accessed. This would stop bad borrowers from accessing further funds. Nevertheless, such a policy must be supported by a legislature that introduces mandatory identity cards for all citizens.

Other policies that would reduce mismatching problems and enhance dynamic incentives relate to the introduction of combined offers that include both joint and individual liability by microfinance institutions. This will require MRFC to relax their rule on joint liability by allowing borrowers with dynamic and growing investments who make use of group loans at the beginning to switch to individual credit offers when they are in need of higher loans.

In conclusion the findings on the effect of peer monitoring, social ties and dynamic incentives in mitigating moral hazard suggest that joint liability lending institutions such as the Malawi Rural Finance Company must continue relying on both social cohesion as well the creation of repayment incentives in order to reduce the incidence of moral hazard. In so doing MRFC will be simultaneously addressing problems of low outreach, limited impact and lack of financial self sustainability, all of which are important pillars in the Triangle of Microfinance.

6 MUTUAL INSURANCE IN JOINT LIABILITY LENDINGPROGRAMS, ITS DETERMINANTS AND POLICY IMPLICATIONS

6.1 Introduction

Following the success of microfinance in the past four decades, the poor are no longer viewed as unproductive individuals who can only be helped through welfare programs and subsidies. There is now, enormous evidence that indeed access to credit even at market clearing interest rates enables the poor to become viable actors in the economy. Despite such successes, microfinance faces a number of problems, amongst which the lack of insurance features highly.

Considering that loan transactions are done over time, with a wide range of risks, there is need for some form of insurance for borrowers. Insurance is also important because even good investments may yield low returns in bad years leading to repayment failure. In concurrence with this notion, Sadoulet (2003) observes that insurance is particularly important for the poor microfinance clients for two reasons: First, the poor are subject and vulnerable to substantial amounts of risk. Second, to make up for income shortfalls, the poor engage in risk mitigating strategies which induce a reduction in profitable investments. However, lending to poor households is associated with problems of information asymmetry and limited enforcement, such that lenders are unwilling to provide insurance.

The main reason for the exclusion of the poor from such insurance services is that lending institutions may not be able to audit each individual borrower to separate genuine failures from false claims resulting from moral hazard. The absence of physical collateral among the poor, further contributes to the complexity. However, Sadoulet (2004) notes that the poor are usually risk constrained such that even if they have the collateral, they may not want to put their collateral at risk. This form of limited liability induces risk taking behaviour among borrowers.

Microfinance practitioners as well as theorists have devoted great attention on 'mutual help' in joint liability lending, while empirical work on the same is rare. Most theories explain how the joint liability mechanism through the provision of intra-group insurance induces, peer monitoring, peer support, peer auditing and peer pressure and when default occurs, the group members are induced to contribute to the payment of the defaulted loan. In this way the group acts as a safety net against default for both borrowers and the lender by allowing members to ensure each other across project specific downside risks. The high repayment rates attained by institutions such as the Grameen Bank have been widely associated with the role of intra-group insurance. In concurrence with this observation, Besley and Coate (1995), contend that the Grameen Banks' success is a result of its ability to induce borrowers to provide mutual assistance in hard times.

Group lending with joint liability lending has not only become a technology of choice for lending institutions, but is also favored by borrowers. Given a choice between individual; and group lending, beneficiaries usually prefer group lending. In a study on Guatemala credit groups from *Genesis,* Sadoulet (2003) observes that borrowers were offered a choice between individual and group loans. Both types of loans carried the same monthly interest rate of 2.5 percent, had the same term and were for the same purpose. Sadoulet notes that the individual and group contracts were identical in every aspect except for the extra joint liability, and yet two thirds of the borrowers chose group loans. The main reason for choosing group loans stemmed from the intra-group insurance that emerges in credit groups. Sadoulet notes that in about 60 percent of the credit groups, at least one member needed help making payment in the past 12 months.

Understanding the way groups perform with regards to risk sharing, is particularly important for two reasons. First, for the moment, despite the high capacity of most MFIs than credit groups (composed of poor and risk-averse borrowers) to absorb credit risks, the MFIs are unwilling to take up this responsibility. It therefore appears that most certainly, groups will continue to be an important source of insurance for loan repayment among the members despite its efficiency and welfare costs. Second, as noted by Wydick (1999), although it is unlikely that fostering this type of intra-group insurance is one of the stated goals of group lending institutions, the positive externalities of having such insurance available to a household are obvious. Thus in the process of establishing borrowing groups, the credit institution is also fostering the development of hundreds of miniature social-security networks that might also be exploited by other development agencies with a community approach.

In most cases it has been assumed that when ever joint liability contracts have been explained to the borrowers, contracts signed, and loans disbursed, members should be willing to offer mutual insurance. This is, however, not true as there are situations where some group members will renege their insurance promise. In Malawi for example, Diagne *et al.* (2000) find that out of about 100 credit groups that received loans from the Malawi Rural Finance Company (MRFC) in 1999, only 42 percent of the groups indicated full willingness to contribute to repay loans of defaulters in their groups. This is a clear example of a situation where the joint liability mechanism is not functioning as expected. When intra-group insurance fails, it defeats the main foundations upon which joint liability lending is built. The unwillingness to insure each other by group members is the unwillingness to pay the joint liability value of the loan, which could result into losses for the lending institution and further the exclusion of the poor from financial markets.

The objective of this chapter is, therefore, to examine the extent to which intra-group insurance occurs in credit groups and investigate determinants of the willingness of group members to offer such insurance. This allows us to test the significance of peer selection, peer monitoring, covariance of output and dynamic incentives, in enhancing mutual insurance. The rest of the chapter is arranged as follows: section two reviews mutual insurance activities in microfinance schemes within Malawi, while section three presents the empirical model. Section four describes the data used in the analysis, while results and discussions are presented in section five. Conclusions and policy implications are presented in section six.

6.2 Mutual Insurance Activities in Joint Liability Lending in Malawi: A Review

As noted by Burritt (2006), while moral hazard can be exclusively addressed through dynamic incentives and collateral as well as monitoring activities, such measures do not address the fundamental risk of bad returns and the consequent loss of future access to credit. This justifies the need for some form insurance for borrowers. In Malawi, despite the realization by MFIs that households demand a wider range of services above loans, non has come forward to offer sustainable insurance mechanisms to protect borrowers again income loss. This leaves borrowers with very limited risk management strategies such that the mutual insurance provided through joint liability remains the only risk sharing mechanism at their disposal. Mutual insurance in credit groups, however, has a lot of limitations because the rural credit markets in Malawi are characterized by high levels of systemic risks. Such risks include production risks resulting from droughts as well as price risks associated with a fall in prices for microfinance products such as Tobacco. Such risks are forms of covariate shocks which affect all households and group members at the same time making it difficult for the intra-group insurance schemes to perform effectively. A number of members in these mutual insurance groups have shown willingness to offer such forms of insurance by promising to make contributions to repay defaulted loans of their peers. Indeed there are instances when such loans have been paid by peers. As study by Diagne *et al.* (2000) revealed that in more than 60 percent of the groups where loans were defaulted, repayment was made by group members through their contributions. Nevertheless, the difficulty arises when defaulted loan are too big for group members to contribute to repay the loan. Under such circumstances, individuals tend to renege their insurance promises. Studies have shown that in some cases only 40 percent of the individuals in groups may be willing to contribute towards the repayment of defaulted loans. Problems also arise when members in a group realize that the non-payment of loans by other members resulted from moral hazard. The incentive to contribute towards repaying such loans is usually lost.

6.3 Empirical Model

Guided by the theoretical framework in Chapter 4, several variables that are associated with the willingness of individuals to offer mutual insurance to group members were generated from the data set. The dependent variable capturing the willingness to offer mutual insurance is binary in nature and, therefore, a Probit model was chosen to estimate the relationship between the explanatory variables and the willingness to offer mutual insurance.

The model specification is as follows:

$$\Pr(y=1 \mid x)=\alpha+\sum_{i=1}^{Pr=2}\beta_{1i}x_{1i}+\sum_{i=1}^{Scr=4}\beta_{2i}x_{2i}+\sum_{i=1}^{pm=3}\beta_{3i}x_{3i}+\sum_{i=1}^{st=5}\beta_{4i}x_{4i}\sum_{i=1}^{pp=2}\beta_{5i}x_{5i}+\sum_{i=1}^{Dinc=3}\beta_{6i}x_{6i}+$$
$$+\sum_{i=1}^{Im=3}\beta_{7i}x_{7i}++\sum_{i=1}^{Rikp=4}\beta_{8i}x_{8i}+\sum_{i=1}^{Ctr=8}\beta_{9i}x_{9i}$$

Where:

x_1´s are a set of variables (Pr=2) that measure factors of production
x_2´s are a set of variables (Scr=4) that measure the quality of screening
x_3´s are a set of variables (pm=3) that measure the quality of peer monitoring
x_4´s are a set of variables (St=6) that measure the strength of social ties
x_5´s are a set of variables (Pp=2) that measure the quality of peer pressure
x_6´s are a set of variables (Dinc=3) that measure the quality of dynamic incentives
x_7´s are a set of variables (Im=3) that the proxy the degree of incentive match
x_8´s are a set of risk pooling variables (Rskp=4) that measure the cost of insurance
x_9´s are a set of variables (Ctr=8) that are control variables

Description of Variables in the model

Dependent Variable

In order to test the hypotheses outlined in literature regarding factors that explain the incidence of mutual insurance in groups, I start by capturing the willingness of group members to provide mutual insurance if a member defaults a loan. The willingness to contribute to repay defaulted loans was elicited on an individual basis targeting the leaders of the group and 2 other group members. From there I create a dependent variable, MUTUAL, which is equal to 1 if it was reported that members were always willing to provide mutual insurance, and 0 if members were only will under certain conditions or never willing at all.

Explanatory variables

From the theoretical framework discussed earlier, the empirical specification is based on nine categories of explanatory variables whose full descriptions and a priori expectations of their effect on the willingness to offer mutual insurance are defined below. The explanatory variables, covariance of out put as a risk pooling factor, cost of insurance, peer selection, peer monitoring, screening, variables that capture the extent of social ties, factors of production, dynamic incentives and variables that capture matching problems.

a) Covariance of out put, as a risk pooling factor

Varian (1990) and Rashid and Townsend (1992) explore the significance of mutual insurance among group members in the presence of idiosyncratic shocks, and if borrower returns are not highly correlated and observe that mutual insurance is beneficial to group members. I test the validity of their proposition by incorporating such variables in my empirical model. The covariance of output among group members is captured by two variables. First, COVLOSS which measures the coincidence of idiosyncratic shocks such as crop loss from bad weather, illness or death among group members. It is a measure of the probability of having group members facing shocks at the same time. COVLOSS was captured by asking group leaders about whether each group member faced crop loss or income loss due to shocks in the past 2 years. The variable was constructed as a probability that two respondents chosen at random from the same group reported having economic shocks in the same year. Consider G_{sz} as the number of members in a credit group and S_{sy} as the share of group members who reported facing an economic shock in year y. The probability is equal to

$$\frac{(\sum_{y=1}^{2} s_{sy}^{2}) - 1/G_{sz}}{1 - 1/G_{sz}}$$

Second, COVOCCUP, which is an indicator of the occupational homogeneity within the group, measures the probability that two randomly chosen group members have the same occupation. The index is computed in the same way as above. I assume that the capacity of members to share risks increases with occupation heterogeneity as it is associated with covariance of output in the group.

b) Cost of insurance

COVLOANVALUE is the measure of the cost of mutual insurance to group members once a member defaults. It is a measure of the variation in loan sizes among group members calculated as a coefficient of variation Loan size heterogeneity can work against mutual insurance because of the unequal costs of insurance. The cost can be too high if the paying members with small loan sizes are expected to pay defaulted loans for members with larger loans. In addition group loan size heterogeneity is not conducive to peer monitoring as it makes it difficult for group members to monitor their peers. I therefore expect higher loan variation to have a negative impact on the willingness of members to provide mutual insurance.

c) Factors of production

The inclusion of factors of production is based on the intuition that higher productivity increases the payoff which will enable members to get returns above the critical amounts required for repayment. Having returns above the critical payoff also increases the likelihood that members can pay the joint liability value when one of the group members defaults. Two variables that are used to capture group productivity are, the average land holding size of group members in acres, (AVGLAND) and the average years of education of the group members (EDUCATION). I expect that both variables will have a positive impact in enhancing mutual support.

d) Screening

First I capture whether or not there are some non-members that were rejected by the group at group formation, (SCREEN). My a priori expectation is that the likelihood of intra-group insurance should be high in groups with evidence of screening. In addition there are three variables that capture the extent to which peer selection is taking place during the group formation process. I include the variable PEERSELECT as a dummy variable (1=formation through peer selection, 0=others), which captures whether or not a group was self-formed by village members. I expect that the likelihood of willingness to provide mutual insurance will be high in groups that were formed through peer selection.
I include two extra variables to capture the extent of screening. FASCREEN is a dummy variable capturing the formation of groups by the Extension workers, while VHSCREEN is another dummy variable capturing the formation of a group by a village chief. The two (village chiefs and extension workers) have significantly different roles in the society. I expect the willingness to offer mutual support to be strong in groups that were formed by chiefs because chiefs usually act as problem solvers in the village and thus there influence on mutual insurance activities should be positive, however, the effect of the Field Assistant is undetermined.

e) Social ties

Generally, I expect the willingness to offer mutual insurance to be an increasing function of social ties. I use four variables to capture the magnitude of social ties within a borrowing group. VILLAGENUMBER measures the number of villages from which group members come. The larger the number of villages relative to the group sizes the smaller the social ties and thus I expected the willingness to offer mutual assistance to be low in groups that are composed of members from many villages. PMFAMVG measures the presence of some members that come from the clan or family of a village chief in a group. Village chiefs are continuously involved in problem solving in the village and have a great influence on the operations of MRFC loans. I expect that the willingness to provide mutual insurance is likely to be high in credit groups that have a link with village chiefs through members of the groups. The presumption is also that relatives of the village chief would want to be seen as good examples in the village because of their linkage to the clan of the chief and therefore less likely to be willing to solve problems that arise from non-repayment of the loan by group members. POLITCLAN measures the presence of group members that are from the clan of a politician. I expect some political influence on groups that have social ties with politicians, although I don't have a predetermined expectation as their influence on intra-group insurance.

CHAIRFAMILY represents the number of group members that belong to the family of a group chair person. I expect that the willingness to provide mutual assistance will be high in groups that have some members that are related to the group leader. This is because when a group fails to repay a loan, group leaders shoulder part of the blame, and as such a higher number of relatives from the group leader in a group may encourage group members to assist each other when a repayment problem arises. The presence of such individuals also signifies the presence of strong social ties among group members which is also good for the general performance of the group.

f) Peer monitoring

The variable GCOMPDNI measures the percent of group members not knowing group composition, while GLONCDNI measures the proportion of group members that don't know the characteristics of the loan. I expect the willingness to offer intra-group insurance to increase with improved information flow within the group captured by the two variables. PMJOINTENT captures the presence of group rules that promote joint enterprise ownership. This is a dummy variable and it is equal 1 when it is reported that the group has rules that promote joint enterprise ownership, and 0, otherwise. I expect the willingness to provide mutual insurance to be high in groups that encourage joint enterprise ownership. This is because joint enterprise ownership promotes togetherness and makes auditing or state verification easy. Thus when a member reports a repayment problem, peers should easily verify this and be able to assist him or her as along as the defaulter provides genuine reasons for the failure to repay.

g) Dynamic incentives and further access to credit

Dynamic incentives are based on stated preferences and willingness to pay as opposed to the actual behavior. In the survey dynamic incentives were captured by using a revealed preference approach. As indicated in chapter five respondents were asked to choose between three options in the vent of a repayment problem in the group as follows:

1. Contribute to repay in full the loans of defaulters, and be part of a new group where the defaulters are excluded
2. pay another 10% penalty and be part of a new group where the defaulters are excluded
3. Accept a lower loan size next time and be part of a new group where the defaulters are excluded

In the regression analysis CONTRIBPAY is equal one when the first option is chosen. I expect mutual insurance to be high among groups that are willing to pay a full amount of defaulted loans because of the high value they attach to access to future credit from MRFC. PASTACA captures the presence of at least one member in a group, who was from the past failed credit program where people defaulted and therefore the program was discontinued. The presence of such members in a group should decrease the degree of cooperation and willingness to provide mutual insurance as they may not attach a high value to credit access from the current institution following their past experience in a failed credit program.

h) Matching problems

Matching problems are captured by two variables in the model. First I include a measure of the age of the group (LONCYCLE). Theoretically, the age of a credit group is negatively associated with repayment. Paxton (1996) notes that as the age of the group increases, group members acquire different skills and they develop divergent credit requirements. The matching problems arises when the demand and supply for credit among group members can no longer match which could lead to default by some members whose supply of credit is not incentive compatible. In most cases group lending starts with high repayment rates. However, this declines with time. Therefore, I expect the willingness for members to offer mutual insurance to decrease with an increase in the loan cycles. Second, I include a variable that captures the presence of new members in a group (NEWMMBAVG) at the beginning of the loan cycle which leads matching problems. I expect that the presence of a matching problem in a group will reduce togetherness and hence reduce the willingness to offer mutual insurance.

i) Control

The following control variables were included:
GPSIZE is a measure for the size of the group. Theoretically group size may affect intra-group insurance and repayment in a number of ways. Smaller group sizes are good for easy monitoring and thus may lead to higher repayment rates. However, larger groups can give better insurance on their members. Thus, the net effect of group size on mutual insurance in ambiguous. CREDLIMIT is the maximum amount of credit a group can access at any time and its impact on mutual insurance is ambiguous. In addition, I include program dummies for the maize group (MAIZE), Cotton group (COTTON), and non farm income generating activity group (NONFARM). Additional location dummies were also included in the regression to control for variations in the sites of the study. Descriptive statistics for both the dependent variable and the explanatory variables and their expected effects on the willingness to offer mutual insurance are described in Table 6.1.

Table 6.1 Descriptive statistics and expected signs of regression variables

Variables	Description	Mean	S.D	Exp sign
Dependent variable				
MUTUAL	Whether group members are always willing to contribute to repay defaulted loans (1=yes, 0=no)	0.45	0.49	
Independent variables				
Factors of production				
AVGLAND	Average land holding of group members in acres	3.17	1.471	+
EDUCATION	Average years of formal education of group members	4.72	1.533	+
Screening				
SCREEN	Whether some individuals who wanted to join the group rejected	0.439	0.490	+
FASCREEN	Group was formed by the Agricultural extension worker (1=yes, 0=no)	0.46	0.499	-
PEERSELECT	Whether group was initiated by peers (1=yes, 0=no)	0.241	0.428	+
VHSCREEN	Group was formed by the Village headman (1=yes, 0=no)	0.12	0.321	-
Peer monitoring				

JOINTENTERP	Members have joint enterprises (1=have joint enterprises)	0.6	0.533	+
GCOMPNAI	Percentage of group members not knowing group composition	0.066	0.147	-
GLONCNAI	Percentage of member not knowing loan characteristics			-
Social ties				
VILLAGENUMBER	Number of villages from which members come	2.76	2.039	-
PMFAMVG	At least one member is from the family of a village headman (1=yes)	0.82	0.383	-+
POLITCLAN	Number of members from the clan of a politician	0.61	1.083	-+
CHAIRFAMILY	Number of members from the family of club chair person	1.50	3.012	-+
GENDERHOMO	Whether gender composition of the group is mixed (1=yes, 0=no)	0.57	0.496	+
Dynamic Incentives				
CONTRIBPAY	Whether would be willing to pay full cost of defaulters loan (1=yes, 0=no)	0.46	0.500	+
PAST SACA	At least one member was from past failed credit programs (1=yes, 0=no)	0.78	0.415	-
Incentive Match				
NEWMMBAVG	Number of new members in the group	1.41	2.732	-
LONCYCLE	The loan cycle for which loan was received (1-5)	2.74	1.051	-
Risk pooling /covariance				
COVLOSS	Measure of coincidence of idiosyncratic shocks	-0.04	0.366	-
COVOCCUP	Measure of Occupational homogeneity within the group	0.27	0.325	-
Cost of insurance				
COVLOANVALUE	Measure of loan Variation within group members (CV)	0.35	0.293	-
Control Variables				
GPSIZE	Number of members at the start of the season in a credit group	16.84	5.563	+
CREDLIMIT	Average Credit limit in a group per individual	4642	3822	-+
MAIZE	Dummy for maize credit group (1=maize, 0=otherwise)	0.19	0.393	-
COTTON	Dummy for cotton credit group (1=maize,0=otherwise)	0.042	0.201	-
NON-FARM	Dummy for non-farm credit group (1=maize 0=otherwise)	0.30	0.462	-+

Source: Own calculation from IFPRI/RDD survey

6.4 Data

The study is based on data collected by the International Food Policy Research Institute (IFPRI) described in Chapter 3. In the survey, group leaders were asked whether individuals in a group were willing to pay loans of defaulters when ever default occurred, and when ever that was possible, how much they were willing to contribute.

Willingness to contribute to repay defaulted loans

As indicated in Figure 6.1, and in Table 6.2, although 91 percent of the group leaders indicated that group members understood that they were obliged to contribute to repay loans if members in the groups defaulted, only 48 percent of the respondents reported that members in the group were always willing to contribute to repay loans of members that failed to repay in order to continue accessing credit from MRFC. About 21 percent reported that group members would never agree to contribute to repay the defaulted loans, while 31 percent reported that their members could only agree to repay if the amount was small enough.

Figure 6.1: Willingness to contribute to repay defaulted loans

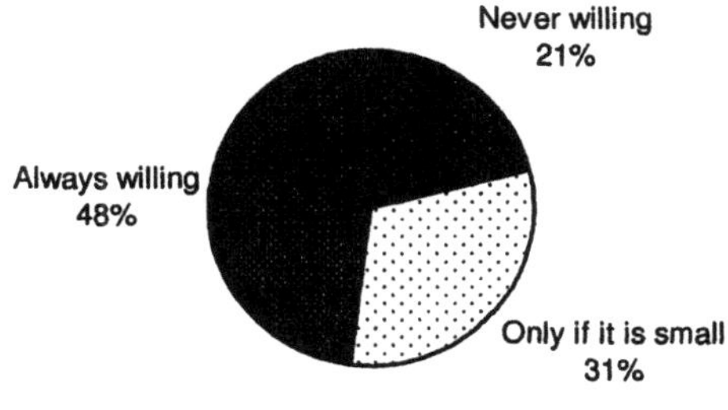

Source: Own calculation from IFPRI/RDD survey

An observation on the willingness to contribute to repay defaulted loans across districts also revealed some interesting phenomenon. As indicated in Figure 6.2,

Rumphi district registered a higher rate (72%) of individuals that were always willing to contribute to repay defaulted loans than other districts. The majority of groups in Lilongwe (52.6%) reported that group members could only be willing to contribute to repay defaulted loans if the amount was small enough. Zomba had the highest proportion of groups (29%) that indicated that their members would never contribute to repay defaulted loans.

Figure 6.2 Willingness to repay defaulted loans by district

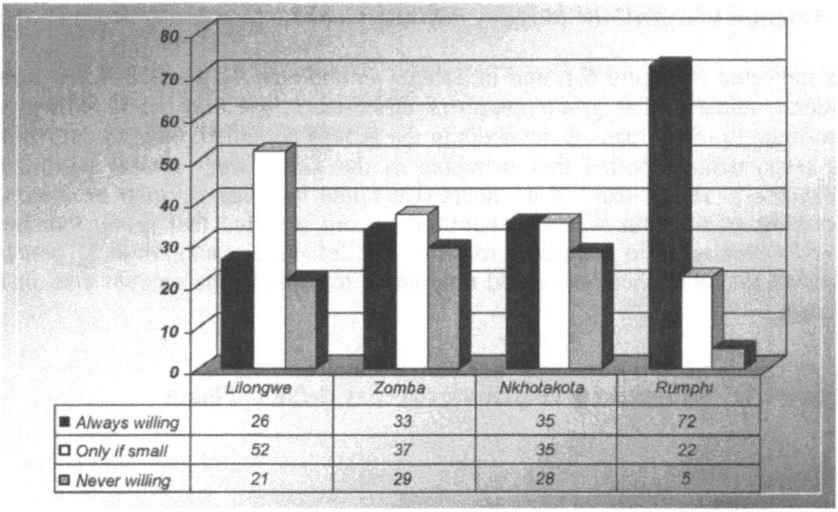

Source: Own calculation from IFPRI/RDD survey

A comparison across credit programs in Table 6.2 indicates that members belonging to maize credit groups are less likely to be always willing to repay the defaulted loans (25%), as compared to tobacco groups (56%) and non-farm business groups (54%).

When asked on how much group members would be willing to contribute to repay the defaulted loans in order to maintain their access to credit, the average amount reported is MK518, which is about 12 US dollars or 32 percent of the average loan size per member[10]. As indicated in Figure 6.3 members belonging to tobacco groups were willing to contribute a higher proportion of their loan sizes (40%) than non-farm (29%), maize (20%) and cotton/rice groups (12%). Although this is beyond the interest of this study, a detailed study on the characteristics of individuals within the group that are willing to contribute to pay

[10] exchange rate 1US$=44

defaulted loans would be a great contribution to the joint liability lending literature. Due to limitation in the data, this aspect was not explored.

Table 6.2 Willingness to pay defaulter's loan by type of credit group

Willingness to offer insurance	Tobacco (%) (n=46)	Maize (%) (n=16)	Cotton (%) (n=8)	Non-farm (%) (n=28)	All (98)
Whether understood repayment of defaulter's loan	93	90	75	90	91
Always willing	56	25	25	54	48
Willing only if small	24	50	50	36	31
Never willing	20	25	25	10	21
Average amount willing to contribute (MK)	680	351	210	435	518

Source: Own calculation from RDD/IFPRI Rural Finance Survey

The distribution of the amount of money that individuals are willing to pay as a proportion of total loan is presented in a kernel density in Figure 6.4. As can be observed from the figure, the majority are only willing to contribute up to 20 percent of the total loan value.

Figure 6.3 Amount of money peers are willing to contribute as a proportion of total loan.

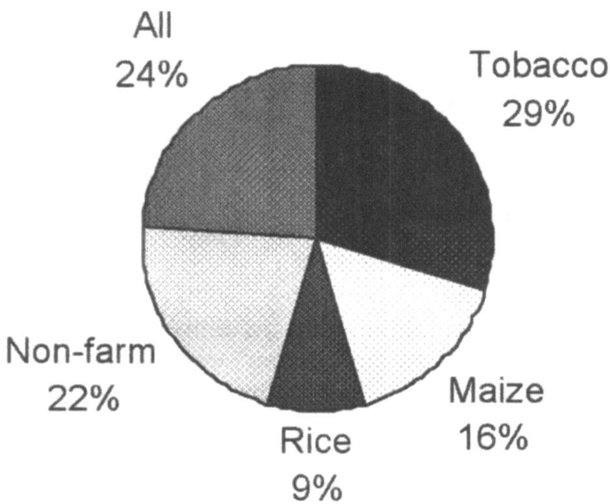

Source: Own calculation from IFPRI/RDD survey

The knowledge of the value of joint liability that group members are willing to pay is of interest to lending institutions because it is an indicator of the amount of loan portfolio at risk. For example, in this study, members are only willing to contribute about 32 percent of the total loan value to pay defaulters loan. Adding a 15 percent compulsory deposit to the contribution gives us a total contribution of about 47 percent of the loan value per person. This implies that at least 47 percent of the loan is insured by the group members. Taking a two borrower-scenario illustrated in most theoretical frameworks on group lending as an example, if one member fails to raise enough to repay his or her loan, it means that the remaining 53 percent of the loan amount must be paid by the defaulting partner. Nevertheless, since the defaulting partner also has a 15 percent compulsory collateral deposit, it means that the defaulting partner has to raise at least 38 percent of the total loan value in order for the group loan to be fully repaid.

Figure 6.4 Distribution of the willingness to contribute as a proportion of the total loan received

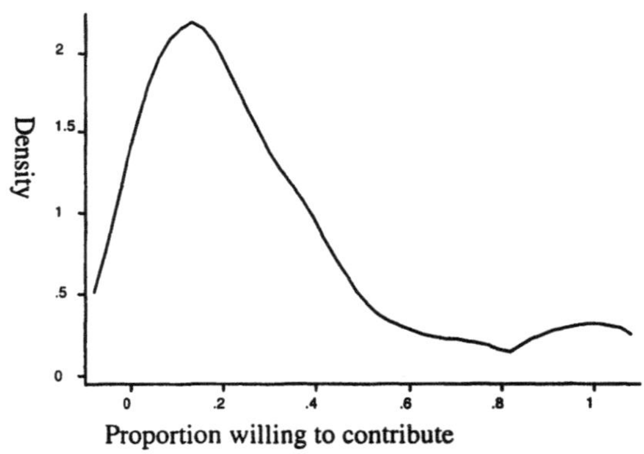

Source: Own calculation from IFPRI/RDD survey

A payment of less than 38 percent by the defaulting member leads to group default and it is a recipe for strategic default since the cost of contributing to repay a defaulted loan by the non-defaulting member exceeds the perceived benefits of doing so. Extending this line of thinking to a group of more than 2 members, at least half of the group members must fully repay their loan, while defaulting members must raise at least 38 percent of the loan value from their investment if group default is to be avoided.

Characteristics of individuals for which peers are willing to contribute

A relational analysis of the type of loans and characteristics of peers for which group members are willing to contribute to repay their defaulted loan produced some interesting findings as well. As indicated in Table 6.3 peers are more willing to contribute to repay defaulted loans only when the loan amounts are significantly small. The results in Table 6.3 Indicate that members are only willing to contribute to repay a defaulted loan when it is small enough. Members for which peers indicated willingness to help in repaying their loan had a significantly ($P<0.05$) lower average loan size (MK 2081.91) than those for which peers were unwilling to help repay their loan (MK2840.98).

Table 6.3 Characteristics of members for which peers are willing to help

Characteristic of group members	Statistic
Average loan size for which members are	
Willing to contribute (MK)	2081.91 (1226)*
Not willing to contribute (MK)	2840.98 (1553)
Gender	
Male (%)	31
Female (%)	21
Relation to respondent	
Relative	44**
Friend or neighbor	16
Age in relation to respondent	
Much older	43.8
Slightly older	25
Same age	0
Slightly younger	16.7
Much younger	28.6
Past membership status	
Past SACA (%)	48**
Non Past SACA (%)	11
Past repayment record in 4 years	
Always repaid on time (%)	35*
Was sometimes late (%)	10

Source: Own calculation form RDD/IFPRI Rural Finance Survey

The gender of a group member did not seem to influence others to help in repaying a delinquent loan. Interestingly, members appear to be more willing to help in the repayment delinquent loans for group members to whom they are related (44%) than mere group members (16%). Beside, members are more willing to help those with a clean past repayment record (35%) than those who sometimes paid late (10%). Members from past SACA are more likely to be helped by some one (48%) than those that were not from past SACA credit programs (11%). It is not possible to ascertain why this was the trend, however one possibility is that the past SACA had a stronger network within credit groups resulting from their previous involvement in the SACA credit program than the others that we usually new members in the group. This assumption is particularly justifiable because microfinance has the potential of building social capital which can then be used by the beneficiaries to achieve their development goals.

Other characteristics for which the relational analysis was conducted include social status and education of a group member, wealth of member and occupation of a group member. In general there appeared to be a lack of association between these characteristics and the willingness of peers to contribute to repay defaulted loans.

Evidence of intra-group insurance

Intra-group insurance is usually an ex-post repayment outcome which must only occur in groups that face an internal repayment problem. In this study and as indicated in Figure 6.5 about 60 percent of the groups reported that at least one member in their groups faced a repayment problem such that they did not repay their loans by the due date. Any loans not repaid by the due date are considered as Portfolio at Risk (PAR) and microfinance Institutions strive to keep their PAR as low as possible. PAR is not considered as a defaulted loan such that it could be recovered through enforcement of the repayment contracts by either the lender or the peers.

None of the rice groups had made full repayments by the due date. The internal repayment problems were also quite evident in non-farm income and maize groups where 65.2 percent and 61.9 percent of the groups, respectively, failed to fully repay their loans before the due date. The proportion of tobacco groups showing repayment problems was lower (53.8%) than both non-farm income and maize groups. When an internal repayment problem occurs, group members may contribute money to repay the defaulted loan. It sounds ironical to note that although repayment problems were highest among maize and non-farm income groups, members in such groups are less willing to offer mutual insurance. These findings suggest that the repayment problems faced by such groups also affect the ability of peers to fulfil the risk sharing promises when a repayment problem occurs. In most cases internal repayment problems among tobacco groups are attributed to delays at the Auction floors where tobacco is sold.

Figure 6.5: Presence of internal repayment problems by due date

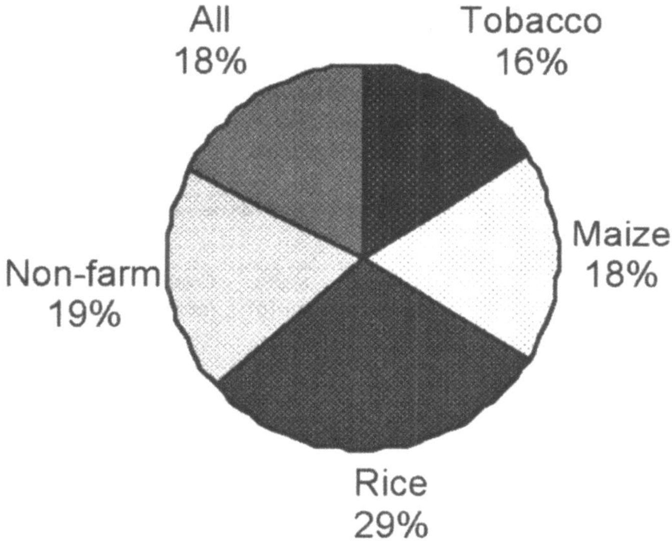

Source: Own calculation from IFPRI/RDD survey

This study finds a strong evidence of occurrence of intra-group insurance among groups that faced internal repayment problems. As indicated in Table 6.4, results indicate that about 63 percent of the defaulted loans were repaid through contributions from group members. About 28 percent of the defaulted loans were repaid from group savings. Both, group contributions as well as group savings are major components of intra-group insurance. Only 13 percent reported that payments were made through by selling assets of defaulters.

Payment of defaulted loans through contributions by group members is highest among tobacco groups (75%) than in other groups. This could be attributed to the higher returns that farmers realize from growing tobacco compared to other crops such as maize. The information collected by IFPRI, however, lacks data on enterprise margins; as such this suggestion is speculative. Nevertheless, the fact that tobacco groups pay their loans through the Auction Holdings where tobacco sales are conducted leaves full paying members that would want to renege their mutual insurance promises with very little room for escaping. Thus, group members that would want to renege their insurance promises are forced to repay on behalf of those with poor returns without their final approval.

Anecdotal stories on why members, particularly, from non-tobacco groups did not repay defaulted loans revealed that even when some members were willing to repay for the defaulters, in most cases they were left with very little money after repaying their own loans. Also it was revealed that in certain circumstances defaulted loans were difficult to be repaid by club members when the defaulter was a group leader. For example, when a village chief defaults, group members had to find ways of repaying the loan without embarrassing or humiliating the chief. This procedure may require the approval of other non-members that are related to the chief before allowing group members to contribute in the repayment of the defaulted loan.

Table 6.4 Ex-post group repayment outcomes and means of repaying defaulted loans

	Tobacco (n=46)	Maize (n=16)	Cotton (n=8)	Non-farm business (n=28)	Total (n=98)
Delinquency rates (%)	14	27	42	31	23
Means of repaying defaulted loans					
Not paid	25	50	57	21	30
Paid by other members	75	44	29	58	63
Paid from group savings	31	19	14	33	28
Paid from sale of assets of defaulter	8	31	29	8	13
Paid by CA/BDA	0	6	0	0	1
Other	2	6	29	13	7

Source: Own calculation form RDD/IFPRI Rural Finance Survey

Peer expectations, confidence and trust

The willingness of group members to repay defaulted loans may also be affected by the expectations that they have on their peers regarding the extent to which they think their peers (non defaulters) are likely to comply with the contractual obligation of repaying loans of defaulters. In this study respondents were asked to explain how confident they were at the beginning of the loan season, that if some members defaulted, those members who repaid their loans would contribute to pay the loans of defaulters. In general, results indicate that members do not have confidence in each other and that there is some degree of doubt regarding the honesty of their peers.

Table 6.5 Ex-ante expectations of members on the likelihood that non-defaulters would repay defaulted loans without complaining

How confident that non defaulters would repay loans of defaulters	Tobacco (n=46)	Maize (n=16)	Cotton/ Rice (n=8)	Non-farm business (n=28)	Total (n=99)
0	0	0	3	3.8	1.4
Less than 50 %	23	22	34	27	24
Between 50 and 99%	74	56	61	65	69
100%	3	22	2	4	5

Source: Own calculation form RDD/IFPRI Rural Finance Survey

As indicated in Table 6.5, only 5 percent of the respondents indicated that they were 100 percent confident that the non-defaulting members of the group would repay defaulted loans. About 25 percent strongly doubted that non defaulting members would contribute, with a degree of confidence of less than 50 percent. A bout 69 percent of the respondents indicated their confidence levels of between 50 and 99 percent. There are no significant differences in the variations in confidence levels between types of credit groups. The results suggest that there still remain a great deal of information asymmetry among group members as shown by the lack of confidence and trust among peers. One source of scepticism was the fact that respondents felt that the profits made from their enterprises were generally small such that it was difficult for one to repay their loan and then contribute to repay a peer's loan.

6.5 Results and Discussions

The main objective of this section is to investigate the role of group dynamics on group member's willingness to provide mutual insurance. The results from a Probit estimation are presented in Table 6.6. In concurrence with the a priori expectations, the sign for the within group coefficient of variation for the loan size (COVLOANVALUE), which is a proxy for the cost of insurance was negative and significant. Figure 6.6 shows the relationship between the willingness to contribute to repay defaulted loans and the variation in the size of the loan (COVLOANVALUE). From the figure, groups with a higher variation are less likely to be willing to offer mutual support in form of repaying defaulted loans than groups where the variation in loan sizes among the group members is small enough. A higher variation in loan size is an indicator of a higher cost of insurance.

The covariance of occupation (COOCCUP) was weakly significant and negative. This suggests that a higher correlation in the occupation of group members, which is a proxy for the correlation of output increases the probability that they would face similar idiosyncratic shocks at the same time which would make it difficult for members to be willing to assist each other.

Figure 6.6 Predicted probability of intra-group insurance by loan size variation

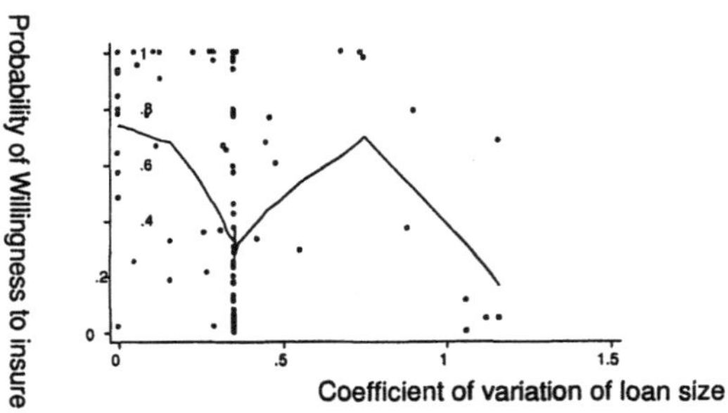

Source: Own calculation from IFPRI/RDD survey

One of the variables capturing factors of production, the average land holding size for the group (PROARABLE) had a significant and positive impact on the willingness of members to provide mutual insurance. The results conform to the a priori expectations as households with larger land holdings are also likely to be rich. In addition they are also likely to be more productive which enables them to get enough returns from their investment (in the case of agricultural investments) and, therefore, this enhances their repayment capacity. The higher repayment capacity is a prerequisite for members to support each other in the event of idiosyncratic shocks that may reduce the repayment capacity of other members. Such findings seem to suggest that households that are wealthier (in terms of education and land) have a stronger ability and willingness to share risks. Nonetheless, MRFC has to be cautious in targeting such households because this would lead into a mission drift.

All screening variables, except one performed poorly. Results indicate that members in groups that were initiated by the village chief (SCRVGHEAD) are more likely to provide mutual insurance. This suggests that traditional leaders play a crucial role in problem solving. Thus although peer selection is recommended, the involvement of a traditional leader in the early stages of group formation appears to play a positive role in enhancing the performance of credit groups, especially when the group faces repayment problems. Leaders can influence group members to make altruistic decisions of contributing to repay defaulted loans of peers. However, this could only function well if the traditional leader is honest and has significant influence in the community, which is usually the case with most village chiefs.

Four of the social ties proxies are significant. Groups composed of members from many villages (VILLAGENUM) are less likely to have stronger ties among the members and therefore the likelihood of mutual assistance is also low. Groups with some members that are related to the village chief

(PMFAMVG) and group chairperson (CHAIRFAMILY) have a higher probability of exercising mutual insurance. The coefficients for the two variables are positive and significant at 5 percent and 1 percent, respectively. The significance of the two would suggest that the presence of such members in a group increases interdependency, and problem solving, and openness, both of which have a positive effect on group morale and group cohesion.

The presence of members that are related to a politician (POLITCLAN) has a significant and negative effect on the willingness to offer mutual insurance. This is not surprising in the case of Malawi because in most instances, politicians, especially, those in the opposition side have been associated with information distortion about the sources of the loan. As reported in Evans (1997) some politicians in Malawi have in the past told borrowers that the loan they get from MRFC is supposed to be a grant. This weakens the commitment of borrowers to their contractual obligations as well as the interdependency between group members. Besides, the presence of members with strong political links reduces the degree of openness between group members, particularly if some members within the group also support a different political party. In sum the finding suggests that politicians may not be helpful in solving repayment problems at group level and that reliance on traditional leaders within the community once a group falls into repayment problems may be the right option.

The significant and positive coefficient of full joint liability option, which is a proxy for dynamic incentives, is not unexpected. This suggests that groups that value highly the access to further credit (as revealed by willingness to pay a full value of the defaulted loans in order to maintain further access), are more likely to be willing to contribute to repay defaulted loans for their peers. As indicated in Figure 6.7, 48 percent of the respondents indicated that they were always willing to contribute to repay in full the loans of defaulters in order to maintain access to a higher amount of future loan from MRFC. Those that were unwilling to pay a full value of the defaulted loan, but were ready to pay only a 10 percent penalty of the defaulted loan accounted for 39 percent of the sample. Interestingly, there are still others (13%) that were ready to accept a lower loan in the next loan cycle and were unwilling to contribute to repay loans of defaulting members of the group. The other proxy variable for dynamic incentives, PASTSACA, was not significant. The peer monitoring proxies PMJOINTENT, GCOMPDNI, and GLONCDNI, performed poorly, as they are insignificant and have mixed signs.

The presence of new members in the group (NEWMMBA) as proxy for matching problems had a negative and significant effect on the willingness to offer mutual insurance. When new members join the group, they bring in new skills. As a result, their loan requirements are different from the other group members. MRFC has a policy of increasing the amounts of loans for each subsequent loan cycle and also observes a three-tier variable interest rate structure, in which prime customers pay the lowest rate, repeat customers pay a rate that is 2 percent higher than prime and first time customers pay 3 percent above the prime customer rate.

Figure 6.7 Willingness to maintain access to higher future loans

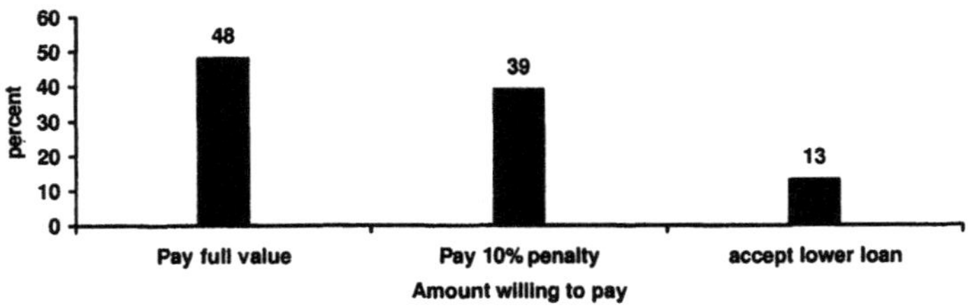

Source: Own calculation from IFPRI/ RDD Survey

The introduction of new members implies an increase in the variation of loan sizes, as well as an in increase in the variation of the cost of the loan as new members pay higher interest rates. A combination of the two raises the cost of insurance for some members such that they may be unable to provide mutual assistance to a defaulting individual with a larger loan or indeed with a higher interest rate. Besides, the matching problem arising from the inability of the lending institution to match loan demand with loan supply for all the group members at once, leads to what Tuckman (1965) calls the adjourning behaviour. This leads to the termination of task behaviours and disengagement from relationship, both of which have a negative impact on the willingness of group members to assist each other.

Nonetheless, in Malawi the high competition that microfinance clients face from traders bas been cited as the main reason why clients, for example, from FINCA in their fourth loan cycle are taking the same size of loan and sometimes even less than they did in the previous cycles. Gallardo (2000) notes that the competition is about holding to the same part of the market which is not growing as fast as the number of sellers in it. In such a case, therefore, the adjourning behaviour could be a result of the inability of microfinance Institutions to meet the financing needs of its clients. As rightly noted by Gallardo (2000), it is important for microfinance practitioners in Malawi a closer understanding of the microfinance clients´ financing needs and how household savings and credit fit into the complex household financial portfolio where household expenses for basic needs, education and micro-business are integrated with contingencies for emergency and medical needs. Besides, it is important to conduct a detailed investigation of factors that lead to the lack of profitability for the non-farm enterprises.

Maize and non-farm income groups returned negative and significant coefficients. This suggests that mutual insurance is less likely to occur in maize and non-farm income groups. One reason could be that the maize crop as well as non-farm income are far less profitable than tobacco, such that it is less likely that members in the such groups will get returns that are higher than the critical values required to make a repayment of their loan before they can consider contributing to repay loans of defaulting group members. This is in concurrence with the observation by Gallardo (2000) who observes that there is a noticeable lack of profitable opportunities for non-farm micro- enterprises.

Table 6.6 Determinants of intra-group insurance- probit estimates

Variable	Coefficient	Coefficient	Z-statistic	$\frac{dy}{dx}$ [11]
Cost of insurance	CVLOANVALUE	-1.254**	-1.94	-2.020
Covariance	COVLOSS	-0.338	-0.46	-0.510
	COVOCCUP	-1.335*	-1.81	-1.810
Production factors	PRODARABLE	0.360**	2.31	2.330
	PRODLEVELSCH	-0.014	-0.09	-0.090
Screening	SCREEN	0.399	0.85	0.890
	SCRFA	0.304	0.4	0.400
	PEERSELECT	0.631	0.82	0.870
	SCRVGHEAD	1.660**	2.36	2.350
Social ties	VILLAGENUM	-0.334**	-2.16	-2.150
	PMFAMVG	1.308**	2.26	2.270
	POLITCLAN	-0.748*	-1.71	-1.850
	CHAIRFAMILY	0.362**	2.3	2.300
Peer monitoring	PMJOINTENT	-0.272	-0.49	-0.670
	GCOMPDNI	-1.186	-0.91	-0.890
	GLONCDNI	4.092	1.03	1.000
Dynamic incentive	CONTRIBPAY	1.457***	3.21	3.230
	PASTSACA	-0.779	-1.53	-1.530
Matching problem	NEWMMBAVG	-0.237*	-1.79	-1.770
	LCYCLE	-0.323	-1.7	-1.600
Control variables	GPSIZE	-0.069	-1.6	-1.540
	MAXIDLMG	0.000	1.64	1.580
	MAIZE	-3.643***	-4.1	-4.130
	COTTON	-1.608	-1.56	-1.570
	NONFARM	-1.155**	-2.09	-2.070
	LILONGWE	-1.215	-1.52	-1.450
	ZOMBA	-0.279	-0.48	-0.430

[11] The marginal effects measure the changes in a regressor on the conditional probability that $y=1$. The marginal effect of regressor x_i is expressed as follows: $\frac{d\Pr(y=1\mid x)}{dx_i}=\phi(\beta' x_i)\beta_j$, where β_j is the sign of the marginal effect

Table 6.7 continued

	NKHOTA	-0.306	-0.21	-0.180
Constant	_CONS	1.846	1.17	1.130
Total observations		99		
Observation with dependent =0		54		
% Correctly predicted		84.85		
Wald chi2 (23)		66.09		
Prob > chi2		0.0043		
Pseudo R2		0.536		

Source: Own calculation from IFPRI/RDD survey 1999
Note: * P<0.10; ** P<0.05; *** P<0.01 ,

This suggests the need for the diversification of activities by allowing non-farm groups and maize groups to access tobacco loans as well. This suggestion arises from the fact that previous studies (e.g. Gallardo 2000) have shown that microfinance clients in Malawi, who appeared to be successful in business, were involved in multiple activities. For example Gallardo noted that a woman could do petty trading in a market place, run a shop from her house, and sell milk from a zero grazing operation with one cow.

Besides, non-farm income groups indicated that they were mostly unwilling to contribute because of the difficulty in auditing peers on the reliability of information they provide to the group regarding the returns to the business. They indicated that some members may lie about the profitability of their businesses and they found it difficult to verify the information. Through anecdotal stories it was learnt that group members found it easier to monitor the performance of crops in the field than to monitor a non-farm business.

6.6 Conclusions and Policy Implications

The aim of this chapter was to empirically analyze determinants of intra-group insurance. Using group level data from Malawi I find that although about 90 percent of the borrowers indicated that they understood that they were obliged to contribute to repay loans of defaulters in the group, only 48 percent expressed a full willingness to do so. An investigation into factors that affect the willingness of group members to offer intra-group insurance has revealed interesting insights and a good number of variables tested conformed to the a priori expectations.

The significance of factors of production and social ties is not unexpected. I find that through high levels of production factors and pre-existing strong social ties, groups function as insurance networks. Groups composed of members with larger land holdings and that are from the same village are more likely to participate in intra-group insurance activities such as contributing to repay loans of defaulters. Besides the study shows that groups composed of members that are related to a village chief, and those that that were formed by the village chief are more likely to be willing to help each other when there is a repayment problem. In contrast, groups composed of members that are related to some politicians were unwilling to help each other in the event of a repayment problem.

Further, results indicate that groups that attach a higher value to accessing future loans from MRFC are more willing to provide intra-group insurance than those that do not. The findings have also revealed that the presence of new members in a group, which potentially introduces a matching problem, works against mutual insurance.

The cost of insurance, captured by the variation in loan size among group members, reduces the capability and willingness of members to provide mutual insurance. The findings on risk diversification are fairly consistent with theory and signify the importance of risk pooling factors in enhancing the group's ability to provide mutual insurance. Specifically, the findings show that high correlation of output leads to a reduction in the willingness of members to offer mutual support. All peer monitoring variables do not play a significant role in intra-group insurance activities. The implication of these findings for group lending as a tool for poverty alleviation is that, risk diversification, social ties, dynamic incentives and factors of production such as land holding size are a recipe for successful intra-group insurance

These finings lead to a number of policy recommendations. First as noted by Sadoulet (2004), considering the unwillingness of MFIs to share the risks of income losses with borrowers, it is likely that intra-group insurance will remain the single major source of insurance for the poor borrowers that have no collateral. As such MRFC must seriously consider investing into a detailed exploration into strategies for enhancing the effective functioning of the intra-group insurance activities.

In order to strengthen the willingness of group members to offer intra-group insurance MRFC has to encourage clients to form groups composed of members from the same village as groups composed of members from several villages are unlikely to exhibit strong social ties required for intra-group insurance.

The positive effect of village chiefs suggests that MRFC has to continue using the traditional leaders in influencing members in groups to help each other. MRFC, currently, attaches great importance to village chiefs as they are supposed to sign for any loan that MRFC gives to groups in each village. Although such leaders may not be important in mitigating other risky behaviour among borrowers, they are quite influential in bringing members together when there is a repayment problem because each member has some respect for the chief. Their involvement in the day today running of the affairs of the village gives them an upper hand in mobilizing group members to repay defaulted loans as each member may want to be in good books with the chief.

The other key recommendation relates to the variation in the size of the loan among group members. It is important for MRFC to pay attention to the variation in loan sizes per group by making it as small as possible in order to reduce the cost of intra-group insurance which might arise when a group member with a larger loan size fails to repay his or her loan. Those with small loans will be unwilling to shoulder the cost of repaying large loans.

The willingness to provide insurance is weak in maize and non-farm income groups. Although this study failed to find explicit reasons for such a trend, some borrowers cited low profitability in non-farm and maize loans as the main cause of the low willingness to assist each other. MRFC should, therefore, consider diversifying the loan package so that clients are allowed to borrow for tobacco production, which is more profitable, as well as for maize production or for non-farm business activities.

Nevertheless, most credit groups in Malawi are exposed to systemic risks related to production and prices which make intra-group insurance ineffective when they occur. In this study I found that in some cases members were unwilling to assist each other because they all had lower returns resulting from drought. MRFC should, therefore, see this as a good justification for the introduction repayment insurance schemes that might be related to the types of shocks that borrowers face. For example borrowers would be requested to start paying weather based insurance premiums to insure themselves against losses resulting from bad weather. This offers a more reliable form of insurance than the existing intra-group insurance that can only insure borrowers against a limited amount of idiosyncratic shocks.

7 THE IMPACT OF ACCESS TO CREDIT ON THE ADOPTION OF HYBRID MAIZE

7.1 Introduction

Food security in Malawi is mainly defined in relation to the availability of maize, the main staple in the country. It is for this reason that the Malawi's agricultural policy for the past two decades, emphasized the production of hybrid maize, a capital intensive and high yielding technology as a substitute to the local maize varieties. Efforts to diversify away from maize into other food crops have failed largely because maize being a C4 plant produces more calories per unit of land area than all other food crops grown in Malawi. It is, therefore, likely that Malawi will continue to rely on maize as a major food crop. In addition the policy emphasis has been on tobacco, a labor and capital intensive cash crop. A combination of the two crops continues to be seen as a potential option for improving the income and food security of rural households in Malawi (Zeller *et al.*, 1998).

The provision of micro-credit to farmers is widely perceived as an effective strategy for promoting the adoption of improved technologies. It is believed that access to credit promotes the adoption of risky technologies through the relaxation of the liquidity constraint as well as through the boosting of household's-risk bearing ability. With an option of borrowing, a household can do away with risk reducing but inefficient income diversification strategies and concentrate on more risky but efficient investments (Eswaran and Kotwal, 1990).

Despite the widely acknowledged importance of credit in relaxing the liquidity constraint, the poor have been discriminated against access to such a valuable resource because of the potential risks and costs associated with administering credit to the poor. Such forms of credit market failure, which are quite pervasive in rural communities in developing countries, affect household behaviour in a number of ways. For example, Eswaran and Kotwal (1986) cited in Vakis *et al.* (2004) show how the labour and credit market failures imply that households with different asset positions relative to labour endowment follow different strategies of labour deployment and use this in turn to establish social classes. Household behaviour under perfect markets implies separability between production and consumption decisions (Singh, Squire and Strauss, 1986). Nevertheless, under imperfect markets production and consumption decisions are non-separable. This implies that for one to correctly model household production decisions, one has to know whether or not a household is behaving according to separability on non-separability decision rules (Vakis *et al.*, 2004).

Recognizing the potential contribution of credit in enhancing the adoption of hybrid maize among smallholders, the government of Malawi has been pursuing a credit policy that seeks to promote hybrid maize production. The government of Malawi, through the Smallholder Agricultural Credit Administration (SACA), started providing joint liability loans to smallholder farmers as far back as 1973, three years before the Grameen Bank was created (Diagne *et al.,* 2000). The credit whose main purpose was to promote smallholders' production of high value crops (first maize, then later in the 1990s also tobacco) was mainly given to farmers in the form of in-kind loans such as fertilizer and seed. However, despite such concerted efforts by the government, and more recently non-governmental organizations in promoting the cultivation of hybrid maize, its adoption remains low. By 2003, more than half of the total maize land was allocated to local varieties (Government of Malawi, 2004). It is often asserted that in addition to taste preferences an on-farm storage constraints (Smale, 1995), and to risk aversion (Simtowe *et al.,* 2006), credit constraints are widely responsible for the low adoption of hybrid maize due to its requirements for costly inputs.

A substantial amount of adoption literature has reported on the impact of access to credit on adoption, and a good deal of it showing that credit has a positive impact on adoption. For, example, Feder and Umali (1993) and Cornejo and McBrid (2002) review factors that affect technology adoption, and they highlight access to credit as a key determinant of adoption of most agricultural innovations. Nevertheless, most studies that have looked at the impact of credit have generalized their analysis by assuming that credit access should always lead to positive impact outcomes. Such studies have ignored household behaviour with regards to whether or not the household is credit constrained. In reality, however, there are circumstances in which access to credit may have no impact on the choice of activities and the welfare of the household. Credit access will only be effective for the credit "constrained" – thus those with access to remunerative consumption, production and investment opportunities who are unable to pursue the opportunities for lack of financial resources. A lack of access to credit may not necessarily imply an unmet credit need (*de* Janvry *et al.*, 1997). In the same way, the marginal contribution of credit is likely to be high in households that have a larger binding credit constraint than in those that are less constrained. Besides, previous studies have ignored the significance of considering separability in production decisions at household levels. Considering separability in production decision models is important because the comparative statics for households facing a market failure such as credit constraints are different from those without a market failure, such that models that do not take into account such differences will lead to inconsistent parameter estimates (Vakis *et al.*, 2004). In Malawi, as else where, all credit impact studies have not taken into account the potential inconsistency that may result from such incorrect modelling. Knowledge of whether or not access to credit enables a household to make its production and consumption decisions separably is also crucial as it enables us to capture other potential constraining factors, such as complementary market failures and other factors that might make credit ineffective to beneficiary households.

Building on the economic theory of the agricultural household model under credit market failure, this chapter aims at investigating the extent to which access to credit enables smallholder farmers to adopt hybrid maize production in Malawi. The study uses a Double-Hurdle model in estimating the determinants of adoption due to a presumption that factors that influence the household's decision to adopt are different from those that affect the extent of adoption. Using the direct elicitation approach developed by Diagne, Zeller Sharma (2000), households are classified into credit constrained and unconstrained regimes. The effect of access to credit on the adoption of hybrid maize is estimated using a switching regression approach by taking into account the selection bias associated with categorizing the sample into constrained and unconstrained regimes. I start by estimating the probability of being credit constrained, followed by an estimation of the impact of access to credit for the two regimes of households (credit constrained and unconstrained), while accounting for selection bias.

A distinction is made between *'access'* to micro-credit, *'participation'* in the micro-credit market and being credit *'constrained'*. A household has *access to micro-credit* from a particular source if it is *able to borrow* from that source (Diagne and Zeller, 2001). A household *participates* if it *actually borrows* from that source of micro-credit. Thus, a household can have access but choose not to borrow, i.e., does not participate in the credit market. A household is credit *constrained* if its demand for credit exceeds the supply of credit (Gilligan *et al.*, 2005, Japelli, 1990). I test for separability in both the constrained and the unconstrained regimes using a farm labour demand model. Data used in this study is from Malawi collected by the International Food Policy Research Institute (IFPRI). The rest of the chapter is arranged as follows: in section two I present a review of maize production in Malawi and the role of credit. In section three I present the empirical approach used. The data used for the estimation is described in section four. In section 5 I present and discuss results, while section 6 concludes.

7.2 Maize Production in Malawi: A Review

A significant feature in Malawi's agriculture is the dominance of maize in the farming systems. It is estimated that more than 70 percent of the arable land is allocated to maize production (Government of Malawi, 2004). It is also noted that despite efforts to diversify away from maize, the land allocated to maize continues to rise. Carr (1997) notes that the continued rise in the land allocated to maize could be attributed to the fact that maize is a C4 plant[12], such that it produces more calories per unit land area than other crops grown in Malawi. With the decline in farm size, small holders have allocated more of their land to maize. Nevertheless due to the short and single farming season, combined with the lack of inputs that accompany the production of maize, yields of maize remain low leading to food insecurity for more than 60 percent of the households who run out of food 4 months before the next harvest(World bank, 1996). The natural response by the government of Malawi has been the introduction of hybrid maize suited for both the climate and food preferences of farmers. Due to the continuous decline in soil fertility, farmers developed special interest in the use of fertilizer such that by 1995 over 90 percent of the maize was fertilized (CIMMYT, 1995).

As a way of achieving the policy of intensifying maize production through the use of hybrid maize seed and fertilizer, the government embarked on an ambitious credit program based on joint liability lending. Agricultural extension officers were given a task of overseeing the functioning of the credit groups and monitoring loan repayment. Supported by the Malawi Congress Party (MCP), the ruling party at that time, Conroy (1992) notes that this exerted pressure on farmers to repay, enabling Malawi to register the highest repayment rates of 95 percent for a number of years. In his paper "a green revolution frustrated" Carr (1997) notes that the rapid increase in hybrid maize seed and fertilizer use which was encouraged by a sharp rise in the supply of credit to smallholder farmers led a number of observers in the World Bank and CYMMT to refer to developments in Malawi as being a Green Revolution. In her paper "Maize is Life: Malawi's delayed Green revolution", Smale (1995) expected that there would be a continued increase in both the area allocated to hybrid maize as well as the yield. The reality though is that the land allocated to hybrid maize remains low.

Figure 7.1 presents the trend in the share of land allocated to hybrid maize from 1984 to 2003. Although there is appositive trend in land allocated to hybrid maize (as shown by the increase from about 8 percent in 1984 to 30 percent in 2003), there has been a number of fluctuations resulting from both policy influences as well as natural disasters such as drought. The steady increase in the share of hybrid maize area was halted in 1994 when it fell to 18 percent due to the collapse of the Small holder Agricultural Credit Administration (SACA). Zeller *et al.* (1998) note that, while 400,000 farmers received credit in 1992 only 34,000 did so in 1994. This led to an increase in the share of small holder land area planted to non-maize crops such as cassava and pulses. Zeller *et al.* (1998) observe that the response of farmers to the perceived advantages of drought-resistant crops, the sudden collapse of the public system for distributing credit for

[12] C4 plants are plants found principally in hot climates whose initial fixation of carbon dioxide in photosynthesis is by the hsk pathway. The presence of the hsk pathway permits efficient photosynthesis at high light intensities and low carbon dioxide concentrations. most species of this type have little or no photorespiration

maize production, and the government policy orientation towards diversifying smallholder crop production may all have played a role in this outcome.

Nevertheless, the increasing trend picked up after 1994 due to the large scale distribution of free fertilizer and hybrid maize seed. A sharp fall was experienced in 2001 and 2002 but 2003 saw a recovery to 30 percent of the land allocated to hybrid maize. From the review it is clear that more has to be done if the government policy of expanding the production of hybrid maize to more than half of the total maize land area is to be achieved.

Figure 7.1 Share of maize land allocated to hybrid maize production

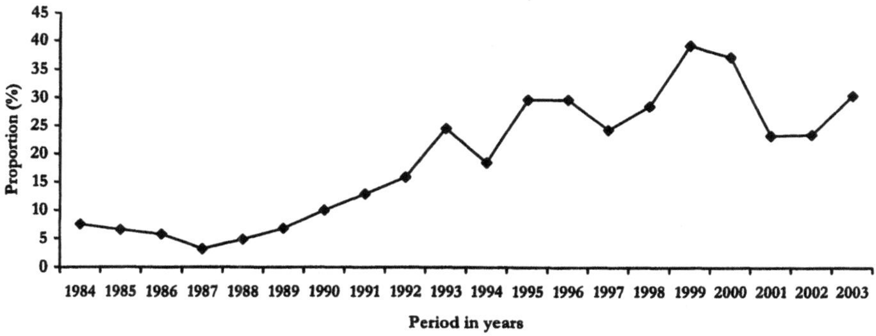

Source: Own calculation from IFPRI/RDD survey

A research on the role of credit on adoption of hybrid maize which takes into account the household credit constraint status is pertinent in that it will inform credit policy makers on the type of farmers to target for credit (or on the role of credit in fostering hybrid maize production).

7.3 Empirical Framework

7.3.1 Determinants of credit constraints

My empirical strategy starts by categorizing households into credit constrained and unconstrained regimes. The elicitation approach allows us to capture whether or not a household is credit constrained by directly asking the household whether they needed more credit for its investment activities. Through a series of questions it is possible to know whether or not a household had excess demand (ED) for credit in a given recall period. The procedure allows for the treatment of excess demand for credit (ED) =(Demand –Supply), as a latent variable for each household *h*. Following this procedure it is not possible to assess the magnitude of the constraint, instead only an indicator of whether or not the household is credit constrained is observed (Gilligan *et al.*, 2005). The specification for the two categories of households can thus be written as follows:

$$k_h = 1 \text{ if } ED^*_h = X_h^{'}\alpha + u_h \geq 0 \qquad (7.1)$$

$$k_h = 0 \text{ if } ED^*_h = X_h^{'}\alpha + u_h \leq 0$$

Where:

X_h represents household and farm characteristics that determine credit demand as well as characteristics of the household and the lending institution that determine the supply of credit

u_h is a random error term with zero mean capturing stochastic factors affecting both the demand and supply

In order to identify determinants of credit constraints, I estimate a model in equation 7.1 to identify factors associated with the likelihood of a household to be credit constrained in which both the demand and supply factors enter the model. This is also used as a test for the reliability of the self-reported credit constraint status.

The likelihood of household reporting credit constraints is assumed to be determined by a latent variable y* which can be expressed as follows in a regression relationship:

$$y_i{*} = \beta'_i X_i + \mu_i \qquad (7.2)$$

where X is a vector of characteristics, which, it is hypothesized that they affect the likelihood of being constrained, β'_i is a vector of coefficients for variables associated with credit constraints and μ_i .is the error term.

In practice y* is unobservable. What is observed is a dummy variable defined as

$$y = 1 \qquad \text{if } y_i{*} > 0 \qquad (7.3)$$

$$y=0 \qquad \text{otherwise}$$

Because of the assumption of a cumulative normal distribution of the error terms, the estimation of determinants of credit constraints is done using the Probit model.

7.3.2 The impact of access to credit on the adoption of hybrid maize

Based on the theoretical framework presented in Chapter 4, the underlying assumption in assessing the effect of credit on adoption is that adoption S is a function of a vector, X consisting of exogenous variables and endogenous credit access, K, such that:

$$S = S(X^{'}, K, ; \beta) + \varepsilon_i \qquad (7.4)$$

In this specification credit access K is endogenous because factors that affect the household's access to credit K may also affect the household's share of land allocated to hybrid maize. In order to solve this problem Zeller *et al.* (1998) recommend a simultaneous modelling of both the adoption decision and access to credit. As such, an extra equation is required to estimate the predicted access to credit, K expressed as

$K = K(X', w; \gamma) + \omega_i$

The theoretical framework outlined earlier postulates that credit access K is only an important variable for adoption among households that are credit constrained. The adoption of hybrid maize by a credit constrained household can thus be specified as follows:

$$S^c = S^c(X', K,; \beta) + \varepsilon_i \quad (7.5)$$

$$K = K(X', w; \gamma) + \omega_i \quad (7.6)$$

Where:

X' is a vector of characteristics that affect both the adoption decision and the endogenous credit access, K,

$w =$ is a vector of instruments correlated with credit access but not with adoption,

ε_1 and ε_2 are random error terms, where as

β, γ are vectors of coefficients.

As for the unconstrained households, since it is assumed that credit access does not affect their decision to adopt hybrid maize, credit access, K, should have no impact on adoption. The specification is as follows:

$$S^u = A^u(X,; \nu) + \eta \quad (7.7)$$

where: ν and η are a coefficient to be estimated and the error tem, respectively. The estimation of equations for the two regimes, thus the credit constrained regime and the unconstrained regime is done using a switching regression approach. Estimating the two equations separately is used as a counterfactual test of whether or not credit access affects adoption among constrained households. In the empirical estimation the predicted access to credit is included as one of the explanatory variables in both regimes.

7.3.3 The switching regression model

In order to test the impact of credit on adoption, I use equation 1 as a criterion function for whether or not a household is constrained and S to represent the dependent variable for adoption to estimate an endogenous switching regression model as specified in Maddala (1986) of the following form.

$$S_h^c = W_{1h}'\phi_1 + v_{1h} \text{ if } k_h = 1 \quad (7.8a)$$
$$S_h^u = W_{2h}'\phi_2 + v_{2h} \text{ if } k_h = 0 \quad (7.8b)$$

where

$\phi_i = [\delta_0, \beta_1 .... \beta_n]$

$W_{ih}' = [X_h', \hat{K}]$

$v_{ih} = \varepsilon_i$ for i=1 if the household is credit constrained and i=2 if unconstrained.

The endogeneity in a switching regression comes from the fact that it allows for correlation between the error terms in the credit constraint criterion function (7.1) and the equations of interest (7.8a) and (7.8b). Thus the error terms v_{1h}, v_{2h}, and, u_h are assumed to be jointly normally distributed with zero mean and the following covariance matrix.

$$\sum \begin{bmatrix} \sigma_{11} & \sigma_{12} & \sigma_{1u} \\ \sigma_{12} & \sigma_{22} & \sigma_{2u} \\ \sigma_{1u} & \sigma_{2u} & \sigma_{uu} \end{bmatrix}$$

The switching regression model accounts for the fact that each household has a non-zero probability of being credit constrained in each period, that this probability varies depending on household characteristics, and that only one realization of these probabilities is observed in each period (Gillgan *et al.*, 2005). Consistent estimates of parameters ϕ_1 and ϕ_2 can be obtained by following a two step Heckman procedure of estimating the credit constraint equation in (7.1) as a Probit and estimating equation 7.8a and 7.8b separately, while correcting for the selection bias by including the inverse Mills ratio from equation 7.1 as a regressor in the two equations.

7.3.4 Empirical estimation of adoption

Following Feder, Just and Zilberman (1985) adopters are defined as households that reported that they grew hybrid maize. The extent of adoption is defined as degree of use of a technology, which for this study is taken as the proportion of maize land that is allocated to hybrid maize. The decision of whether or not to adopt hybrid maize variety and how much land to allocate to hybrid maize can be estimated using a censored Tobit model (Zilberman and Just 1984) or a P-Tobit model (Deaton and Irish (1984). A Tobit is an econometric model in which the dependent variable is censored. In the original model of Tobin (1958), for example, the dependent variable was expenditures on durables, and the censoring occurs because values below zero are not observed. The Tobit model assumes a latent variable y* that can be expressed in the following functional form:

$$y_i^* = \beta x_i + \mu_i \tag{7.9}$$

where y^* is a latent variable that truncates adoption of hybrid maize, x is a vector of farm household characteristics, which, it is hypothesized that they affect the adoption decision, and β is a vector of coefficients to be estimated. μ_i is the error term which is assumed to have a truncated normal distribution, yielding a Tobit model. The model has two advantages. First it permits the investigation of the decision of whether to adopt and the level of adoption (Adesina and BaiduForson, 1995) and its coefficients can be disaggregated to determine the effects of change in one variable on changes in the probability of adoption and the expected intensity of adoption.

The specification for hybrid maize adoption and non-adoption, measured by the censored random variable is written as follows for hybrid maize adopters:

$$y_i = y_i^* \text{ if } y_i^* > 0 \text{ or } \beta x_i + \mu_i > 0 \tag{7.10}$$

and as follows for those who did not grow hybrid maize:

$$y_i = 0 \text{ if } y_i^* \leq 0$$

The probability function for non- adopters is given by:

$$pr(y_i{*} = 0) = \Phi\left(\frac{\beta x_i}{\sigma}\right) \tag{7.11}$$

while the density function for the adopters is:

$$f(y_i / y_i^* > 0) = \frac{f(y_i)}{pr(y_i^* > 0)} = \frac{\frac{1}{\sigma}\phi\left(\frac{y_i^* - \beta x_i}{\sigma}\right)}{\Phi\left(\frac{\beta x_i}{\sigma}\right)} \tag{7.12}$$

where $\Phi(.)$ and $\phi(.)$ are the standard normal cumulative and probability density functions (cdf and pdf), respectively.

The log-likelihood function for the Tobit model (Moffat, 2003) is as follows:

$$LogL = \sum_0 \ln\left[1 - \Phi\left(\frac{x_i{'}\beta}{\delta}\right)\right] + \sum_+ \ln\left[\frac{1}{\delta}\phi\left(\frac{y_i - x_i{'}\beta}{\delta}\right)\right] \tag{7.13}$$

in which "0" indicates summation over zero observations in the sample, while "+" indicates summation over positive observations.

However, the main weakness with the Tobit model is that it only allows one type of zero observation, namely *a corner solution*, since it is based on the implicit assumption that zeros arise only as a result of the respondent's economic circumstances (Martínez-Espiñeira, 2006). In the same context Moffat (2003) observes that in some cases there are household that would never take some positive values, (thus they would never adopt under any circumstances because they consider the technology to be inferior), then the use of a restrictive Tobit model without considering the group that would never adopt may give biased results. Deaton and Irish (1984) propose a relaxation of this restriction by considering the probability that one would never adopt. With respect to this study, let us assume that the proportion of households that are potential adopters of hybrid maize is *p*, such that the proportion of households that would never adopt hybrid maize is *(1-p)*. The Tobit model would apply for the group of potential adopters while it wouldn't for the "never adopters" since the intensity of adoption would be automatically zero. This gave rise to the P-Tobit model with the following likelihood function (Moffat 2003):

$$LogL = \sum_0 \ln\left[1 - p\Phi\left(\frac{x_i'\beta}{\delta}\right)\right] + \sum_+ \ln\left[p\frac{1}{\delta}\phi\left(\frac{y_i - x_i'\beta}{\delta}\right)\right] \qquad (7.14)$$

Thus in addition to estimating β and δ the P-Tobit also estimates the p.

Nevertheless, as noted by Martínez-Espiñeira (2006), the P-Tobit model fails to analyze the factors that will make a respondent more or less likely to adopt a technology. A further generalization allows for the parameter *p* to vary according to respondent's characteristics. This gives rise to the Double-Hurdle model. The underlying assumption in the Double- Hurdle approach is that individuals make two decisions with regard to their willingness to grow hybrid maize. The first decision is whether they will allocate a positive amount of land to hybrid maize at all. The second decision is about the share of land that they will allocate, conditional on the first decision. The two decisions are, therefore, whether to grow hybrid maize and how much to grow. The importance of treating the two decisions independently lies in the fact that factors that affect one's decision to adopt may be different from those that affect the decision on how much to adopt. This implies that households must cross two hurdles in order to adopt. The first hurdle needs to be crossed in order to be a potential adopter. Given that the households is a potential adopter, their current circumstances then dictate whether or not they do in fact adopt- this is the 'second hurdle' (Moffat 2003). The Double-Hurdle model allows for the possibility that these two decisions are affected by a different set of variables. The advantage with this approach is that it allows us to understand characteristics of a class of households that would never adopt hybrid maize. Thus the probability of a household to belong to a particular class depends on a set of household characteristics.

Originally proposed by Cragg (1971), the double hurdle model has been recently applied in a variety of areas. Martínez-Espiñeira (2006) cites the use of the Double -Hurdle model by Burton, Dorset and Young´s (1996), who model US food expenditure away from home; Yen and Jones (1997) who apply the model to alcohol consumption and US household consumption of cheese, respectively. Moffat (2003) used the model to model loan default. The Double-Hurdle model is a parametric generalization of the P-Tobit model in which the decision to adopt and the intensity of adoption are determined by two separate stochastic processes and therefore two equations. The first equation in the Double-Hurdle relates to the decision to adopt and it can be expressed as follows:

$$d_i = 1 \text{ if } d^*_i > 0 \text{ and } 0 \text{ if } d^*_i \leq 0 \qquad (7.15)$$

$$d^* = z_i'\alpha + \varepsilon_i$$

d^*_i is latent adoption variable that takes the value of 1 if a household grew hybrid maize and 0 otherwise, z is a vector of household characteristics and α is a vector of parameters;

The second hurdle, which closely resembles the tobit model is expressed as:

$$y_i = y_i^* \text{ if } y_i^* > 0 \text{ and } d_i^* > 0$$

$$y_i = 0 \text{ otherwise}$$

$$y^* = x_i'\beta + u_i \qquad (7.16)$$

where y_i is the observed response on how much land one allocated to hybrid maize, x is a vector of the household characteristics and β is a vector of parameters.

The decision of whether or not to adopt hybrid maize and about how much land to allocate to hybrid maize can be *jointly* modelled, if they are made *simultaneously* by the household; *independently*, if they are made *separately*; or *sequentially*, if one is made first and affects the other one as in the dominance model (Martínez-Espiñeira, 2006). If the independence model applies, the error terms are distributed as follows:

$$\varepsilon_i \div N(0,1)$$

$$u_i \div N(0,\delta^2)$$

If both decisions are made jointly (the Dependent Double - Hurdle) the error term can be defined as

$$\varepsilon_i \mu_i) \div BVN(0,\Upsilon)$$

$$\text{Where} : \Upsilon = \begin{bmatrix} 1 & \rho\delta \\ \rho\delta & \delta^2 \end{bmatrix}$$

The model is said to be a dependent model if there is a relationship between the decision to adopt and the intensity of adoption. This relationship can be expressed as follows:

$$\rho = \frac{\operatorname{cov}(\varepsilon_i \mu_i)}{\sqrt{\operatorname{var}(\varepsilon_i)\operatorname{var}(\mu_i)}} \tag{7.17}$$

if $\rho = 0$ and there is dominance (the zeros are only associated to non-participation, not standard corner solutions) then the model decomposes into a Probit for participation and a standard OLS for y.

Following Smith (2003) I assume that the error terms ε_i and μ_i are independently and normally distributed[13] and thus I have the following expression:

$$\begin{pmatrix} \varepsilon_i \\ u_i \end{pmatrix} N \left[\begin{pmatrix} 0 \\ 0 \end{pmatrix}, \begin{pmatrix} 1 & 0 \\ 0 & \delta^2 \end{pmatrix} \right]$$

And finally, the observed variable in a Double-Hurdle model is $y_i = d_i y_i^*$

The log-likelihood function for the double hurdle model is:

$$LogL = \sum_0 \ln\left[1 - \Phi(z_i'\alpha)\Phi\left(\frac{x_i'\beta}{\delta}\right)\right] + \sum_+ \ln\left[\Phi(z_i'\alpha)\frac{1}{\delta}\phi\left(\frac{y_i - x_i'\beta}{\delta}\right)\right] \tag{7.18}$$

Empirical results by both Moffat (2003) and Martínez-Espiñeira (2006) reveal that the Double-Hurdle model gives superior results to those obtained from Tobit and P-Tobit models. Thus in this study I estimate the decision to adopt and the extent of adoption using a Double-Hurdle model.

7.3.5 Test for separability

In economic theory the problems of production decisions, consumption decisions and labour supply are usually analyzed separately through the behaviour of three classes of agents, namely producers, consumers and workers. Following Sandoulet and *de* Janvry (1995), the three problems are integrated in a single household problem. The use of farm household models is favoured in adoption studies because they integrate in a single institution the decision regarding production, consumption and reproduction overtime (Sadoulet and *de* Janvry, 1995). The agricultural household model, therefore, serves as a theoretical framework for analyzing the production and consumption decisions

[13] See Smith (2003) for a theoretical analysis of why there might little gain from modeling dependence

either sequentially (separable model) or simultaneously (non-separable) (Swaminathan, 2003).

Separability implies that production decisions of the household are not affected by consumption and labour supply decisions. However, through the profit effect, consumption and labour supply decisions are affected by production decisions. Separable models can be solved recursively by first, solving the production problem to obtain factor demands, output supplies and optimal profit. Second, given the maximized level of profit the consumption problem is solved. In the presence of market failure, the assumption of separation between consumption and production decisions breaks down. The production and consumption problems are solved simultaneously. It is important to take into account separability in modelling household decision-making because as noted by Singh *et al.* (1986), wrongly assuming separability when the situation merits non-separability changes the comparative statics while parameters for demand and supply will be statistically inconsistent.

In this study, in order to test the reliability of the self reported credit constraints as well as understand differences in household's decision making between constrained and unconstrained households, I test for separation using a farm labour demand model. Theoretically, when markets and information are complete, household production and consumption decisions are decisions are separable (Singh *et al.*, 1986). The intuition is that if a farmer has access to as much labour as needed at market clearing wage rates and can obtain credit needed to hire the workers, the optimal demand for labour on the farm will not be affected by the number of potential workers in the household. Following Benjamin (1992), the farm labour demand equation for household *h* in period *t* can be specified as follows:

$$L_{ht} = \delta_0 + \delta_1 w_{vt} + \delta_2 A_{ht} + \delta_3 n_{ht} + \delta_4 X_{ht} + \omega_{ht} \qquad (7.19)$$

where:

L_{ht} is the total number of labour days on farm by household members and hired workers, w_{vt} the wage rate paid by households for the farming activities until harvest

A_{ht} is area of land cultivated, by household

X_{ht} Variables controlling for managerial ability (such as age, and education of household head), access to labour saving technologies and distance to markets

n_{ht} is a vector of variables representing the household structure including household size and composition (share of prime adult males and females)

δ_3 is a parameter representing the joint test for separability of production and consumption decisions. It should be equal to zero in order to accept separability.

ω_{ht} is a random error term

The model has power as a test for credit constraints as well as if farmers commonly hire workers for cash wages and use credit to finance the transactions, or if they would like to in the absence of credit constraints. The use of a farm-labor demand model in testing for credit constraints has advantage over other models such as the output supply model used by Ferder *et al.* (1990) and cited by Gilligan *et al.* (2005) because the effect of credit access on output supply operates through demand for factors such as labour and fertilizer.

The farm-labour demand model is chosen in testing for credit constraints due to such advantages over other models. In this data set the test for separability using the farm labour demand model is more appropriate among the tobacco farmers because, being a labor and intensive crop tobacco farmers have to hire extra labour to meet the labour demand.

A switching regression model as mentioned by Maddala (1986), similar to the specification in equation (7.8), is used to test for separability. As noted in Gilligan et al. (2005), the model can be use to test both the accuracy of self-reported credit constraints and it has power in identifying constraints by allowing parameter estimates in each model to differ in credit constrained and credit unconstrained regimes. Based on the criterion function specified in equation (7.1) for whether or not a household is credit constrained, the following endogenous switching regression is estimated:

$$L_{ht} = W_{1ht}^{'}\phi_1 + v_{1ht} \text{ if } k_{ht} = 1 \qquad (7.20)$$

$$L_{ht} = W_{1ht}^{'}\phi_1 + v_{2ht} \text{ if } k_{ht} = 0$$

where

$$\phi_1 = [\delta_0, \delta_1, \delta_2, \delta_3, \delta_4]$$

$$W_{iht}^{'} = [w_{vt}, A_{ht}, n_{ht}, X_{ht.}]$$

$v_{iht} = \omega_{iht}$ for i=1 if the household is credit constrained and i=2 if unconstrained.

7.4 Data

The data used in this analysis draws from a survey of households conducted by the International Food Policy Research Institute (IFPRI), and the Department of Rural Development at Bunda College of Agriculture in 1996 (for details see Diagne and Zeller, 2001). Only 3 modules were of relevance to this study, namely, household demographics, crop and livestock production and credit and savings. The data is available from on request from the International Food Policy Research Institute (IFPRI).

The analysis starts by categorizing households into credit constrained and unconstrained regimes. A number of approaches for identifying credit constraints have been cited in literature. Such approaches fall into two categories, namely the indirect methods and the direct methods. Indirect methods are based on tests of theoretical models involving credit constraints while direct methods are based on responses to qualitative questions about credit constraint status collected in surveys (Gillgan *et al.,* 2005). The indirect methods involve comparisons of parameter estimates for specific outcomes across constrained and unconstrained groups. The most widely used models for indirect test include consumption smoothing models, and farm labour demand models[14]. Vakis *et al.* (2004) propose a superior approach for identifying credit constrained households by using a mixture distribution approach to estimate the probability that a farm household behaves according to non-separability using a 1997 Peruvian data collected by the World Bank.

In the IFPRI survey, from which data for this study is drawn, they used a direct method in identifying credit constrained households. The direct method involves a direct elicitation in which respondents are asked questions on their perceptions of constraints. Using survey questions that are usually qualitative in nature, respondents are asked about the current credit demand in order to identify households facing credit constraints. The early application of the approach was by Jappelli (1990). Jappelli classified households in the US 1983 survey of Consumer Finances as credit constrained if they had a loan application rejected or did not apply for a loan because they believed they faced a probability of rejection. Feder *et al.* (1990) cited in Gilligan *et al.* (2005) classified households in China as credit constrained if they stated the willingness to use more credit at prevailing interest rates if it were available. In a similar context, Diagne, Zeller and Sharma (2000) classified a household as credit constrained if it had reached a perceived credit limit for any loan sources or if its members said that they could not obtain credit. In general, therefore, all elicitation approaches rely on survey questions that identify whether or not a households demand for credit exceeds supply available to the household.

The demand for credit may exceed supply for credit for a number of reasons. First, the demand could exceed supply due to quantity rationing. Quantity rationing occurs when a lender sets credit limits that are lower than the household credit demand, usually resulting from moral hazard concerns and enforcement problems. Second, high transaction costs may also restrict the supply of credit to the households. Third, the demand for credit may exceed the supply for credit due to risk rationing, also referred to as the ´discouraged borrower's´ scenario´. Going by the definition of Boucher *et al.* (2005), Risk rationing occurs when lenders, constrained by asymmetric information, shift so much contractual risk to the borrower that the borrower voluntarily withdraws

[14] For details see Jacoby (1994)

from the credit market even when she or he has the collateral wealth needed to qualify for a loan contract. The private and social costs of risk rationing are similar to those of more conventional quantity rationing. Like quantity-rationed individuals, risk rationed individuals will retreat to lower expected return activities.

Some individuals will avoid getting enough credit or never get credit at all due to fears of low returns on its investment. This will happen among risk-averse households that will adopt a low risk and low investment strategy in order to avoid defaulting on the loan. In the IFPRI survey, the following questions were used to identify credit constrained households:

1. Had any member in your household wanted to join a credit organization and applied for membership but his or her application was rejected?
2. If yes what was the reason for rejection?
3. If a household a member received any loan was he /she given the same amount as amount as asked for?
4. Did the household make any loan applications that were completely rejected?
5. If no applications were made, why did you not ask for any loan in the past 4 months?

Using this approach it was possible to identify credit constrained households and the sources of credit constraints.

7.5 Results and Discussions

7.5.1 Sources of credit constraints

Considering that designing credit contracts with incentives that are constraint compatible is a complex process, microfinance institutions are continuously exploring strategies for identifying and targeting credit constrained households with the limited poverty assistance funds that are made available to them by donors. The extent to which a microfinance institution targets its financial services to the poor is one of the key indicators of performance by most donors. In this regard, Zeller *et al.* (2006) note that profitable microfinance institutions will not have served their original objectives if the poorest are not among their clients. Indeed in the case of credit, targeting households that are credit constrained implies an improvement in economic efficiency since the impact of credit is expected to be high among credit constrained households than among the unconstrained households. The analysis on determinants of credit constraints is motivated by the concern that even well designed credit programs will have limited or no impact at all if they fail to reach those that genuinely need credit.

We talk of credit market failure when individuals that are interested in borrowing from a particular source are unable to do so because of high expected disutility from borrowing from such credit sources. There are a number of reasons why credit markets may fail for the poor. First credit markets may fail because the cost of borrowing, reflected in interest rates, size of the loan and transaction costs related to participation, are too high compared to expected returns also known as quantity rationing (Boucher *et al.*, 2005). Markets may also fail if borrowers are unable to borrow as much as they would like to due to over-rationing. This eventually leads to the withdrawal of potential borrowers from participating in credit markets. Second credit markets may fail for the poor due to lack of credit suppliers that are interested in providing credit to the poor as a result of moral hazard concerns and the lack of collateral by the poor. In addition, it is naturally too costly to deal with poor people whose loans are usually too small. Markets may also fail for the poor due to some other non-price rationing also know as risk rationing.

In sample data, about 55 percent of the households indicated that they faced credit constraints. As indicated in Figure 7.2, the majority of households that were credit constrained were discouraged borrowers (48%). There are a number of reasons why households may be discouraged from borrowing most of which relate to the perception individuals have towards the lender. In this study most discouraged borrowers indicated that they did not make any attempts to apply for loans because they expected their applications to be rejected by the lender. About 20 percent of the credit constrained household mentioned quantity rationing as their source of credit constraints[15]. These are households that applied for credit but did not get the same amounts that they had requested. Risk rationing resulting from individuals not borrowing at all or not borrowing enough due to fear of failure of default was reported by 18 percent of the credit constrained households. Only 13 percent reported full rejections of loan applications.

The discussion on sources of credit constraints indicates that most potential beneficiaries have a negative perception of the way microfinance institutions distribute the loans. Anecdotal stories on why some credit constrained households did not apply for loans revealed that they were afraid of rejections. The implication is that microfinance institutions need to improve their image to the public in order to attract potential borrowers that would otherwise become good and faithful customers. This will require investments in civic education regarding the customer requirements and procedures that MFIs undertake in the selection and screening of borrowers.

[15] In theory, quantity rationing should include both, loans that were fully rejected as well as those that were partially rejected (in which respondents received some positive amount of credit less that what they had requested).

Figure 7.2 Sources of credit constraints among credit constrained households

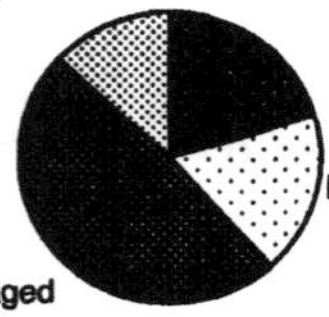

Source: Own calculation from IFPRI/RDD survey

7.5.2 Determinants of credit constraints

Definition of variables for determinants of credit constraints

In order to identify determinants of credit constraints, equation 7.1 is estimated using a Probit model in which the dependent variable is dichotomous (1=constrained household, 0=otherwise). The aim is to identify factors associated with the likelihood that a household will be credit constrained in which both the demand and supply factors enter the model. This is also used as a test for the reliability of the self-reported credit constraint status. The explanatory variables in the model include household demographic characteristics, socioeconomic characteristics, as well as community variables that capture the remoteness of the area where respondents live. Variables included and their expected impact on the household demand for credit, the household's supply or access to credit and the credit constraint status are presented in Table 7.1.

Table 7.1 Expected effects of specific characteristics on credit constraint status

	Demand for credit	Access to credit	Probability of being credit constrained
Age of a household head	+	+	+/-
Years of education of household head	+/-	+	+/-
Gender of a household head	+/-	+/-	+
Number of adult males(>15 years)	+/-	+/0	+/-
Number of adult females(>15	+/-	+/0	-

years)			

Table 7.2 continued

Quartile number 1 value of assets	-	-	+/-
Quartile number 2 value of assets	-	-	+/-
Quartile number 3 value of assets	+/-	+/-	+/-
Quartile number 4 value of assets	+	+	+/-
Quartile number 5 value of assets	+	+	+/-
Membership in a credit program	+/-	+/-	+/-
Total household land area per capita	+	+	+/-
Land area per capita squared	-	-	-
Value of land	+	++	-
Proportion of land for hybrid maize	+		
Proportion of land for tobacco	+	++	-
Distance to parents of household head	+/-	+/-	+
Distance to the commercial bank	0	-	+
Distance to the trading center	0	-	+

Source: Own calculation from RDD/IFPRI Rural Finance Survey

I expect both the demand and supply of credit to a household to increase with the age of a household head. Demand for credit increases as a response to the rise in the size of investments that household heads undertake as they grow older and get more experienced. Where lenders consider age as an indicator of experience, it is likely that access to credit will also increase with age. Therefore, the impact of age on the probability of being credit constrained will depend on the magnitude of the two opposing outcomes and can not be predetermined. Education of a household head can have a positive effect on demand for credit if education leads to households to acquire skills that are required to mange bigger investments that will require more credit. On the supply side education may have competing effects. First it can have a positive effect if it is used as an indicator of productivity and thus lenders may be willing to lend more to educated people with the anticipation that the risk of default is much lower. Second, it might have a negative effect if credit programs are pro-poor focus and thus the target the poor and illiterate individuals. Thus the net effect of education on the probability of being credit constrained can not be predetermined.

With regards to gender, I expect that male headed households will demand more credit than female headed households because male headed households also have access to other production resources that require credit supplementation than female headed households. However, on the supply side I expect that female headed households will have more access to credit because most microfinance institutions in the rural communities have a gender bias towards women. Considering that male headed households may also be capable of self financing it is not possible to predetermine the expected impact of gender on the probability of being credit constrained.

As noted by Gilligan *et al.* (2005), the number of adults in a household increases demand for credit for consumption but reduces demand for labor on farm if factor markets are imperfect. However, having more adults in a household could imply that a household has more income earners and therefore this increases their capability of self financing leading to a reduction in demand for credit. On the supply side a larger number of adults in a household implies more potential borrowers and thus increases credit supply. The overall effect on credit constraint status is ambiguous. In order to capture the impact of gender, I separate the counts of adults into males and females. I include the wealth of the household captured by 5 ranks of household wealth based on the asset value. I expect that households that are poor will have less demand for credit, while their access to credit may be increased due to the poverty lending programs that target the poor. As such, the net impact on the household credit constraint status is not predetermined.

The size of cultivable land and its square is included as an indicator of demand for credit arising from the demand of production inputs. Thus, I expect that land area will have an increasing effect on demand for credit and, therefore, increasing the probability of being credit constrained. On the other hand, the inclusion of the value of land enables us to capture the supply effect of land. It is expected that for lenders interested in collateral, they will use land value as an indicators of how much credit should be supplied and thus I expect a negative relationship with the probability of being constrained. The distance to parents of a household head and spouse are included as proxies of length of residency of the household in the area (those whose parents live far away are more likely to have migrated into the area). They also can be used as proxies for the ease with which a household can engage in inter-household economic and social activities (Zeller *et al.*, 2001). Distance to the Commercial bank and the trading centers increases the probability of a household being credit constrained by raising transaction costs of obtaining loans.

Area allocated to hybrid maize and a dummy variable for tobacco growing households are included as control variables. The interest in including these variables is to explore potential bias in access to credit by farmers growing a commercial crop, tobacco. The impact of participation in a credit program on the probability of being constrained is predetermined. A negative relationship could imply that participation in a credit program makes it much easier to obtain more credit, a possible indication of barriers to entry into credit borrowing (Gilligan *et al.* 2005). A positive relationship would imply that getting sufficient credit is more difficult than initial access to credit an indication of high levels of quantity rationing.

Household characteristics by credit constraint

Table 7.2 indicates household characteristics desegregated by credit constraint. Unconstrained households have relatively larger households (5.6 persons) than constrained households (4.8 persons). Households with no binding credit constraints have older heads of households than those with binding constraints. They have a much smaller proportion of female headed households (19%) compared to households that have some credit binding constraint (38%). There are no significant differences in most other household characteristics between constrained and unconstrained households.

Table 7.3 presents maximum likelihood Probit estimates of the determinants credit constraints. The model chi-square, which measures the goodness of fit of the model is significant at 1 percent level, signifying a good fit. Most parameter estimates returned expected signs. The age of household head had a negative and marginally significant (10%) impact of the likelihood of a household being credit constrained. This implies that the supply of credit exceeds their demand as age progresses. The average age for the sample population was 43 years and it is mainly household heads above this age that have excess supply of credit probably because of their accumulated social capital which enables them to access credit from different sources.

The probability of being credit constrained significantly declines (at 5% level) with gender of a household head. Thus male-headed households are less likely to be credit constrained than female-headed household. The wealth of a household has no effect on the likelihood that a household will report credit constraints although the parameter estimates carry the expected signs. Households currently participating in credit programs are less likely to be credit constrained than those that do not, implying that it is more difficult to get accepted as a credit program participant (an indication of barriers to entry), than its is to get enough credit once one becomes a member.

These findings comply with an earlier discussion in which it was noted that quantity rationing was not a major source of credit constraints. Rather, the main source of credit constraints is the fear that individuals may not get accepted once they apply for credit and thus they are discouraged from applying for membership in credit programs because of the perception that once they apply their applications would be rejected.

Table 7.3 Household characteristics by credit constraint

	Constrained (n=223)	Unconstrained (n=181)	All (n=404)
Household size	4.8	5.6	4.7
Adult equivalent household size	3.7	4.5	3.6
Dependency ratio	0.5	0.5	0.5
Age of household head	42	45	43
Number of female adults	1.3	1.5	1.3
Number of male adults	1.1	1.4	1.1
Female headed households (%)	38	19	29
Years of schooling of household head	2.8	4.2	3.3
Years of schooling spouse	2.4	2.6	2.3
Total land holding	1.5	2.67	1.63
Land pressure	1.2	1.4	1.3
Main Occupation of household head			
Farming	70	76.3	72
Household worker	5.5		3.3
Wage laborer	6	7.9	10
Trade	6	7.9	7.0
Other self-employment	10.5	2.6	10.3

Source: Own Calculations from IFPRI/RDD Rural Finance Survey

A similar study by Gilligan *et al.* (2005) found that households that participated in credit programs in the Philippines were less likely to report credit constraints than non-program participants and indication that there were barriers to entry into the credit program.

Tobacco farmers are less likely to face credit constraints than those that do not grow tobacco. This can be explained by the fact that there is a deliberate bias by MFI to support the production of tobacco because of its high profitability, which enables tobacco-growing households to get enough credit when ever they need it. Nevertheless, it is also possible that tobacco growing households are richer households considering that the crop is capital intensive such that households that decide to grow the crop do so after realizing that they can afford the finance its production. As an indicator of remoteness of the location, I find that households that are far away from the commercial bank are more likely to report credit constraints than those close to the commercial bank. Normally commercial banks are located in administrative centres where several other microfinance institutions that provide credit are based. The further away from the location the more costly it is for a house to apply and access loans.

Table 7.4 Determinants of credit constraints		
Independent variable	**Coefficient**	**T-statistic**
Age of a household head	-0.02*	-1.77
Years of education of household head	-0.09**	-2.01
Gender of a household head (1=male)	-0.80**	-3.30
Number of adult males(>15 years)	0.01	-0.04
Number of adult females(>15 years)	-0.15	-1.04
Quartile number 2 value of assets	-0.09	-0.24
Quartile number 3 value of assets	-0.05	-0.12
Quartile number 4 value of assets	-0.20	-0.46
Quartile number 5 value of assets	0.49	1.13
Membership in a credit program	-2.34***	-9.60
Total household land area per capita	0.94	1.20
Land area per capita squared	-1.13**	-2.52
Value of land	0.00	-0.06
Proportion of land for hybrid maize	0.31	0.79
Table 7.5 continued		
Proportion of land for tobacco	-1.08**	-2.37
Distance to parents of household head	0.01	0.83
Distance to the commercial bank	0.05*	2.00
Distance to the trading center	-0.02	-0.62
Mangochi	-1.39	-1.08
Nkhotakota	0.04	0.05
Rumphi	0.98	1.14
Dedza	-0.43	-0.83
Constant	2.51	3.30
No. obs	402	
Chi square	177.8	
Prob Chi2	00	
-Log likelihood	-92.42	
Pseudo R2	0.49	
Percent correctly predicted (%)	80.6	

Source: Own calculation from RDD/IFPRI Rural Finance Survey

7.5.3 Determinants of adoption of hybrid maize

7.5.3.1 Household characteristics by hybrid maize adoption status

Descriptive statistics for selected variables included in the adoption model differentiated by the adoption status are presented in Table 7.4. They include socio-economic characteristics such as age, sex and education level of a household head. I also include wealth status indicators such as land size, the value of assets, amount of off farm income and market access factors (supply related factors) such as credit, distance to markets, and access to the extension services. My a priori expectation is that wealth proxy variables will have a positive effect on the adoption of hybrid maize (Feder *et al.*, 1985). I expect that access to credit will increase adoption among credit constrained households through the relaxation of the liquidity constraints. I expect farmers that are close to input and output markets as well as close to extension service centres to adopt hybrid maize due to the reduction in transaction costs.

Descriptive statistics indicate that adopters have high off-farm incomes (MK 3050) than non-adopters (MK 2167). At the time of the survey, 1 US-dollar was worth 44 Malawi Kwacha (MK). There are no marked differences in terms of gender, age and education of household head between adopters and non-adopters. However, adopting households are significantly (at 5 percent level) larger (4.9 persons) than non adopters (4.3 persons). It is also observed that adopting households have significantly larger ($P<0.05$) land holdings (1.8 hectares) than non adopters (1.5 hectares). With regards to wealth, adopters are wealthier with significantly larger asset values (MK 2762) than the non adopters (MK 1006). In addition, adopters have significantly higher levels of access to formal credit than non-adopting households. A larger proportion of non-adopters (86%) than adopters (50%) rely on agriculture as their primary occupation. Other major sources of livelihoods for adopters are self employment (10%) and wage employment (15%).

With regards to the adoption intensity, about 28 percent of the maize land among the sample households was allocated to hybrid maize. This compares well with the national average of 30 percent reports by the National Statistics Office (2004). The distribution of adoption intensities for, (i) the credit constrained with no access to credit (ii) the credit constrained with access to credit and (iii) unconstrained households are presented in kernel densities in Figure 7.3. The average adoption intensity was lowest among the credit constrained with no access to credit (25%). Households that were credit constrained but had some access to credit had slightly higher adoption intensities (27%). However, unconstrained households had the highest average adoption intensity of 29 percent.

Table 7.6 means of selected variables, differentiated by adoption status for hybrid maize

Variable	Adopters (n=161)	Non-adopters (n=243)	Total (n=404)
Yearly off-farm income (MK)	3050.40	2167.86	2694
Male- headed (%)	71.4	67.5	70
Age of household head(years)	45	47	46
Years of schooling of household head	3.6	2.8	3.3

Table 7.7 continued

Years of schooling of spouse	2.6	2.1	2.4
Household size	4.9	4.3	4.7
Number of adult males (15-64 years)	1.2	1.1	1.1
Number of adult females(15-64 years)	1.4	1.3	1.3
Land holding size in hectares	1.8	1.5	1.7
Number of persons per hectare cultivated	1.4	1.2	1.3
Credit access (MK/year)	346	232	300
Percentage of households owning livestock	53	65	58
Value of assets owned (MK)	2762	1006	2036
Occupation of household head			
Farming	50	86	65
Household worker	3	4	3
Wage laborer	15	3	10
Trade	10	2	6
Other self-employment	17	1	11
Unemployed	1	2	1.2
Other	4.1	1.5	3.0

Source: Own calculation from RDD/IFPRI Rural Finance Survey

Figure 7.3 Kernel density distributions of adoption intensities for hybrid maize

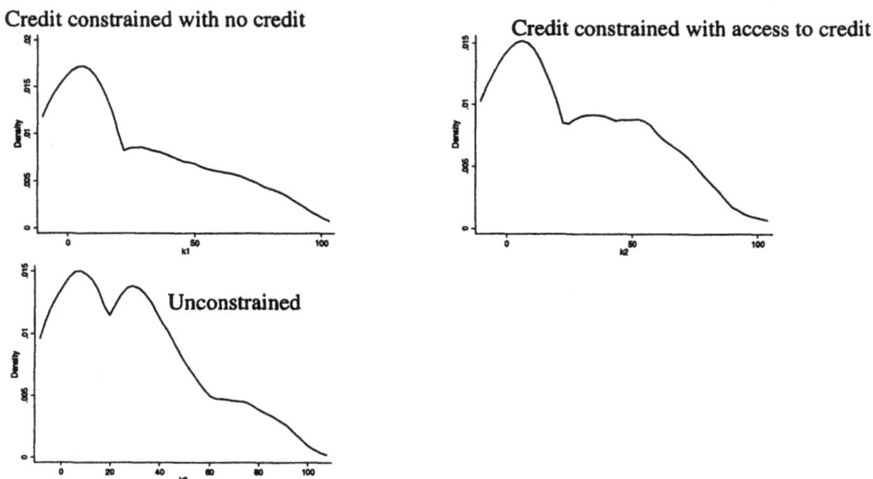

Source: Own calculation from IFPRI/RDD survey

7.5.3.2 Full sample estimates of determinants of adoption

Table 7.5 presents results from the double hurdle model of determinants on adoption. In addition to credit variables I include other variables that are theoretically linked to technology adoption. I estimate three separate equations and observe differences in the impact of credit between credit-constrained and unconstrained households. Columns 1 and 2 present estimates of the adoption model for the full sample of farmers. Results show that access to credit has a positive and significant effect on the probability of adoption, while its effect on the extent of adoption is not significant. The implication from this finding is that access to credit increases the likelihood that a household will potentially adopt hybrid maize but conditional on adoption, access to credit does not lead to high levels of adoption. One explanation to the insignificant effect of credit on the extent of adoption in the full sample could be that the credit provided is not high enough to significantly improve the intensity of adoption. This is consistent with the finding by Diagne and Zeller (2001) that the credit limits granted by formal lenders in Malawi were relatively small in relation to the amount of credit demanded. Zeller and Diagne (2001) therefore recommend to gradually increase loan sizes to repeat borrowers. The other explanation could be that not all credit is used for the production of hybrid maize which is also confirmed by Diagne and Zeller (2001). Nevertheless, the finding that credit significantly increases the likelihood of adoption is inline with a priori expectations and in concurrence with findings from a number of studies that have shown that the lack of access to credit significantly inhibits the adoption of high yielding varieties even when fixed pecuniary costs are not large (Feder *et al.*, 1985).

Other than credit, a number of other variables returned significant signs in the full sample estimates. The amount of off- farm income had a positive and significant effect on the likelihood of adoption but it returned a negative and significant effect on the extent of adoption. Theoretically, off-farm income can help to overcome a working capital constraint or may even finance the purchase of a fixed investment type of innovation. Empirical evidence of similar findings has been reported by Feder *et al.*, (1985). These results imply that households with high off-farm income have a higher potential of becoming adopters, thus they are more likely to pass through the first hurdle than those with less off-farm-income. However, conditional on adoption households with high off farm income will allocate smaller portions of land to hybrid production. One reason is that households with high off-farm incomes are located in Nkhotakota and Mangochi districts where maize is not a prime crop and where households derive most of their livelihoods from fishing in the lake or fish selling such that the amount of off-farm income earned is not reinvested into hybrid maize production. The average off-farm incomes for Nkhotakota and Mangochi were MK 5808 and MK 4440, respectively. These incomes were twice as high as the average off-farm income for the sample of MK 2600.

Regarding the age of the household head, results indicate that it has a negative and significant effect on the probability of adoption. The age of household head had no effect on the extent of adoption. Old age happens to be one of the human capital characteristics that have been frequently associated with non-adoption in most adoption studies. Among the several reasons that could explain the negative effect of age on adoption is the fact that older farmers have a tendency to stick to their old production techniques and that they are usually unwilling to accept change. In addition young people are associated with a higher risk taking behavior than the elderly. At the time of the survey, more than 60 percent of the heads of households were more than 40 years old.

The size of a household has a positive and significant effect on the probability of adoption. However, it has a negative and significant effect on the extent of adoption for hybrid maize. The positive effect on the probability of adoption can be explained by the fact that labour is an important input in the production of maize and therefore, larger households have abundant labour required for maize production. The negative effect of household size on the extent of adoption can be explained by the fact that once the decision to grow hybrid maize is made based on abundant labour available, the extent of adoption will depend on the ability of the household to finance the purchase of inputs required for the cultivation of hybrid maize. This is particularly true because hybrid maize requires more capital for the purchase of fertilizer and seed than it requires labour because it is not labor intensive. Households that received free inputs in form of fertilizer and seed were more likely to adopt hybrid maize than those that did not but conditional on adoption, free inputs had no effects on the extent of adoption. This can be explained by the fact that the amount of free inputs distributed in form of fertilizer and seed are usually the same across households and that they are usually enough for the cultivation of very small portions of land of about 0.25 acres.

Land pressure, which is measured as the number of persons per hectare has a negative and significant effect on the probability of adoption, but conditional on adoption households with more individuals per hectare allocate more land to hybrid maize. Experience has shown that households with high land pressure are also likely to be poor households hence less likely to finance the purchase of costly innovations. However, upon surpassing the first hurdle, households with high land pressure will intensify their adoption of an improved variety to maximize productivity required to meet their food and cash requirements from the small size of land. In most adoption literature, high land pressure has been described as a prerequisite for agricultural intensification.

Table 7.8 Determinants of adoption- Double- hurdle estimates

Variable	Pooled of full sample (n=404)		Credit Constrained (n=223)		Credit unconstrained (n=181)	
	First hurdle	Second hurdle	First hurdle	Second hurdle	First hurdle	Second hurdle
	Coefficient (Standard error)	Coefficient (Standard error)	Coefficient (Standard error)	Coefficient (Standard error)	Coefficient (Standard error)	Coefficient (Standard error)
Off farm income	0.0011***	-0.0012***	0.0001	-0.0024***	0.0000	-0.0004
	(0.0001)	(0.0003)	(0.0001)	(0.0006)	(0.0001)	(0.0003)
Gender (1=male)	-0.1048	0.4032	-0,5364	6.7265	-0.8836	18.5642**
	(0.2463)	(4.6639)	(0.4079)	(5.3282)	(0.6020)	(7.7599)
Age household head	-0.0148*	-0.2382	-0.0131	-0.4992**	-0.0039	-0.3825*
	(0.0076)	(0.1455)	(0.0176)	(0.2389)	(0.0143)	(0.2036)
Asset value	0.0001	0.0005	0.0004**	-0.0008	0.0000	0.0002
	(0.0001)	(0.0004)	(0.0002)	(0.0008)	(0.0001)	(0.0003)
Household size	0.2684***	-3.0063**	0.3866***	-2.8244	0.1470	-3.8909***
	(0.0732)	(1.3570)	(0.1266)	(2.0886)	(0.1645)	(1.1912)
Total land holding	-0.0419	-1.6460	-0.4282**	0.0544	0.8746***	-2.2721**
	(0.1119)	(1.4963)	(0.2108)	(2.8510)	(0.2307)	(1.1093)
Education head	0.0466	-1.3151	-0.2748	-0.6274	-0.7890	-9.6408*
	(0.2157)	(5.3272)	(0.5051)	(7.3753)	(0.5566)	(5.0293)
Free inputs	0.9796**	3.2644	0.6274	12.7164***	1.0161	-13.3996**
	(0.3832)	(3.7366)	(0.8003)	(4.3385)	(0.8043)	(6.2884)
Tobacco growing	-0.0586	-6.3529	0.9890	-5.4611	-1.0685**	6.0363
	(0.3450)	(6.7016)	(0.7466)	(12.6465)	(0.4776)	(5.3914)
Distance to extension office	-0.0116	1.4238	-0.3370**	1.0640	0.0425	1.1292
	(0.0411)	(1.1182)	(0.1564)	(2.4644)	(0.0951)	(0.8765)
Distance to market	-0.0023	0.5269	-0.0855	0.3529	0.0304	1.2907**
	(0.0250)	(0.5717)	(0.0696)	(0.4953)	(0.0628)	(0.5407)
Formal credit	0.0013***	0.0016	0.0001	0.0334***	0.0000	0.0013
	(0.0004)	(0.0020)	(0.0005)	(0.0123)	(0.0001)	(0.0012)
Informal credit	-0.0003	0.0019	0.0000	0.0017	0.0006	0.0040
	(0.0006)	(0.0059)	(0.0014)	(0.0106)	(0.0005)	(0.0038)
Land pressure	-0.2389***	4.5916***	-0.3476***	5.7717***	-0.1953*	3.9224**
	(0.0554)	(1.5095)	(0.1146)	(2.1543)	(0.1135)	(1.7802)
Mangochi	1.6047***	17.3987**	-0.3120	21.2384*	2.7333**	20.2055**
	(0.4126)	(8.6653)	(0.8298)	(10.9443)	(1.1144)	(8.3566)
Nkhota	0.5178	-5.1923	-2.1100*	2.4047	1.1728	20.8476*
	(0.5400)	(11.2355)	(1.2297)	(13.0428)	(1.1626)	(12.1804)
Rumphi	0.5078	-7.4643	-0.4602	-20.3768	4.0824**	4.4304
	(0.6550)	(11.4892)	(2.2966)	(18.6330)	(1.7858)	(11.186)
Dedza	-0.7269**	-20.7612**	2.2634	-60.8863***	0.5016	-17.5358**
	(0.2986)	9.4830)	(1.4331)	(11.5352)	(0.5316)	(7.6329)
_cons	0.0404	48.5584***	3.2837*	46.3980**	-3.0855**	53.7061***
	(0.6098)	(15.6481)	(1.9231)	(19.5353)	(1.4051)	(19.5569)
/lnsigma		3.18238***		3.17436***		2.8668***
		(0.0574)		(0.0710)		(0.07489)
Sigma		24.1040***		23.91169***		17.58148
		(1.3842)		(1.6260)		(1.3168)
No. of obs		404		223		181
Chi-square		112.31***		208***		120.22***
LL-function		-1152.109		-609.131		-532.6219

Source: Own calculation from RDD/IFPRI Rural Finance Survey

Note: * P<0.10; ** P<0.05; *** P<0.01,

Results indicate that households in Mangochi and Dedza are more likely to allocate larger portions of land to hybrid maize than households from other districts. The remaining explanatory variables such as gender, education, land holding as well as markets access variables such as distance to market and distance to extension office were not significant in the full sample estimates.

7.5.3.3 Constrained versus unconstrained households

Columns 3-4 and columns 5-6 present estimates of the switching regression model for the credit constrained and credit unconstrained households, respectively.16 Results from the credit constrained regime in columns 3 and 4 indicate that credit has a positive and significant effect on the extent of adoption of hybrid maize but it had no effect on the likelihood of adoption. The implication from these findings is that once credit constrained households decide to adopt hybrid maize, credit significantly increases their ability to finance the purchase of inputs required for the production of hybrid maize which leads to an expansion of the area under hybrid maize. Therefore, conditional on adoption, credit constrained households with higher amounts of credit allocate more land to hybrid maize production. In the study area in particular, formal credit is provided for the production of tobacco as well as for off-farm employment activities.

In concurrence with the null hypothesis that credit will have no effect on the adoption of hybrid maize among unconstrained households, results in columns 5 and 6 reveal that indeed credit had no effect on both the likelihood of a adoption as well as the extent of adoption in the unconstrained regime. The value of assets which was used as a proxy for household wealth had a positive and significant effect on the likelihood of adoption in the credit constrained regime but it had no effect on the likelihood of adoption in the unconstrained regime. Land holding size reduces the likelihood of adoption in the credit constrained regime while it increases the likelihood of adoption in the unconstrained regime. This is not a surprising finding because as observed by Weil (1970) the negative relationship between adoption and land holding size may be caused by credit constraints. Weil suggests that capital may be more available for larger farms, so that even though all farms may wish to adopt, larger farms are more likely to do so. Thus, households with larger holdings are also likely to be wealthier, with increased ability for self financing the purchasing of inputs but when such households are credit constrained then their adoption rate is negatively affected. The negative effect of land holding on the extent of adoption inn the unconstrained regime implies that smaller farmers exhibit higher

[16] The results for the switching regression model are estimated using a Heckman selection model to estimate parameters in each regime while adjusting standard errors accordingly. Estimates of the first stage probit model on credit constraints were presented earlier.

intensities of hybrid maize adoption than larger farms. Feder et al. (1975) suggested that the phenomenon may arise because small farms will farm land more intensively to meet subsistence needs

The gender of household head was significant only in the unconstrained regime. Thus male headed households that were not credit constrained allocated larger proportions of their land to hybrid maize cultivation than female headed households. Of interest in the unconstrained regime is the fact that while land holding increases the likelihood of adoption, it negatively affects the extent of adoption. While the land allocated to tobacco was insignificant in the constrained regime, results show that tobacco growing households that are unconstrained are less likely to grow hybrid maize. Free input distribution among unconstrained households does not necessarily translate into increased hybrid maize production. The main reason is that the majority of unconstrained households that received free inputs were from Mangochi and Nkhotakota where maize farming is not popular. Hence, because of such mis-targeting of credit to on average wealthier households, the expected effects on hybrid maize adoption and production were not materializing.

7.5.4 Test for separation of production and consumption decisions using the on-farm labor demand model

A test for separability of consumption and production decisions was conducted using the labour demand model.

Figure 7.4 Distribution of the intensity of labor use in man days per acre

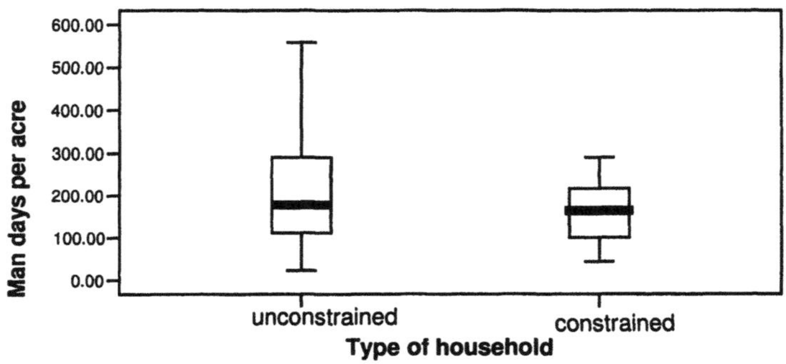

Source: Own calculation from IFPRI/RDD survey

Examining Figure 7.4 we see that the distribution of labour intensity use for credit unconstrained households has a larger mean (216 man days) than the distribution of labour intensity use for credit constrained households (148 man days). In this section I investigate whether the differences in labour intensity use between the two categories of households can be attributed to the differences in the household demographic structure or access to credit.

Table 7.6 presents OLS estimates of the farm labour demand model in which the dependent variable is the total man days worked on the farm. The estimates are meant as a test for separation of consumption and production decisions as well as a test for credit constraints. The a priori expectation is that labour demand should be independent of household demographics if production and consumption are separable. Columns 1 and 2 show pooled sample estimates. The results reveal that the number of adult males aged between 15 and 64 has a significant and positive effect on labour demand. These results suggest that in general households in the study area make production and consumption decisions simultaneously. The number of males and females aged more than 60 has a negative impact on labour demand although neither of them is significant. As expected in developing countries where child labour is sometimes used for farm production, the number of boys and girls aged between 7 and 14 years has a positive effect, although it is not significant. In line with a priori expectations the size of land operated returned a positive and significant effect. The wealth of a household proxied by the value of assets also had a positive and significant impact on labour demand. Richer households are more likely than poor households to hire labour. A joint F-test of significance of the six household demographic factors on labour demand rejected the null hypothesis of no effect at 5 percent an indication that households in the sample generally face some sort of market failure. At this stage of the analysis we can not state with certainty whether or not the lack of separability is a result of liquidity or credit constraints.

Testing the extent to which credit constraints cause non-separability

Although there could be other causes of this failure of separation such as labour market imperfections, our interest is to test the extent to which credit constraints contribute to such a failure. We do that by estimating a switching regression model of credit constrained and credit unconstrained regimes whose results are presented in column 3-4 and 5-6, respectively. The switching regression on which results are based is specified in equation (3). The sample is split based on reported credit constraints. The hypothesis under test here is that the amount of labour supplied for farm production activities will vary with the demographic structure of the household if a household has liquidity constraints and that the demographic structure will have no effect on labour supply among unconstrained households. Results in columns 3 and 4 indicate that the number of adult males aged between 15 and 64 years has a positive and significant effect on labour demand in the constrained regime while its effect is insignificant in the unconstrained regime (column 5 and 6).

Table 7.9 Determinants of on-farm labor demand

Dependent variable: Total labor days on farm	Full sample		Credit Constrained		Credit unconstrained	
Independent variables	Coefficient	Std. errors	Coefficient	std. errors	Coefficient	Std. errors
Wage	0.916	3.240	2.009	1.442	-2.655	6.216
Average years of schooling	-1.477	12.596	- 11.442**	5.519	1.031	22.56
Population males older than 64	-104.737	85.742	-0.552	28.012	-83.259	154.5
Population females older than 64	-94.766	88.862	-50.161*	28.909	-182.069	147.2
Population boys 7 to 14	14.699	23.666	9.283	9.205	1.492	39.77
Population girls 7 to 14	17.560	20.124	-1.323	8.975	35.492	30.89
Population males 15 to 64	58.904**	26.329	34.203**	14.522	59.214	41.23
Population females 15 to 64	12.883	24.771	-2.176	5.240	74.200	55.57
Sex of head	15.032	54.241	-1.887	16.015	70.894	115.6
Area sown/planted in acres	76.551***	19.632	12.441	8.533	99.447**	33.56
Age of head	2.776	1.842	0.843	0.625	3.214	3.247
asset value	0.018***	0.005	0.003	0.003	0.022**	0.008
Distance to ADMARC	-3.067	4.631	-13.648	8.652	-3.313	6.392
1=Nkhotakota district	107.415	67.258	33.638	205.316	95.582	111.5
Dedza	10.463	85.104	72.428	213.665	73.322	147.1
1=Dowa district	-98.9418	89.41512	8.237		-63.326	152.5
LAMBDATOB	-44.4652	47.91321	12.488	110.893	-61.498	54.78
(Constant)	-91.077	126.49	142.453	61.436	-185.830	239.7
No observations	115		48		67	
R-squared (pooled)	0.51		0.75		0.56	
Joint F-test for demographic variables	0.05		0.05		0.207	

Source: Own calculation from RDD/IFPRI Rural Finance Survey
Note: * P<0.10; ** P<0.05; *** P<0.01

Further, a joint F-test of significance of the six demographic variables on labour demand rejected the null hypothesis of no effect in the constrained regime at 5 percent and could not reject the null hypothesis in the unconstrained regime. This suggests that the lack of access to credit in the constrained regime prevents households from hiring extra labour and hence they rely on family labour. It must be pointed out, however, that although credit constrained households show nonseparabilty, as noted in Gillgan *et al.* (2005), it is difficult to separate the contribution of credit market imperfections from labour market imperfections in such a test for separation. This is because even when households are not credit constrained they may be unable to hire labour if the labour markets in the area are under developed.

The presence of separation among the unconstrained group is in concurrence with a priori expectations. Tobacco is by nature a labour and capital intensive crop such that households wanting to grow the crop will ensure that they have access to liquidity before they can do so. In the sample, a higher proportion of tobacco farmers (58%) were unconstrained compared to 44 percent for the entire sample. Further, the difference in the effect of household demographic variables on labour demand between constrained and unconstrained regimes suggests that credit constraints are partly responsible for the failure of separation in the constrained group. Therefore, results on the test for separation justify the earlier model specification in the analysis of adoption in which I took into account potential separation.

Results further indicate that factors that affect labour supply in credit constrained households are not important in unconstrained household. For example, the size of land and the value of asset increases labour supply in unconstrained regimes but they have no effect on constrained households.

7.6 The impact of Credit on Risk Attitudes towards Fertilizer-use on Maize

Farming, especially, under rain-fed conditions remains a risky enterprise. Uncertainties in context of crop production arise because either the yields or prices or both are uncertain (Dillon 1977). Production risk is mainly associated with uncertainties in climate, particularly, precipitation and, to some extent, temperature. A number of studies have shown that production risk is the major constraint to technology adoption in the rain fed ecosystems. In Malawi, for example, maize production is one such risky enterprise where in most cases farmers must invest resources in fertilizer application before it is clear whether or not the use of fertilizer will be effective.

In concurrence with this notion Pandey (2004) points out that modern varieties (MVs) have not realized their full potential because year-to-year yield variability makes it risky for farmers to apply economically optimal levels of inputs. In Malawi maize response to fertilizer varies from year to year, due stochastic disturbances mainly resulting from weather. As away of managing the production risk ex-ante farmers that are risk-averse may avoid to apply the profit-maximizing or optimal level of fertilizers.

Access to credit is seen as one of the most efficient risk coping mechanism among peasants. Eswaran and Kotwal (1990) observe that credit relaxes liquidity constraints and it boosts a household's-risk bearing ability. They note that with the option of borrowing a household can do away with risk reducing but inefficient income diversification strategies and concentrate on more risky but efficient investments. In concurrence with this notion, de Janvry et al. (1999) contend that households can reduce exposure to consumption and production risk through risk management (interventions which are ex-ante relative to income realizations) and through risk coping (ex-post relative to income), and there is hence a trade-off between the two. Since risk management has an opportunity cost on expected income, improved access to risk coping instruments may allow households to take higher risks in production and achieve higher expected incomes (Binswanger and Rosenzweig, 1993; Morduch, 1992). Thus access to risk coping instruments such as flexible credit, by the poor has been used, as a way of raising expected incomes.

Motivated by a hypothesis that access to credit boosts the risk bearing ability of households, this section investigates the effect of access to micro-credit on risk attitudes. The key hypothesis is that households that lack access to credit or are credit constrained are more risk-averse towards fertilizer-use than those with access to credit. The analysis is based on fertilizer use for maize production.

7.6.1 Framework for risk preference

Risky returns occur in the context of crop production because either the yields or prices or both are uncertain (Dillon 1977). Often, uncertainties arise from the influence of the uncontrolled variables whose levels are unknown. If the probability of distribution of a return relative to the uncontrolled variables can only be specified conditional on controlled variables, the choice and level of controlled variables will influence the distribution of the return. Therefore in such a case, the choice and levels of controlled inputs should allow for risk effects. An individual is said to be risk-neutral if the utility of the expected value is equal to the expected utility. In such cases the individual is said to have a linear utility function. An individual is said to be risk-averse if his or her NM utility function is strictly concave, thus if the utility of the expected value is greater than the expected utility. Similarly an individual is said to be a risk-lover if his or her NM utility function is strictly convex (Takayama, 1993).

The analysis on risk attitudes is guided by production model under risk (Groom et al., 2006). The model starts by considering a risk-averse farmer who produces a single crop with output q. Let p denote the output price, $f(.)$ is the production function, f is the fertilizer input, x_0 is the vector of other inputs and r is the vector of input prices. Applying fertilizer to maize (f) is considered to be an important input for production to occur. Assuming that inputs are chosen to maximize the expected utility of profit EU (π), the total profit of a farm activity is:

$$\pi = \sum_{i=1}^{n} pf(f,.x_0) - r_f f - r' x_0, \qquad [7.6.1]$$

The von Neumann-Morgenstern utility function U(π) represents risk preferences of a farmer. The farmer's utility maximization problem is:

$$\underset{x_0 f}{Max}\, EU(\pi) = \underset{x_0 f}{Max} \sum_{i=1}^{n} pf(f, x_0) - r_f f - r' x_0 , \qquad [7.6.2]$$

Allowing for risk aversion and assuming the cost of private risk bearing to be R, then the farmer's problem is to maximize the certainty equivalent of profit given as:

$$EU(\pi) = U[E(\pi) - R], \qquad [7.6.3]$$

where, R is the risk premium which measures the maximum amount that the risk averse individual is willing to pay to have the sure return rather than the expected return from the uncertain prospect (Takayama,1993). It is assumed that R>0, i.e., that the farmer prefers a risk-less world. The risk exposure also depends on inputs, f, x_0, thus R(f, x_0). From equation (7.6.3), maximizing expected utility is equivalent to maximizing the certainty equivalent,

$$E[\pi(f, x_0)] - R(f, x_0), \qquad [7.6.4]$$

Assuming that the risk R is represented by a random variable ξ with distribution *G*(.), then the farmer maximization problem of expected utility of profit without considering any constraint can be written as:

$$\underset{x_0 f}{Max}[E(U(\pi)] = \underset{x_0 f}{Max} \int U(pf((\varepsilon, f, x_0) - r_f f - r' x_0) dG(\varepsilon), \qquad [7.6.5]$$

where U(.) is the *von Neumann-Morgenstern* utility function. The first order condition associated with use of fertilizer f defines the marginal risk premium with respect to fertilizer.

$$\partial R / \partial f = p \times E\left({(\partial f(\varepsilon, f, x_0)} \big/ {\partial f} \right) - r_f , \qquad [7.6.6]$$

The first order condition for fertilizer can be written as follows:

$$E[r_f U'] = E\left\{ P \frac{\partial f(\varepsilon, f, x_0)}{\partial f} U' \right\} \qquad [7.6.7]$$

$$\frac{r_f}{p} = E\left[\frac{\partial f(\varepsilon, f, x_0)}{\partial f} \right] + \frac{\mathrm{cov}(U'; \partial f(\varepsilon, f, x_0) / \partial f)}{E(U')},$$

where U′ is a change in the utility of profit as a result of a change in profit

$\left(\partial U(\pi)/\partial\pi\right)$.

For a risk-neutral farmer the ratio of the two prices in equation 7.6.7 is equal to the expected marginal product of fertilizer input, which is equal to the first term in the right hand-side of equation 7.6.7. The second term in the right hand-side of equation 7.6.7 measures deviations from the risk-neutrality case and it is different from zero when a farmer is risk-averse. The term is proportional and has an opposite sign to the marginal risk premium with respect to fertilizer specified in equation 7.6.6.

7.6.2 Econometric estimation of risk attitudes

Based on Antle (1987), a moment based approach is used to estimate risk-attitude parameters maize farmers. We assume that a farmer maximizes a function of moments of the profit distribution. We firstly estimate the risk-premium of each farmer associated with the use of fertilizer which is later incorporated in the adoption models that are specified in the later stages. Following this approach, the farmer's program becomes:

$$\text{Max } E[U(\pi)] = [f(\mu_1(X), \mu_2(X), \ldots \mu_m(X)] \qquad [7.6.8]$$

where μ_j, j=1,2……, m is the mth moment of profit.

The first order condition of the program is approximated by the following Taylor expansion, in matrix form. Following the Taylor expansion which is not specified here, one can derive the marginal contribution of input j to the expected profit as follows:

$$\frac{\partial u_1(X)}{\partial X_j} = \theta_{1j} + \theta_{2j}\frac{\partial u_2(X)}{\partial X_j} + \theta_{3j}\frac{\partial u_3(X)}{\partial X_j} + \ldots\ldots + \theta_{mj}\frac{\partial u_m(X)}{\partial X_j} + u_j \qquad [7.6.9]$$

where $\theta_{2j} = -\alpha_{2j} \times (1/2!), \theta_{3j} = -\alpha_{3j} \times (1/3!), \theta_{mj} \times (1/m!)$ and u_j is the usual econometric error term. A nice feature of this model is that the parameters $\theta_{2j} and \theta_{3j}$ are directly interpretable as Arrow-Pratt and down-side risk-aversion coefficients respectively (Koundouri et al., 2006).

The Arrow-Pratt (AP) absolute risk aversion coefficient is defined by:

$$AP_j = -\frac{E(U''(\pi))}{EU'(\pi)} \cong -\frac{\partial F(X)/\partial\mu_2(X)}{\partial F(X)/\partial\mu_1(X)} = 2\theta_{2j} \qquad [7.6.10]$$

A positive AP coefficient means that the farmer is risk-averse. Down –side (DS) risk- aversion is measured by

$$DS_j = \frac{E(U''(\pi))}{EU'(\pi)} \cong \frac{\partial F(X)/\partial \mu_3(X)}{\partial F(X)/\partial \mu_1(X)} = -6\theta_{3j} \quad [7.6.11]$$

A positive DS coefficient means that the farmer is averse to down-side risk (Groom et al., 2006). Usually the higher moments have less influence on the dependent variable, as such this analysis will concentrate of the first three moments (i.e mean, variance and skewness) The risk premium is computed by:

$$RP = \mu_2 \frac{AP_j}{2} - \mu_3 \frac{DS_j}{6} \text{ for each } j, \quad [7.6.12]$$

where μ_2 and μ_3 are , respectively a measure of the second- and third-order moments of the distribution. The risk premium derived from the process is used as an explanatory variable in the adoption model.

The empirical estimation of the analysis of these moments can be conducted as follows:

$$\pi_1 = f_1(x_{i}.....x_j, \beta_1) + v_{1\Pi} \text{ for the expected value of profit, } \mu_1 \quad [7.6.13]$$

where $v_{1\Pi}$ is an error term distributed with mean zero, E($v_{1\Pi}$)=0. Let β_1^{LS} be the least square estimator of β_1 in (7.13) giving the least squares residual

$$v_{1\Pi}^{LS} = \pi_1 - f_1(x_{i}.....x_j, \beta_1^{LS}). \quad [7.6.14]$$

Consider the following model specification

$$(v_{1\Pi}^{LS})^2 = f_2(xi........xn, \beta_2) + v_{2\Pi}, \quad [7.6.15]$$

for the expected value of the variance of profit (μ_2). The least square estimation of (7.14), gives β_2^{e}, a consistent estimator of β_2 (Antle, 1983). It follows that $f_2(xi........xn, \beta_2^{e})$ is a consistent estimator of the variance of profit, $Var(v_{1\Pi})$. Using the same procedure you can estimate skewness (μ_3).

Following Groom et al. (2006) derivatives to each moment with respect to fertilizer cost are estimated. A 2 SLS equation[17] of the estimated derivative of the expected profit is finally fitted on derivatives of higher moments for the seed cost. The parameters associated with the second and third moments, denoted by ϑ_{2j} and ϑ_{3j}, respectively are used as proxies for the Arrow-Pratt (AP) and the down side (DS) risk aversion measures as stated above.

Results in Table 7.7 indicate that farmers applied 53.64 kg/ha of fertilizer. Credit-constrained households used less fertilizer (34.78 kg/ha) than the

[17] I use rainfall intensity, rainfall variation, the value of agricultural assets and soil quality as instruments

unconstrained households (76.89 kg /ha). The results also reveal that the average maize yield for the sample was 1407.2 kg/ha. Credit constrained households had significantly lower yields (1178.53 kg/ha) (p>0.05) than the unconstrained households (535.36 kg/ha). The yield difference could be attributed to differences in the intensity of fertilizer use. Interestingly, there were no significant differences in gross margins between constrained and unconstrained households. The average return per hectare of maize for the sample was MK1271.85. This implies that the use of fertilizer, while increasing yield, does not lead to significant better performance to the constrained than the constrained in terms of gross margins per hectare, which is in contrast to the conventional hypothesis the access to credit improves incomes for the borrowers. Similar studies in Malawi, for example, Diagne and Zeller (2001) have shown that credit used on maize production is not profitable.

Table 7.10 Fertilizer use, yield and gross margins for maize

Variable	constrained	Unconstrained	Total
Fertilizer (kg/ ha)	34.78	76.89*	53.64
Yield (kg/ha)	1178.53	1680.48*	1407.2
Gross margin (MK)	1261.14	1284.86	1271.85

Source: Own calculation from IFPRI/RDD data
*Significant difference at (P>0.05)

7.6.3 Risk attitudes towards the use of fertilizer

Table 7.8 shows econometric results of risk parameters which measure the risk attitude of framers towards the use of fertilizer as an input in the production of maize. The results are in compliance with the expectation of risk aversion behaviour among smallholder farmers towards fertilizer-use. First, the constant is insignificant which implies that the farmers efficiently use fertilizer and that farmers have a profit maximizing behaviour.

Table 7.11 Risk aversion Indicators

Risk parameter	Coefficient	t-value
Constant	-0.006108	-0.271
Q2 (associated with AP)	2.05526**	2.203
Q3 (associated with DS)	-1.419432***	-2.987

Source: Own calculation from IFPRI/RDD data
, * represent significance at 5% and 1%, respectively.

A negative and significant constant implies that farmers are underutilizing the input under consideration, while a positive coefficient signifies overuse of the input. By definition we should not observe a significant constant term in the model linking the derivatives of moments with respect to each input (Groom et al., 2006).

Table 7.8 shows that the parameter associated with Arrow –Pratt (θ_2) is positive and significant which indicates that farmers are averse towards the use of larger quantities of fertilizer. Further, Table 7.8 shows that the parameter associated with downside-risk aversion, (θ_3), which measures the cumulative probability of getting lower returns, has the expected sign and is significant which implies that farmers are also averse to down-side risk associated with the use of fertilizer. Risk aversion on fertilizer use can have serious implications on productivity and hence food security. These findings point to the need for exploring strategies for improving efficiency in the production of maize.

Risk attitudes and access to credit

A relative risk premium, which is a measure of the proportion of profit that each farmer would be willing to pay in order to avoid the risk associated with the use of fertilizer, is calculated using the empirical framework discussed above. The study finds that farmers are generally risk averse with the risk premium, expressed as a percentage of the expected profit averaging around 3 percent. This implies that on average households in the sample will pay a premium of around 3 percent to ensure their income per annum.

Figure 7.5 Risk premium of credit constrained and unconstrained households

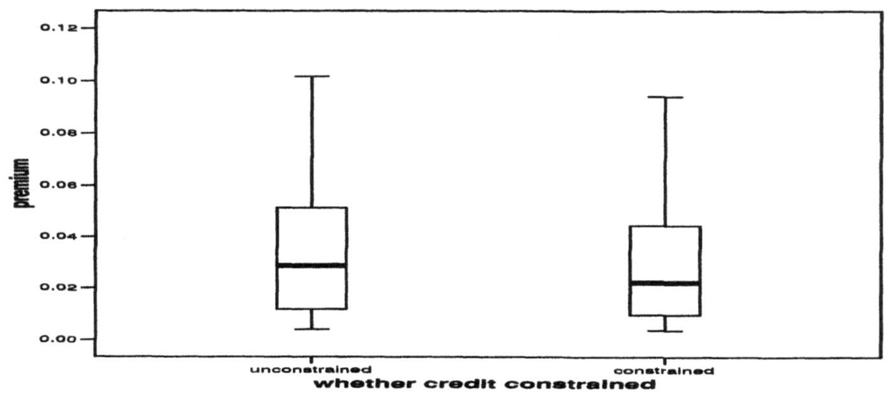

Source: Own calculation from IFPRI/RDD survey

When disaggregated by credit constraint status, Figure 7.5 shows that the risk premium among households without credit constraints is higher (4%) than those with credit constraints (3%). This implies that households without credit constraints are more cautious, preferring relatively low but steady income, a finding that contradicts a priori expectations of the influence of credit or liquidity in reducing risk aversion. Nonetheless, higher levels of risk aversion within the unconstrained group could be an indication that credit makes households to become more cautious about their investment to ensure that they are able to service the loan. This finding is quite relevant to the situation in Malawi where interest rates on loans appear to be too high for households that invest the loan on a less profitable maize crop.

7.7 Conclusions and Policy Implications

The current policy emphasis on credit as a development tool coupled with the limited availability of funds for credit implies that targeting credit to those that really need it has become a crucial issue. In addition, it is theoretically expected that credit provided at market interest rate results into marginal benefits among credit constrained households but does no welfare enhancement for unconstrained households. Therefore, achieving high economic efficiency in credit allocation requires targeting credit- constrained households.

This chapter has investigated the impact of access to credit among households that vary in their credit constraint status. As a test of the reliability of self reported credit constraints I estimated the probability that a household will face credit constraints and tested for separation in the constrained and unconstrained regimes using a on-farm labor demand model. Using a switching regression approach I investigated determinants of adoption of hybrid maize using a Double-Hurdle model due to a presumption that factors that affect the decision to adopt hybrid maize may be different from those that influence the extent of adoption.

Results on determinants of credit constraints indicate that most of the estimated parameters conform to a priori expectations. The significance of age and education of household head in reducing credit constraints implies that either the availability of credit is biased towards, older and educated household heads, or there could be other factors that enable older and educated individuals to finance their production through other sources. The implication is that credit policies need to encourage the supply of credit to the young and less educated who are more likely to be credit constrained. The significance of gender of the household in reporting credit constraints implies that female headed households have to be given some priority in accessing the limited funds that are supplied in the form of credit. While such efforts are already in place in Malawi, the rapid growth of female headed households resulting from HIV/AIDS and other causes implies that deliberate efforts must be made to increase access to credit by women and female headed households, in particular.

Membership in credit programs significantly reduces credit constraints implying that there are barriers to participation in credit programs. Thus, once members get accepted into the programs they tend to get enough credit. However considering that most individuals reporting credit constraints belonged to the discouraged borrower's category, it implies that lending institutions need to improve their image to the public about their criteria for selecting beneficiaries. It is unlikely that MFI can meet the demand for credit considering the capacity and financial constraints they face, however, the need for scaling up their outreach is obvious. Tobacco households are less likely to report credit constraints. This could result from the bias MFIs have on the commercial crop. Considering the importance of tobacco to Malawi's economy it will be important to continue supporting the production of this crop through credit since farmers may not initially have the resources to self finance the production of tobacco. The significant and negative impact of the distance between households and the commercial bank, which is a proxy of the remoteness of the location, implies that the transaction costs of obtaining credit are a major limiting factor for accessing credit. Efforts of establishing credit branch offices in rural areas need to be stepped up.

Results on the test for separation using the on-farm labour demand model, consistent with theory, indicate that the household demographic structure has a significant effect on labour supply among households facing credit constraints. Although the lack of separation in credit-constrained households might result from other market failures such as imperfect labour markets, results of the positive impact of credit on adoption should be taken as evidence that credit constraints are responsible for the lack of separation. In general these findings justify the need for credit targeting and the need for considering issues of separation when assessing the effect of access to credit.

Results on determinants of hybrid maize adoption reveal that factors that influence the decision to adopt hybrid maize are not necessarily the same factors that affect the extent of adoption. Results also indicate that factors that affect adoption decisions among credit constrained households are different from those that affect adoption in the unconstrained regime. For, example, while credit had a positive effect on adoption in the constrained regime, it had no effect among unconstrained households. The effect of land size on adoption is another example of variables with an opposite effect between the two regimes. Results indicated that while larger land holdings lead to increased adoption among the unconstrained regime, it has a negative effect on adoption in the constrained regime probably due to credit constraints. An interesting lesson from this study is that it is important to consider the two stages of adoption separately when assessing strategies for promoting agricultural technologies because factors that affect the decision to adopt are different from those that affect the decision on the extent of adoption.

The fact that access to credit led to a higher and positive effect on the adoption of hybrid maize among credit constrained households justifies the need for targeting credit to credit constrained households in order to achieve high economic efficiency. Second, most of the formal credit from formal credit institutions in Malawi to rural households is in the form of in-kind credit, namely fertilizer and seeds either for hybrid maize and tobacco. My results show that – unless such credit is provided to credit-constrained households – the current practice of loan delivery aimed at increasing hybrid maize production fails to achieve the objective of increasing hybrid maize share. Farm households receiving such in-kind credit simply at best substitute own financing for credit, or worse, they will on-sell the hybrid maize seed and fertilizer presumably at a loss, or use it for other crops. In any case, formal credit institutions in Malawi may reconsider the practice of in-kind loans, considering that the net welfare benefit of cash credit for rural farm households with multiple sources of income, investment and consumption opportunities is likely to be higher than the one generated by in-kind credit.

Third, the results indicate that although credit access increases the likelihood of adoption, it does not influence the extent of hybrid maize area cultivated. This indicates that loan sizes may be too small for making a significant impact on smallholder crop production and household welfare. The formal institutions may reconsider their practice of giving standardized loan sizes, and adopt a more demand-oriented flexible policy that rewards repeat borrowers with impeccable repayment records with gradually increasing larger loans. Among hybrid maize farmers, this change in policy is likely to increase the area of hybrid maize grown in Malawi. Fourth, only less than 6 percent of smallholders in Malawi have currently access to credit. Expanding the existing rural credit system to more smallholders will be crucial for fostering the adoption of higher-value food and cash crops, such as hybrid maize.

Also to be noted is that, poverty in rural Malawi is widespread and deep. The poorest of the poor among rural farm households need to be targeted through safety net schemes – not credit- in order to enable these households to adopt higher value crops while ensuring food security after droughts or other natural disasters. Hence, credit is only of relevance to a subset of rural households in Malawi. Other constraints, such as extreme vulnerability and poverty, or lack of market access and road infrastructure, need to be addressed by other policy instruments.

The finding that the risk-aversion towards the use of fertilizer increases with access to credit suggests that credit is not the only constraint in the area of study. Other factors such as access to output markets, conducive output prices and the choice of the enterprise on which credit is used needs to be looked into seriously for households to benefit from credit. As already indicated costly fertilizers make maize less profitable to the extent that there was no significant difference in the gross margins for maize between unconstrained households that used more fertilizer than the constrained households that used less fertilizer and this is despite the fact that unconstrained households had higher yields.

8 SUMMARY, CONCLUSIONS AND POLICY IMPLICATIONS

8.1 Introduction

The lack of access to formal finance in the developing world, where the majority of people do not have adequate physical collateral to secure loans has been identified as a major constraint to economic growth. In order to address the information asymmetry problem as well as the problem of lack of collateral, microfinance institutions have devised lending mechanisms that are a divergent of the standard bilateral debt contracts involving a borrower and a creditor. Such innovations involve agreements between the lender and a group of borrowers without physical collateral who are linked by a joint responsibility default clause. In such an arrangement, if a member of the group defaults, other members have to pay her/his share of the debt. When group members fail to repay the defaulted loans, the whole group loses access to future financing. The choice of a lending mechanism by the MFI determines whether or not the institution will simultaneously achieve the three goals of 1) high outreach 2) financial sustainability and 3) discernible impact. Although group lending with joint liability has been successful in some countries its performance in Malawi has not been as expected.

This study evaluated the performance of group lending with respect to 1) the impact on beneficiaries with respect to adoption of hybrid maize, and 2) the extent to which beneficiaries comply with their contractual obligations. On the contractual side, the study aimed at assessing the extent to which joint liability lending reduces moral hazard and enhances intra-group insurance once certain prerequisites are met. On the impact side, the study focused on assessing the extent to which access to credit enhances the adoption of hybrid maize. A number of theorists have attempted to explain how collective credit agreements such as joint liability may reduce information asymmetry problems leading to high repayment rates, and discernible impacts, however, empirical studies are not common. In order to address research gaps identified in literature, chapters 5, 6, and 7 dealt with specific issues related to three research objectives raised in chapter 1. The objective of this chapter is to summarize results presented in preceding chapters, to provide conclusions and to suggest policy implications of the results. The rest of the chapter is organized as follows. In the next section, the summary and conclusion of the results on determinants of moral hazard are presented. The summary and conclusions on determinants of intra-group insurance and the impact of access to credit on the adoption of hybrid maize are presented in section 3 and 4, respectively. Policy implications are presented in section 5, while section 6 presents limitations for the research and suggestions for future research.

8.2 Determinants of Moral Hazard

The analysis revealed that risk taking behavior was common among credit group members. The incidence of moral hazard was found to be associated with the process of group formation. The analysis revealed that the likelihood of occurrence of moral hazard was lower in groups that were endogenously formed through peer selection. Peer monitoring through rules that encourage joint enterprise ownership was found to have a reducing effect on the likelihood of moral hazard. The degree of pre-existing social ties captured by the number of villages from which group members come as well as the existence of peer pressure had a negative effect on the incidence of moral hazard. The study further revealed that groups composed of new members as well as groups that had been receiving credit for a number of loan cycles were more likely to face problems of moral hazard mainly resulting from matching problems proposed by Paxton (1996).

With regard to dynamic incentives, results show that the full joint liability as captured in the willingness of group members to pay a full amount of defaulter's loan reduces the incidence of moral hazard. Such a finding suggests that groups composed of individuals that attach higher value to access to future loans from the same lending institution are less likely to default willfully while factors of production had no effect on the likelihood of moral hazard.

8.3 Determinants of Intra-group Insurance

Although joint liability lending is built on the assumption that members should assist each other when they face a repayment problem, this study has revealed that group members are not always willing to assist each other. This section, therefore, focused on investigating factors that influence the willingness of group members to offer mutual insurance. Results reveal that groups composed of members with larger land holdings are more likely to be willing to support each other whenever a repayment problem arises than those composed of members with small land holdings. Groups that were formed by the village chief were more willing to offer mutual insurance than those that were formed by the credit assistant from a lending institution. The presence of pre existing social ties also had an enhancing effect on the willingness to offer mutual insurance. For example, groups that were composed of members that were related to the village chief and those that were related to the chairperson of the group were more willing to offer mutual support. The study revealed that the presence of such members in a group strengthens togetherness in the group. However, the presence of members with political connections weakens the groups' cohesion and thus reduces the willingness of individuals to contribute to repay loans of defaulters. All peer monitoring variables were not important in explaining the willingness of members to offer mutual insurance. The willingness to accept full joint liability had an enhancing effect on the willingness to offer mutual insurance which implies that mutual insurance is likely to be high in groups where group members attach a high value to access to future loans from the same lending institution.

Only one of the variables capturing matching problem was significant. The presence of new members in the group, which potentially introduces a matching problem, had a significant and negative effect on the willingness of individuals to offer mutual insurance. The cost of insurance, captured by the variation in loan size among group members, reduces the capability and willingness of members to provide mutual insurance. Occupational homogeneity which captures the degree of correlation of output indicates that higher correlation of output reduces the capacity for intra-group insurance. Intra-group insurance is less likely in maize groups than in tobacco groups probably due to the low profitability of the crop for which loans are obtained.

8.4 The Impact of Access to Credit on the Adoption of Hybrid Maize

The study further assessed the effect of access to credit on the adoption of hybrid maize among households with differing credit constraints. As a test of the reliability of self reported credit constraints, I estimated the probability that a household will face credit constraints and tested for separation in the constrained and unconstrained regimes using an on-farm labour demand model. A Double-Hurdle model was used to assess the determinants of adoption for hybrid maize in which credit was included as one of the explanatory variables.

Results on determinants of credit constraints indicate that household characteristics such as age and education of household head are negatively associated with credit constraints. Thus, younger and less educated household heads are more likely to face credit constraints. Female headed households were more likely to report credit constraints than male headed households. Membership in credit programs was negatively associated with credit constraints, an indication of barrier to participation in credit programs. Households that were located far from commercial centers were more likely to face credit constraints than those that were close to the commercial centers.

Results on determinants of adoption for hybrid maize indicate that factors that influence the decision to adopt hybrid maize are not necessarily the same factors that affect the extent of adoption. Results also indicate that factors that affect adoption decisions among credit constrained households are different from those that affect adoption in the unconstrained regime. Access to credit had a positive effect on the likelihood of adoption only among credit constrained households and had no effect on the extent of adoption in both regimes. While larger land holdings lead to increased adoption among the unconstrained regime, it had a negative effect on adoption in the constrained regime probably due to credit constraints. The amount of off-farm income had a positive and significant effect on the likelihood of adoption but it returned a negative and significant effect on the extent of adoption in the credit constrained regime.

The age of a household head had a negative and significant effect on the probability of adoption but had no effect on the extent of adoption. The size of a household had a positive and significant effect on the probability of adoption but conditional on adoption it had a negative and significant effect on the extent of adoption. Male headed households that were not credit constrained allocated larger proportions of their land to hybrid maize than female headed households. Households that received free inputs in form of fertilizer and seed were more likely to adopt hybrid maize than those that did not, but conditional on adoption, free inputs had no effects on the extent of adoption. The value of assets, which was used as a proxy for household wealth, had a positive and significant effect on the likelihood of adoption in the credit constrained regime but it had no effect on the likelihood of adoption in the unconstrained regime.

The number of persons per hectare had a negative and significant effect on the probability of adoption, but conditional on adoption, households with more individuals per hectare allocated larger proportions of land to hybrid maize in both the constrained and unconstrained regimes.

A test for separation using the on-farm labour demand model indicated that the household demographic structure had a significant effect on labour supply among households facing credit constraints but it had no effect among unconstrained households suggesting that unconstrained households were making consumption and production decisions separably. The analysis on risk attitudes towards fertilizer-use revealed that households with access to credit were more risk-averse suggesting that other constraints such as poor access to output markets and low output prices, and uncertain weather conditions still exist which make the returns from fertilizer use unpredictable and low.

8.5 Main Policy Implications

The results from this study point to a number of policy issues that are pertinent for enhancing the performance and impact of microfinance in Malawi. Such policies are important prerequisites for microfinance institutions to achieve their simultaneous goals of grater outreach, discernible impacts on beneficiaries and financial sustainability. The results on the role of dynamic incentives imply that such incentives can be used as a discipline device for borrowers that want to take risky actions and that through the creation of proper incentives; borrowers will be persuaded to behave in an honest manner.

The emergence of several microfinance institutions, some with conflicting objectives, has created alternatives for bad borrowers such that defaulters in one credit program would borrow from another credit program without facing any sanctions. This seriously reduces the value such members may attach to accessing credit from a particular institution particularly when they know that they can still borrow from other institutions. A policy initiative that supports the establishment of credit referencing bureaus should be introduced. These bureaus should be responsible for maintaining databases for current, past and potential borrowers. By using credit referencing, MFIs would stop bad borrowers from accessing further funds. Nevertheless such a policy must be supported by legislation that introduces mandatory identity cards for all citizens. Other policies that would reduce mismatching problems and enhance dynamic incentives relate to the introduction of combined offers that include both joint and individual liability by microfinance institutions. This will require MFIs to relax their rule on joint liability by allowing borrowers with dynamic and growing investments who make use of group loans at the beginning to switch to individual credit offers when they are in need of higher loans.

Policies that advocate group formation or the creation of associations for purposes of accessing credit should ascertain that such groupings are endogenously self-formed with minimum intervention from credit officers. The self-formation process will facilitate screening of potentially bad borrowers. The self-section process would also enhance the formation of groups with strong pre-existing social ties, which are important for enhancing the interdependency between group members, which is also needed for strong intra-group insurance. The current government policy of promoting the formation of credit associations and introduction of tougher penalties for defaulters is unlikely to yield tangible results unless supported by a proper group formation process.

While emphasizing on self-selection, MRFC should encourage the participation of village chiefs in the credit groups because in the event of a repayment problem, village chiefs act as problem solvers by encouraging group members to contribute to repay defaulted loans. However, village chiefs should be trained on group management and be sensitized on transparency, good governance and corruption prevention. Such training and sensitization will minimize the risk of chiefs abusing their authority for personal gains through corrupt practices.

In order to strengthen the willingness of group members to offer intra-group insurance, MRFC has to encourage clients to form groups composed of members from the same village since members from different villages are unlikely to exhibit strong pre-existing social ties required for intra-group insurance. Further, it is important for MRFC to reduce heterogeneity in loan sizes among group members because higher heterogeneity leads to higher costs of insurance.

The willingness to provide insurance was weak in maize and non-farm income groups suggesting to need for MRFC to consider starting offering combined loan packages that would allow for group members to borrow for tobacco production, which is more profitable, as well as for maize production or for non-farm business activities.

Since MFIs are unwilling to share default with borrowers, intra-group insurance is likely to remain the major source of repayment insurance for both borrowers and MFIs. However, considering that Malawian borrowers are exposed to a number of environmental risks associated with weather as well as systemic risks such as price variations for their products it might be necessary to introduce repayment insurance schemes for which borrowers would be required to pay premiums to insure themselves against losses. This would offer a more reliable form of insurance as the current intra-group insurance arrangements are ineffective against global or covariate shocks.

In this study, the fact that access to credit had an effect on the adoption of hybrid maize among credit constrained households justifies the need for credit targeting to achieve high economic efficiency. These results show that unless credit is provided to credit-constrained households, the current practice of loan delivery aiming at increasing hybrid maize production and indeed promoting participation in other market activities will not achieve its goals. Unconstrained farm households receiving such credit will simply use the credit for other unproductive purposes.

The results indicate that although credit access increases the likelihood of adoption, it does not influence the extent of hybrid maize area cultivated. This indicates that loan sizes may be too small for making a significant impact on the cultivated area. The formal institutions may reconsider their practice of giving standardized loan sizes, and adopt a more demand-oriented flexible policy that rewards repeat borrowers with good repayment records with gradually increasing larger loans. Among hybrid maize farmers, this change in policy is likely to increase the area of hybrid maize grown in Malawi.

In Malawi, only less than 6 percent of smallholder farmers, currently, have access to credit. Expanding the existing rural credit system to more smallholder farmers will be crucial for fostering the adoption of higher-value food and cash crops, such as hybrid maize. In addition, considering that households in remote areas that are far from commercial centers are more likely to report credit constraints, it is important to promote policy that specifically targets such areas with credit services while also providing other complementary services such as linking them to markets for their products.

Results also revealed that other policies that can potentially reduce liquidity constraints faced by farmers such as the distribution of free inputs should be supported such that as many households can benefit from the initiative because they promote the adoption of hybrid maize. Indeed the poorest of the poor among rural farm households may need to be targeted through safety net schemes – not credit- in order to enable these households to adopt higher value crops or participate in other risky but high return investments, while ensuring food security after droughts or other natural disasters. Hence, credit is only of relevance to a smaller set of rural households in Malawi. Other constraints, such as extreme vulnerability and poverty, or lack of market access and road infrastructure, need to be addressed by other policy instruments.

8.6 Study limitations and Areas for Future Research

The major limitation in this study is associated with endogeneity problems that may potentially arise in empirical chapters 5 and 6. Endogeneity may arise when two or more variables in an equation are simultaneously determined. When endogeneity occurs, there is a correlation between explanatory variables and the error term resulting into inconsistent and biased estimates. In the models used to estimate determinants of moral hazard and intra-group insurance, for example, the right hand variables such as peer selection and peer monitoring may be endogenously determined. One way of correcting for endogeneity is to use instrumental variables but since it is difficult to identify correct instruments, the use of lagged variables when time series data is used has been recommended as a key strategy for correcting this problem (Hermes *et al.*, 2005). This data set used for this study was cross sectional, as such, future research should consider constructing panel data from where lagged variables could be used as instruments to correct for endogeneity.

The other major limitation for this study relates to the analysis on intra-group insurance. In this study, the analysis was based on the willingness to offer insurance. Considering that intra-group insurance is *ex-post* internal repayment problem, it should never occur in groups that never faced internal repayment problems; therefore, an inclusion of groups that never faced repayment problems in the sample can result into misleading results. Thus future research on mutual insurance would focus on the occurrence of mutual insurance among groups that faced internal repayment problems (ex-post repayment), while correcting for the potential selection bias. This could not be done in this study because of the limited number of observations.

9 REFERENCES

ACCION. 2005. UN International Year of Micro-credit. Accessed at http://www.accion.org/unyear.asp.

Adesina A., and A. Baidu-Forson. 1995. Farmers´ Perception and Adoption of New Agricultural Technology: Evidence from Analysis in Burkina Faso and Guinea, West Africa, *Agricultural Economics* 13 (1):1-9.

Aghion de Armendariz B. 1999. On the Design of a Credit Agreement with Peer Monitoring. *Journal of Development Economics* 60 (1): 79-104.

Aghion de Armendariz B., and J. Morduch. 1998. Peer Group Formation in an Adverse Selection Model. Working Paper, University College, London.

Aghion de Armendariz B., and J. Morduch. 2005. The Economics of Microfinance. MIT Press. USA

Aghion de Armendáriz B., and C. Gollier. 2000. Peer Group Formation in an Adverse Selection Model, *The Economic Journal* 110 (1): 632-643.

Ahlin C., and R.Townsend. 2003. Using Repayment Data to Test Models of Joint Liability Lending. Accessed at http://people.vanderbilt.edu/~c.ahlin/research/repay.pdf

Akerlof G.A. 1970. The Market for 'Lemons': Quality Uncertainty and the Market Mechanism, *The Quarterly Journal of Economics*, MIT Press 84(3): 488-500.

Aniket K. 2004. Sequential Group Lending with Moral Hazard. Unpublished Paper. London School of Economics, United Kingdom.

Antle, J., 1987. Econometric Estimation of Producers´ Risk Attitudes. *American Journal of Agricultural Economics*, 69(1): 509-522.

Balkin S. 1993. A Grameen Bank Replication: the Full Circle Fund of the Women's Self-employment Project of Chicago. In: Washid (ED).

Benjamin D. 1992. Household Composition, Labor Markets, and Labor Demand: Testing for Separation in Agricultural Household Models. *Econometrica* 60(2): 287-322.

Besley T., and S.Coate. 1995. Group Lending, Repayment Incentives and Social Collateral. *Journal of Development Economics* 46 (1): 1-18.

Binswanger H., and M. Rosenzweig. 1993. Weather Risk and Composition and Profitability of Agricultural Investments. *Economic Journal*, 103 (1): 56-78

Boucher S., M.R Carter and C. Guirkinger. 2005. Risk Rationing and Activity Choice in Moral Hazard Constrained Credit Markets. University of California, Berkeley, California, U.S.A.

Bratton M. 1986. Financial Smallholder Production: A Comparison of Individual and Group Credit Schemes in Zimbabwe. *Public Administration and Development* 6 (2): 115-132.

Bryla E., Panos V., and T.Pauline. 2001. Making Agricultural Lending Less Risky: Using Market Based Price Risk Management Instruments to

Manage Commodity Price Volatility, Commodity Risk Management Group, World Bank.
Buckley G. 1996. Rural and Agricultural Credit in Malawi. A study of the Malawi Mudzi Fund and the Smallholder Agricultural Credit Administration. *Finance Against Poverty*, Volume 2, eds. Hulme D. and P. Mosley. Routledge, London.
Burritt K. 2006. Expanding Access to Financial Services in Malawi. United Nations Capital Development Fund, Two United Nations Plaza, 26th FloorNew York, NY 10017, http://www.uncdf.org e-mail: info@undp.org
Burritt K. 2003. Microfinance in Turkey. The United Nations Capital Development Fund. http://www.uncdf.org/english/microfinance/sectorDev/UNCDF_TurkeyAssessment.pdf
Burton M., R.Dorsett, and T.Young. 1996. Changing Preferences for Meat: Evidence from UK Household Data, 1973-1993. *European Review of Agricultural Economics* 23 (3): 357- 370.
Carr S.J. 1997. A Green Revolution Frustrated: Lessons from the Malawi Experience. *African Crop Science Journal,* www.bioline.org.br
Che Y. 2002. Joint Liability and Peer Monitoring under Group Lending, Contributions to *Theoretical Economics* 2 (1): 1-13.
Chirwa E.W. 2002. Microfinance and Poverty Reduction in Malawi: What happened to the microfinance revolution? University of Malawi, Chancellor College.
Chirwa E.W. Mvula P.M., Namata.L and E.K Zgovu. 1996. Review of Credit Operations under Social Dimensions of Adjustment (SDA) Project and Other Programs, Report prepared by *Wadonda Consult* for the Ministry of Economic Planning and Development.
Chowdhury P.R. 2005. Group-lending: Sequential Financing, Lender Monitoring and Joint Liability. *Journal of Development Economics* 77 (2): 415–439.
CIMMYT. 1995. Maize Technology in Malawi. Research Report No. 4. CIMMYT.
Coleman J.S. 1993 The Rational Reconstruction of society (1992 Presidential Address) *Am. Socio. Rev.,* 58: 1-15.
Conning J. 1999. Outreach, Sustainability and Leverage in Monitored and Peer-Monitored Lending. *Journal of Development Economics*, 60(1): 88
Conning J. 2000. Monitoring by Delegates or by Peers? Joint Liability Loans under Moral Hazard, William College Center of Development Econ., working paper.
Conroy A.1992. The Economics of Smallholder Maize Production in Malawi with Reference to Hybrid Seed and Fertilizer. Unpublished PhD Thesis. Manchester University

Cornejo J., and W. McBride. 2002. Adoption of Bioengineered Crops. Agricultural Economics Report No. 810. 1800 M Street, NW, Washington, DC

Cragg J. 1971. Some Statistical Models for Limited Dependent Variables with Application to the Demand for Durable Goods. *Econometrica* (39): 829-844.

De Janvry A. R. Murgai. and E. Sadoulet 1999. Rural Development and Rural Policy, University of California at Berkeley and the World Bank. . http://are.berkeley.edu/~sadoulet/papers/Handbook_text.pdf

De Janvry A., M. Fafchamps, M.Raki, and E.Sadoulet. 1992. Structural Adjustment and the Peasantry in Morocco: A Computable General Equilibrium Model. *European Review of Agricultural Economics*, (19): 427-453

De Janvry A., N. Key., and E.Sadoulet. 1997. Agricultural and Rural Development Policy in Latin America. New Directions and New Challenges. *FAO Agricultural Policy and Economic Development Series 2* Rome/Italy http://www.fao.org/docrep/W7441E/w7441e00.htm#Contents

De Meza D., and D. Webb. 2000. Does Credit Rationing Imply Insufficient Lending? *Journal of Public Economics* 78(3): 215-34.

Deaton A.S. and M. Irish. 1984. Statistical Models for Zero Expenditures in Household Budgets. *Journal of Public Economics* 5 (23): 59-80.

Diagne A. and M.Zeller. 2001. Access to Credit and Its Impact on Welfare in Malawi. IFPRI, Washington D.C.

Diagne A., 1998. Default Incentives, Peer Pressure, and Equilibrium Outcomes in Group Based Lending Programs. Working paper, IFPRI, Washington D.C.

Diagne A., and M. Zeller. 2001. Access to Credit and Its Impact on Welfare in Malawi. Research report No. 116, IFPRI, Washington D.C.

Diagne A., C. Simtowe, W. Chimombo, and C. Mataya. 2000. Design and Sustainability Issues of Rural Credit and Savings Programs for the Poor in Malawi : An Action- Oriented Research Project. IFPRI. Washington DC.

Diagne A., M.Zeller and M. Sharma. 2000. Empirical Measurement of Households' Access to Credit and Credit Constraints in Developing Countries: Methodological Issues and Evidence. FCND Discussion Paper, No. 90, IFPRI, Washington D.C.

Dillon, J., 1977. The Analysis of Response in Crop and Livestock Production. 2nd edn., Pergamon Press, Oxford.

Economist Intelligence Unit (EIU). 2004. Country Report Malawi. Accessed at www.eiu.com Economist Intelligence Unit (EIU). 2003. Country Report Malawi. Accessed at www.eiu.com

Eswaran M, and A. Kotwal.. 1986. Access to Capital and Agrarian Production Organization. *Economic Journal* (96): 482-498

Eswaran M., and A. Kotwal. 1990. Implications of Credit Constraints for Risk Behavior, *Oxford Economic Papers*, New Series 42 (2): 473-482

Evans A., and C.Ford. 2003. A Technical Guide to Rural Finance. For World Council of Credit Union (WOCCU), Available at www.woccu.org/development/guide/rf_tech_guide.pdf
Evans J .1997. Beneficiary Impact Assessment of the MRFC Tikolore Program in Nchisi District in Malawi
Feder G., and D.L Umali.. 1993. The Adoption of Agricultural Innovations: A Review, *Technological Forecasting and Social Change* 43:215-239.
Feder G., Just R.E, and Zilberman D. 1985. Adoption of Agricultural Innovations in Developing Countries: A Survey. *Economic Development and Cultural Change*, 3: 255-298.
Feder G., Lawrence J., Justin Y., and L.Xiaopeng. 1990. The Relationship Between Credit and Productivity in Chinese Agriculture: A Microeconomic Model of Disequilibrium. *American Journal of Agricultural Economics* 72 (5): 1151-1157.
Floro S.L and P.A Yotopolous 1991. Informal Credit Markets and the New Institutional Economics The Case of Philipine Agriculture, Boulder: West View Press.
Fuglesang A.D., D.Chandler., and D. Akuretiyagama. 1993. Participation as a Process - Process as Growth: what we can learn from Grameen Bank, Bangladesh. Dhaka, Bangladesh, Grameen trust.
Gallardo J. 1998. Assessment of the Legal and Regulatory Framework for Operations of Microfinance Institutions in Malawi: The World Bank, Washington, DC .
Gallardo J. 2000. Malawi: Critical Issues in Developing Sustainable Microfinance, Finance and Private Sector , Africa Region, The World Bank, Washington, DC .
GEMINI. 2000. The Malawi National Gemini MSE Baseline Survey Malawi
Ghatak M. 1999b. Screening by the Company you Keep: Joint Liability Lending and the Peer Selection Effect, Mimeo. Univ. of Chicago.
Ghatak M. 1999a. Group Lending, Local Information and Peer Selection, *Journal of Development Economics,* 60 (1): 27-50.
Ghatak M., and T. Guinnane 1999. The Economics of Lending with Joint Liability: Theory and Practice, *Journal of Development Economics* 60 (1): 195-229.
Ghate P.B. 1988. Informal Credit Markets in Asian Developing Countries *Asian Development Review* 6(1): 64-85.
Gilligan D., S. Harrower, and A. Quisumbing. 2005. How Accurate are Reports of Credit Constraints? Reconciling Theory with Respondents` Claims in Bukidnon, Philippines. IFPRI, Washington, DC
Gonzalez-Vega C. 2005. Deepening Rural Financial Markets: Macroeconomic, Policy and Political Dimensions. Supported by USAID. Available online: www.basis.wisc.edu/rfc/documents/theme_macro.pd

Government of Malawi. 2002. The Malawi Microfinance Policy, Lilongwe, Malawi
Government of Malawi. 2003a. Malawi Poverty Reduction Strategy Paper (PRSP), Lilongwe, Malawi
Government of Malawi. 2003b. Crop Husbandry Practices 2003, Ministry of Agriculture and Livestock Development Malawi.
Government of Malawi. 2004. Agriculture Statistics Crop Production Estimates, Ministry of Agriculture and Livestock Development Malawi
Groom, B., P.Koundouri C. Nauges and A.Thomas, 2006. The Story of the Moment: Risk-averse Cypriot Farmers Respond to Drought Management. Applied Econ, (In Press)
Guinane T.W. 1994. A Failed Institutional Transplant: Raiffeisen´s Credit Cooperatives in Ireland 1894-1914. *Explorations in Economic History, 31.*
Guinnane T.W. 1993. Cooperatives as Information Machines: The Lending Practices of German Agricultural Credit Cooperatives, 1883-1914. *Economic growth Center Discussion Paper* No 699. Yale University.
Hermes N., R. Lensink, and H. Mehrteab. 2005. Peer Monitoring, Social Ties and Moral Hazard in Group-Based Lending Programs: Evidence from Eritrea, Research Report, Research School, Systems, Organization and Management (SOM), 03E36, Groningen University, The Netherlands.
Holmstrom B. 1979. Moral Hazard and Observability. *Bell Journal of Economics*, 10 (1): 74-91
Jacoby H. 1994. Borrowing Constraints and Progress through School: Evidence from Peru, *Review of Economics and Statistics* (76): 151-160.
Jappelli T. 1990. Who is Credit Constrained in the U.S. Economy? *Quarterly Journal of Economics* 105(1): 219-234.
Koundouri, P Nauges.C and Tzouvelekas. 2005. Endogenous Technology Adoption under Production Risk: Theory and Application to Irrigation Technology.
Kritikos A.S., and D.Vigenina. 2005. Key Factors of Joint- Liability Loan Contracts: An Empirical Analysis. Kyklos. 58 (2): 213-238
Kugler M., and R.Oppes. 2005. Collateral and Risk Sharing in Group Lending: Evidence from an Urban Micro Credit Program, Economics Division School of Social Sciences, University of Southampton SO17 1BJ. UK http://www.socsci.soton.ac.uk/economics/Research/Discussion_Papers
Lweya K.B. 2006. The Implications of Adaptations in Organizational Capacity and Cultures for the Provision of Microfinance in Malawi. PhD Dissertation submitted to University of Reading, UK.
Maddala G.S. 1986. Disequiribrium, Self-Selection and Switching Models. In: Handbook of Econometrics, edited by Giliches, Zvi and Michael D. Intriligator (New York: North Holland).
Maddala G.S. 1997. Limited Dependent and Qualitative Variables in Econometrics, Cambridge University Press, London

Marr A. 2000. A Challenge to the Orthodoxy Concerning Microfinance and Poverty Reduction. School of Oriental and African Studies, University of London, U.K.
Marr A. 2002. Studying Group Dynamics: An Alternative Analytical Framework for the Study of Microfinance Impacts on Poverty Reduction,: *Journal of International Development*, 14(4): 511-534
Martin I., D.Hume, and S.Rutherford.1999. Financial Services for the Poor and Poorest: Deepening Understanding to Improve Provision. Working Paper 9, Institute for Development Policy and Management, University of Manchester, UK, http://www.sed.manchester.ac.uk/idpmpublications/archive/fd/fd_wp09.shtml
Martínez Espiñeira R. 2006. A Box-Cox Double-hurdle Model of Wildlife Valuation: The Citizen's Perspective, *Ecological Economics* 58(1):192-208
Matin I. 1997. Repayment Performance of Grameen Bank Borrowers: The Unzipped State, *Savings and Development* 21 (4):451-472.
Menza Jorge R. 2000. Group and Individual Micro Credit Contracts: A Dynamic Numerical Analysis. Dissertation presented in partial fulfillment of the requirements for the degree 'doctor of philosophy' in the Graduate School of the Ohio State University.
Moffatt P.G. 2003. Hurdle Models of Loan Default. Unpublished Paper. School of Economic and Social Studies, University of East Anglia. Available on-line at http://www.crc.ems.ed.ac.uk/conference/presentations/moffat.pdf.
Mondal W.I., and R.A Tune. 1993. Replicating the Grameen Bank in North America. The Good Faith Fund Experience. In: Walid, A.N.M. (ED). The Grameen Bank: Poverty Relief in Bangladesh . Westview Press, San Francisco
Morduch J.1992. Risk Production, and Saving: Theory and Evidence from Indian Households. Mimeo, Harvard University.
Mosley P. and R.P Dahal. 1985. Lending to the Poorest: Early Lessons from the Small Farmers' Development Program, Nepal. *Development Policy Review* (3):193-207
National statistics Office. 2004. Malawi Demographic and Health Survey, Malawi
of Agriculture, Government of Malawi, Lilongwe, Malawi.
Olomola A.S. 2000. Effects of Membership Homogeneity on the Design and Performance of Informal Finance Groups in Rural Nigeria. A Research Report Submitted to the African Economic Research Consortium (AERC), Nairobi, Kenya.
Pandey S. 2004. Risk and Fertilizer Use in the Rain Fed Rice Ecosystem of Tarlac, Philippines. *Journal of Agricultural and Applied Economics Papers* 44 (4): 581-595.

Paxton J. 1996, Determinants of Successful Group Loan Repayment: An Application to Burkina Faso, PhD Dissertation, Ohio State University.
Plunkett Horace K.C.V.O. 1904. Ireland in the New Century. London : Murray. Pp 300.
Prescott E.S. 1997. Group Lending and Financial Intermediation: An Example, Economic Quarterly, Federal Reserve Bank of Richmond, (4):23-48. Press, Boulder
PWC. 2003. Restructuring and Privatization of MSB and MRFC: Draft Summary Paper on Short-term Restructuring Options of MSB and MRFC. Malawi Privatization Commission.
Rahman. A. 1999. Micro-credit Initiatives for Equitable and Sustainable Development: Who pays? *World Development*, 27(1): 67-82
Rai A.S., and T. Sjostrom. 2004. Is Grameen Lending Efficient? Repayment Incentives and Insurance in Village Economies. *Review of Economic Studies*, (71): 217-234
Rashid M. and R. Townsend. 1992. Targeting Credit and Insurance: Efficiency, Mechanism Design and Program Evaluation, Working paper, University of Chicago, Rural Credit Groups and Related Institutions. Draft report submitted to the Ministry
Rutherford.S. 2002. The Economics of Poverty: How Poor People Manage their Money, Safe Save, Bangladesh.
Sadoulet E. 2004. Access to Financial Services in Development. MFI Handout - 1 - PP C253 – ARE C 253. University of Berkeley, Califonia. http://are.berkeley.edu/courses/ARE253/2004/handouts/PP04-6-MFI.pdf
Sadoulet E., and A. de Janvry. 1995. Quantitative Development Policy Analysis, Johns Hopkins University Press, Baltimore.
Sadoulet L. 2003. Reputation as Insurance: Extending a Range of Financial Services for the Poor. Free University of Brussels. http://papers.ssrn.com/sol3/papers.cfm
Sadoulet L., and E.S.Carpenter. 2001. Endogenous Matching and Risk Heterogeneity: Evidence on Micro-credit Group Formation in Guatemala, Working Paper, ECARES, Université Libre de Bruxelles
Sadoulet L., and S.Carpenter. 1999. Risk-matching in Credit Groups: Evidence from Guatemala. The Role of Mutual Insurance in Group Lending. Department of Economics, Princeton University, Princeton, N.J., U.S.A. Photocopy.
Salanie B. 2000. The Economics of Contracts: premier, The MIT Press, Cambridge, Massachusetts, London, England
Schaefer-Kehnert W. 1983. Success with Group Lending in Malawi. In: J. D. Von Pischke et al. (eds.), Rural Financial Markets in Developing Countries. The World Bank, Washington D.C.

Schutjer W. and M.Van der Veen. 1977. Economic Constraints on Agricultural Technology Adoption in Developing Countries. USAID occasional paper No. 5, page 14. Washington, D.C.
Simtowe F. J.Mduma, MAR.Phiri, A.Thomas, and M.Zeller. 2006. Can Risk Aversion Towards Fertilizer Explain Part of the Non-adoption Puzzle for Hybrid Maize? Empirical Evidence from Malawi. *Journal of Applied Sciences* 6(7):1490-1498 *http://ansijournals.com/jas/2006/1490-1498.pdf.*
Singh I., L.Squire, and J. Strauss. 1986. Agricultural Household Models: Extensions, Applications, and Policy. Baltimore: Johns Hopkins University Press.
Smale M. and P. Heisley. 1994. Maize Research in Malawi Revisited: An Emerging Success Story. *Journal of International Development* 6(6): 689-706.
Smale M., P.Heisey, and H.D.Leathers. 1995. Maize of the Ancestors and Modern Varieties: The Microeconomics of High-yielding Variety Adoption in Malawi. *Economic Development Journal.* 43 (2): 351-368
Smale M. 1995. Maize is Life: Malawi's Delayed Green Revolution. *World Development* 23: 819-831
Smith M.D. 2003. On Dependency in Double-Hurdle Models. Statistical
Stiglitz J. 1990. Peer Monitoring and Credit Markets, *World Bank Economic Review* 4(3): 197-203.
Swaminathan H. 2003. Bargaining and Intra-household Resource Allocation: An Analysis of the Impact of Credit and Land in Malawi. A Dissertation in Agricultural Economics Submitted in Partial Fulfillment of the Requirements for the Degree of Doctor of philosophy at the Pennsylvania State University, the Graduate School College of Agricultural Sciences.
Takayama A., 1998. Analytical Methods in Economics. University of Michigan Press, United States of America
Tchale H .2005. Economic Policies, Soil Fertility Management and Economic Policies, Soil Fertility Management and Sustainable Agricultural Growth in Malawi: A Bio-economic Analysis. PhD Dissertation, University of Bonn, Germany.
Tchale H., and P. Wobst. 2005. Soil Fertility Management Choice in the Maize-based Smallholder Farming System in Malawi, Center for Development Research (ZEF), Department of Economics and Technical Change, University of Bonn, Germany.
Tobin J. 1958. Estimation of Relationships for Limited Dependent Variables, *Econometrica*
Tuckman B. 1965. Developmental Sequence in Small Groups, *Psychological Bulletin* (63): 384-399 accessed at http://146.227.1.20/~jamesa//teaching/group_development.htm#TUCKMAN

UNCDF. 2003. Basic Facts about Microfinance. http://www.uncdf.org/english/microfinance/facts.php
USAD. 2004a. Deepening Malawi's Microfinance Sector Project (DMS), USAID Malawi
USAID. 2004b. Microfinance Sector Assessment in the Republic of Malawi, Lilongwe, Malawi
Vakis.R., de Janvry A., A. Sadoulet., and C. Catero. 2004. Testing for Separability in Household Models with Heterogeneous Behavior. A mixture model approach. University of California, Berkeley.
Van Bastelaer T. 2000. Imperfect Information, Social Capital, and the Poor's Access to Credit, IRIS Center Working Paper No. 234, University of Maryland, Center on Institutional Reform and the Informal Sector (IRIS)
Varian. Hal R. 1990. Monitoring Agents with Other Agents. *Journal of Institutional and Theoretical Economics.* 146 (1): 153-174.
Weil P.M.1970. The Introduction of the Ox Plow in Central Gambia in Mclaughlin, P.F. (Eds.) *African Food Production Systems: Cases and Theory*, Baltimore. The John Hopkins University Press.
Wenner M.W. 1995. Group Lending: A Means to Improve Information Transfer and Loan Repayment Performance. *Journal of Development Studies* 32 (2): 263-281
Woolcock M. 1998. Social Theory, Development Policy and Poverty Alleviation: A Comparative Historical Analysis of Group-Based Banking in Developing Economies. PhD dissertation, Department of Sociology, Brown University.
World Bank. 1996. Malawi Human Resources and Poverty. Report No. 15437 MAI.
Wydick B. 1999. Can Social Cohesion be Harnessed to Repair Market Failures? Evidence from Group-based Lending in Guatemala. *Economic Journal* 4 (109):463-475.
Wydick B. 2001. Group Lending under Dynamic Incentives as a Borrower Discipline Device, *Review of Development Economics,* 5 (3): 406-420.
Yen S., and A.Jones. 1997. Household Consumption of Cheese: An Inverse Hyperbolic Sine Double-hurdle Model with Dependent Errors. *American Journal of Agricultural Economics* (79):246—251.
Zeller M. 1998. Determinants of Repayment Performance in Credit Groups: The Role of Program Design, Intra-group Risk Pooling, and Social Cohesion. *Economic Development and Cultural Change* 6 (3): 599-620.
Zeller M., Sharma M., Henry. C and C. Lapenu. 2006. An Operational Method for Assessing the Poverty Outreach Performance of Development Policies in Africa, Asia and Latin America. *World Development* 34 (3): 446-464.
Zeller M., and R.L.Meyer. 2002. The Triangle of Microfinance: Financial Sustainability, Outreach, and Impact. Johns Hopkins University Press in

collaboration with the International Food Policy Research Institute (IFPRI), Baltimore and London.

Zeller M., Diagne A., and C.Mataya. 1998. Market Access by Smallholder Farmers in Malawi: Implications for Technology Adoption, Agricultural Productivity, and Crop Income. *Agricultural Economics*, 19 (2): 219-229

Zeller M., Sharma M., Ahmed A., and S. Rashid. 2001. Group–based Financial Institutions for the Rural Poor in Bangladesh. An Institutional and Household Level Analysis. Research Report 120, IFPRI, Washington DC

Zilberman D., and R.E Just. 1984. Labor Supply Uncertainty and Technology Adoption. In: R.D Emerson, (Ed.), Seasonal Labor Markets in the United States pp. 200-224. Ames: Iowa State University.

10 APPENDICES

Appendix 5.1: Sample distribution of credit groups by district

	Tobacco (n=46)	Maize (n=16)	Cotton (n=8)	Non-farm business (n=28)	Total (n=99)
Lilongwe	34	27	0	0	20.4
Zomba	26	33	25	29	28
Nkhota kota	2	40	75	7	15
Rumphi	38	0	0	64	36.6

Source: Own calculation RDD/IFPRI 1999 Rural Finance Survey

Appendix 5.2 Selected Demographic characteristics of group members by district

Characteristics	District where survey was conducted				Total
	Lilongwe	Zomba	Nkhotakota	Rumphi	Col %
Sex of respondent					
Male	51.1	47.5	47.9	46.3	47.5
Marital status					
Unmarried	2.2	3.0	1.7	2.0	2.1
Married	95.6	83.2	94.2	87.5	89.3
Widow	2.2	7.9	3.3	6.4	5.4
Divorced		5.0	0.8	3.7	2.8
Ever attended primary school?1=yes,2=no					
Yes	66.7	67.3	64.5	92.3	78.9
No	33.3	32.7	35.5	7.4	21.0
Level of schooling					
Can't read/write Chichewa	31.5	32.0	40.5	8.1	21.9
Read but can't write Chichewa	6.7	5.0	5.0	2.4	4.0
Read/write Chichewa	34.8	24.0	25.6	19.9	23.9
Read but can't write English	2.2	1.0	7.4	2.7	3.3
Read/write English	5.6	8.0	7.4	9.4	8.2
Primary school leaving certificate	13.5	15.0	9.9	37.7	24.9
Junior certificate	3.4	7.0	0.8	12.8	8.1
M.S.C.E.		5.0	0.8	6.4	4.1
Thos with professional training	11.1	20.8	14.9	27.0	21.2
Main occupation of household member					
Agriculture	95.6	87.1	95.8	82.2	87.7
Household work	1.1	1.0		1.7	1.1
Government/private service		3.0		3.0	2.0
Blacksmith	1.1			0.7	0.5
Small trade	1.1	5.9	2.5	8.4	5.7
Contract laborer		2.0		1.3	1.0
Child currently attending school				0.7	0.3

Source: Own calculation RDD/IFPRI 1999 Rural Finance Survey

Appendix 5.3 Correlation coefficients for variables on moral hazard

	prodar~e	prodle~h	scrfa	peerse~t	scrvgh~d	Je	Gpcomp~w	gloncdni	villag~r	pmfamvg	chairf~y
Prodarable	1										
Prodlevelsch	-0.0667	1									
Scrfa	-0.0401	0.0138	1								
Peerselect	0.1371	-0.0727	-0.4624	1							
Scrvghead	0.1402	-0.0982	-0.3098	-0.0575	1						
Pmjenterprise	-0.1959	0.0452	0.1276	-0.0884	-0.0072	1					
Gpcompknow	-0.2543	-0.1619	-0.1309	-0.0028	-0.0572	0.1891	1				
Gloncdni	-0.1174	-0.0823	-0.1188	0.1992	-0.092	-0.089	0.0618	1			
villagenum~r	0.1302	0.1422	-0.0145	-0.0211	0.0211	-0.0792	-0.2096	-0.069	1		
Pmfamvg	0.0351	-0.0992	0.0457	-0.1732	0.0933	-0.0147	-0.2401	-0.0525	-0.0032	1	
Chairfamily	0.0811	0.0143	0.0298	-0.0624	-0.0447	-0.0253	-0.0621	-0.0852	-0.1317	0.2221	1
Pressure	-0.1384	-0.1488	-0.0293	0.0138	-0.1494	-0.0189	-0.1611	-0.0683	0.1382	0.156	-0.1104
Left97	0.0172	-0.0512	0.0117	0.0216	-0.0922	-0.0735	0.0449	0.2837	0.0965	-0.1581	-0.0907
Fulljoint	0.0222	0.0163	0.1285	0.1804	0.0429	-0.0678	-0.0003	0.0715	0.0283	0.1119	0.1129
Pastsaca	0.0745	-0.0729	-0.3429	0.1878	0.1048	-0.0663	0.0304	0.1534	0.2494	-0.0196	-0.0649
New	0.3	0.0368	-0.1451	-0.017	0.1936	0	-0.2249	-0.0123	0.1671	0.4254	0.1741
Lcycle	0.0732	0.0055	-0.213	0.2325	0.0911	0.0843	-0.0355	0.1321	0.2345	-0.0315	-0.1334
Gpsize	0.1251	-0.2314	0.091	0.0709	-0.125	-0.1035	-0.0992	-0.0695	0.0847	0.2866	0.403
Maxidlmg	0.1022	0.2038	-0.1344	0.1175	0.0763	0.0295	0.0376	-0.0717	0.0381	-0.0354	-0.0966
Maize	0.1006	-0.2152	-0.143	0.0786	-0.0598	-0.0189	0.4055	0.1556	-0.1072	-0.1505	-0.122
Cotton	-0.13	0.095	-0.1103	0.1689	0.131	-0.0331	0.2159	-0.1097	0.0474	-0.2884	-0.0601
Nonfarm	-0.1662	0.163	-0.0526	-0.1585	0.0634	-0.0702	-0.0556	0.0447	-0.1713	0.1213	-0.0935

Source: Own calculation RDD/IFPRI 1999 Rural Finance Survey

Appendix 5.3: Correlation coefficients for variables on moral hazard.. continued

	Pressure	left97	fulljo~t	pastsaca	new	lcycle	gpsize	maxidlmg	maize	cotton	nonfarm
Pressure	1										
left97	-0.0089	1									
Fulljoint	0.041	0.0592	1								
Pastsaca	0.0125	0.0512	-0.0405	1							
New	0.0103	-0.0895	0.0886	0.1263	1						
Lcycle	0.1485	0.1221	0.039	0.3307	0.136	1					
Gpsize	0.0017	-0.0148	0.1573	0.016	0.0805	0.0633	1				
Maxidlmg	0.104	-0.1286	0.2291	-0.0918	0.0904	0.1524	-0.1796	1			
Maize	-0.1	0.2147	-0.0717	0.0814	-0.1029	0.0459	-0.1076	0.0973	1		
Cotton	-0.1253	-0.0924	0.0831	0.1538	-0.2707	0.147	0.0229	-0.0719	-0.1253	1	
Nonfarm	0.1725	-0.133	0.1088	-0.0582	0.1024	-0.1483	-0.2544	0.1812	-0.2654	-0.1862	1

Source: Own calculation RDD/IFPRI 1999 Rural Finance Surv

Appendix 5.4 Test for multicolinearity among variables on moral hazard

Variable	VIF	Tolerance (1/VIF)
Nkhota	7.26	0.137703
gpcompknow	5.14	0.19437
Lilongwe	2.97	0.336405
Zomba	2.82	0.354614
Cotton	2.71	0.368969
Scrfa	2.63	0.380575
pmgenderhomo	2.27	0.439843
Womenpg	2.21	0.453502
Nonfarm	2.15	0.465278
Peerselect	2.11	0.473371
Maize	2.07	0.482264
prodlevelsch	2.02	0.496218
Prodarable	1.88	0.532746
Pmfamvg	1.87	0.533832
Scrvghead	1.77	0.564616
Gpsize	1.71	0.583286
New	1.71	0.585705
Pastsaca	1.67	0.598674
Chairfamily	1.64	0.609295
Maxidlmg	1.64	0.610064
Rejected	1.6	0.626766
Villagenum~r	1.56	0.640598
cowealthhomo	1.55	0.644728
Lcycle	1.53	0.652945
Pressure	1.51	0.661356
Fulljoint	1.51	0.663093
Gloncdni	1.45	0.690404
Left97	1.38	0.722767
Je	1.37	0.731628
Mean VIF	2.2	

Source: Own calculation RDD/IFPRI 1999 Rural Finance Survey

Appendix 6.1 Correlation coefficients for variables on intra-group insurance

	Arable7	levelsch	scrfa	scrvil~r	scrvgh~d	covloss	cvloan~e	vilages2	pmfamvg	politc~n	chairf~y
arable7	1										
Levelsch	0.0426	1									
Scrfa	0.1682	-0.0146	1								
Scrvillager	-0.0581	0.025	-0.4957	1							
Scrvghead	0.0085	-0.0553	-0.3098	-0.2	1						
Covloss	0.1868	-0.0594	-0.1333	-0.1114	0.178	1					
Cvloanvalue	-0.0269	-0.0921	0.1488	0.061	-0.1115	-0.2214	1				
Vilages2	-0.1775	0.1209	-0.0174	0.1589	-0.0221	-0.1742	0.145	1			
Pmfamvg	0.2005	-0.0836	0.0457	-0.1399	0.0933	0.2109	-0.0586	-0.1776	1		
Politclan	-0.1682	-0.0042	-0.0665	-0.0459	-0.0347	0.0656	-0.0296	0.0004	0.2187	1	
Chairfamily	0.0241	0.0144	0.0298	-0.0427	-0.0447	0.0329	-0.0274	-0.1398	0.2221	0.2374	1
Pmjointent	-0.2042	-0.0207	0.0225	-0.0929	0.0557	0.0326	0.0493	0.1619	-0.0728	0.1741	-0.1706
Gloncdni	-0.1704	-0.0562	-0.1188	0.1103	-0.092	0.0042	-0.0444	0.1233	-0.0525	-0.0603	-0.0852
Contibpay	0.193	-0.0429	0.2051	0.0401	-0.0716	-0.1238	0.0089	0.0262	0.1295	-0.0655	0.1304
Pastsaca	-0.2538	-0.1047	-0.3429	0.1782	0.1048	0.0991	-0.1522	0.2503	-0.0196	0.0604	-0.0649
New	0.0487	-0.0143	0.0111	-0.0956	0.0354	-0.0307	0.0902	0.1166	0.1859	0.0825	0.0773
Lcycle	-0.0866	-0.0039	-0.213	0.216	0.0911	-0.1546	0.0641	0.2333	-0.0315	0.0649	-0.1334
Gpsize	0.1024	-0.2057	0.091	0.0559	-0.125	0.1249	0.0448	0.001	0.2866	0.2177	0.403
Maxidlmg	0.1755	0.2048	-0.1344	0.091	0.0763	-0.1185	-0.0406	0.0605	-0.0354	-0.1184	-0.0966
Maize	-0.1002	-0.1753	-0.143	0.2211	-0.0598	0.0807	0.017	-0.0324	-0.1505	-0.0026	-0.122
Cotton	-0.1107	0.0263	-0.1103	0.0917	0.131	-0.023	0.0039	0.0873	-0.2884	-0.0602	-0.0601
Nonfarm	-0.0025	0.1883	-0.0526	-0.1459	0.0634	-0.1338	-0.0755	-0.0656	0.1213	-0.1092	-0.0935

Source: Own calculation from IFPRI/RDD survey 1999

Appendix 6.1 Correlation coefficients for variables on intra-group insurance continued

	Pmjoin~t	gloncdni	contib~y	pastsaca	new	Lcycle	gpsize	maxidlmg	maize	cotton	nonfarm
Pmjointent	1										
Gloncdni	-0.1285	1									
Contibpay	-0.3609	0.1024	1								
Pastsaca	0.0584	0.1534	-0.0616	1							
New	0.0309	-0.1368	-0.1696	-0.094	1						
Lcycle	0.1262	0.1321	0.0606	0.3307	-0.1478	1					
Gpsize	-0.1448	-0.0695	0.1749	0.016	0.0858	0.0633	1				
Maxidlmg	-0.0024	-0.0717	0.238	-0.0918	0.0066	0.1524	-0.1796	1			
Maize	-0.0755	0.1556	-0.0548	0.0814	-0.0783	0.0459	-0.1076	0.0973	1		
Cotton	0.0584	-0.1097	-0.0533	0.1538	-0.1762	0.147	0.0229	-0.0719	-0.1253	1	
Nonfarm	-0.2263	0.0447	0.1345	-0.0582	0.027	-0.1483	-0.2544	0.1812	-0.2654	-0.1862	1

Source: Own calculation from IFPRI/RDD survey 1999

Appendix 6.2 Test for multicolinearity among variables on moral hazard

Variable	VIF	1/VIF
Scrfa	3.65	0.273752
Lilongwe	2.68	0.372459
Scrvillager	2.63	0.379724
Nonfarm	2.19	0.456431
Zomba	2.08	0.481239
Chairfamily	1.97	0.508099
Lcycle	1.94	0.516642
Covloss	1.91	0.522936
Contibpay	1.85	0.540082
arable7	1.85	0.540962
Politclan	1.84	0.543968
Screen	1.84	0.544553
Maize	1.82	0.550132
levelsch	1.78	0.562029
pastsaca	1.77	0.565376
gpsize	1.76	0.568416
scrvghead	1.75	0.571013
pmjointent	1.74	0.576234
maxidlmg	1.73	0.579331
pmfamvg	1.7	0.588899
covoccup	1.67	0.59894
vilages2	1.59	0.630075
New	1.54	0.64864
gloncdni	1.45	0.690664
cotton	1.43	0.697914
cvloanvalue	1.35	0.738011
Mean VIF	1.9	

Source: Own calculation from IFPRI/RDD survey 1999

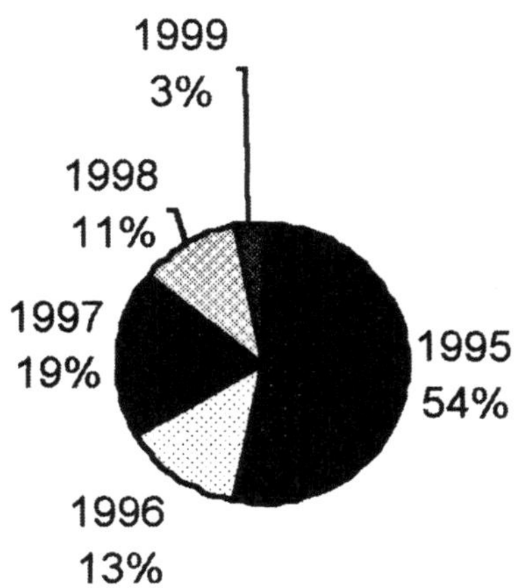

Appendix 6.3: Year when group was formed

Appendix 6.4 GLM estimates of the determinants of the extent of willing to insure

Variable	Coef.	Std. Err.	z	P>z	[95% Conf.	Interval]
LAND	0.2055	0.1458	1.4100	0.1580	-0.0801	0.4912
LEVELSCH	-0.0300	0.1095	-0.2700	0.7840	-0.2447	0.1846
SCREEN	0.8508	0.3605	2.3600	0.0180	0.1443	1.5574
SCRFA	1.6026	0.4117	3.8900	0.0000	0.7956	2.4095
SCRVILLAGER	1.7112	0.4061	4.2100	0.0000	0.9154	2.5071
SCRVGHEAD	1.3457	0.4781	2.8100	0.0050	0.4087	2.2827
COVLOSS	-0.2829	0.4296	-0.6600	0.5100	-1.1250	0.5592
COVOCCUP	0.0666	0.4555	0.1500	0.8840	-0.8262	0.9594
CVLOANVALUE	0.7652	0.5079	1.5100	0.1320	-0.2304	1.7608
VILAGES2	-0.0725	0.0890	-0.8100	0.4160	-0.2469	0.1020
PMFAMVG	-0.0850	0.3576	-0.2400	0.8120	-0.7859	0.6159
POLITCLAN	0.2182	0.1321	1.6500	0.0990	-0.0407	0.4771
CHAIRFAMILY	-0.0263	0.0440	-0.6000	0.5500	-0.1126	0.0600
PMJOINTENT	-0.4403	0.2573	-1.7100	0.0870	-0.9445	0.0640
GLONCDNI	-1.2902	1.2406	-1.0400	0.2980	-3.7218	1.1414
GCOMPNAI	-5.6313	2.6081	-2.1600	0.0310	-10.7430	-0.5195
PAPENATY	0.5071	0.4356	1.1600	0.2440	-0.3468	1.3609
PASTSACA	1.4876	0.3875	3.8400	0.0000	0.7280	2.2471
NEW MEMBERS	0.0000	0.0582	0.0000	1.0000	-0.1140	0.1140
LCYCLE	0.1824	0.1739	1.0500	0.2940	-0.1584	0.5232
GPSIZE	0.0426	0.0287	1.4800	0.1380	-0.0137	0.0989
MAXIDLMG	0.0000	0.0000	1.2100	0.2240	0.0000	0.0001
MAIZE	-1.0848	0.4326	-2.5100	0.0120	-1.9328	-0.2369
COTTON	-3.5976	1.0457	-3.4400	0.0010	-5.6472	-1.5480
NONFARM	-0.4827	0.3772	-1.2800	0.2010	-1.2220	0.2565
LILONGWE	-0.8258	0.5125	-1.6100	0.1070	-1.8303	0.1787
ZOMBA	-0.6897	0.5028	-1.3700	0.1700	-1.6752	0.2958
NKHOTA	2.3292	1.0418	2.2400	0.0250	0.2873	4.3711
_CONS	-4.7687	1.1508	-4.1400	0.0000	-7.0243	-2.5131

Source: Own calculation from RDD/IFPRI survey

Appendix 7.1: Descriptive statistics of variables on determinants of adoption

Variables	Mean	Std. Deviation	Minimum	Maximum
Dependent Variables				
Whether adopted (1=yes, 0=no)	0.596535	0.491201	0	1
Percentage of land under hybrid maize	27.35657	27.32174	0	99
Independent variables				
Yearly off-farm income (MK)	2694.354	7481.599	-28921	77700
Gender of household head (1=male)	0.722772	0.448185	0	1
Age of household head(years)	45.13119	13.58404	20	86
Value of assets owned (MK)	3433.017	8112.252	100	126920
Household size	4.361386	1.931351	1	12
Land holding size(ha)	2.175743	1.956425	0	22
Years of schooling of head	0.759901	0.427673	0	1
Whether receive free inputs (1=yes)	0.160891	0.430079	0	5
Tobacco growing household (1=yes)	0.225248	0.418263	0	1
Distance to Market	6.267327	7.221956	0	23
Distance to the extension office	2.242574	3.60322	0	15
Formal credit access (MK/year)	716.7129	1444.45	0	15998
Informal credit access (MK/year)	176.6856	303.4811	0	2020
Number of persons per hectare cultivated	3.081683	2.640731	0	16
Mangochi	0.24505	0.43065	0	1
Nkhota kota	0.175743	0.381073	0	1
Rumphi	0.190594	0.393257	0	1
Dedza	0.252475	0.434971	0	1

Source: Own calculation from RDD/IFPRI Rural Finance Survey

Appendix 7.2: Parameter Estimates of the expected Profit (Trans-log Specification)

Variable	Coefficient	t-statistic	t-probability
(Constant)	.001	.158	.874
Seed	1.066	90.160	.000
Fertilizer	-.060	-2.644	.009
Labor	-.070	-4.401	.000
Seed squared	-.478	-19.567	.000
Fertilizer squared	-.036	-.792	.429
Labor squared	.042	.977	.329
Seed –fertilizer interaction	.013	.221	.825
Seed- labor interaction	.254	4.791	.000
Fertilizer- labor Interaction	.108	1.696	.091
N	400		
R-Square	0.78		

Development Economics and Policy

Series edited by Franz Heidhues and Joachim von Braun

Band 1 Andrea Fadani: Agricultural Price Policy and Export and Food Production in Cameroon. A Farming Systems Analysis of Pricing Policies. The Case of Coffee-Based Farming Systems. 1999.

Band 2 Heike Michelsen: Auswirkungen der Währungsunion auf den Strukturanpassungsprozeß der Länder der afrikanischen Franc-Zone. 1995.

Band 3 Stephan Bea: Direktinvestitionen in Entwicklungsländern. Auswirkungen von Stabilisierungsmaßnahmen und Strukturreformen in Mexiko. 1995.

Band 4 Franz Heidhues / François Kamajou: Agricultural Policy Analysis – Proceedings of an International Seminar, held at the University of Dschang, Cameroon on May 26 and 27 1994, funded by the European Union under the Science and Technology Program (STD). 1996.

Band 5 Elke M. Förster: Protection or Liberalization? A Policy Analysis of the Korean Beef Sector. 1996.

Band 6 Gertrud Schrieder: The Role of Rural Finance for Food Security of the Poor in Cameroon. 1996.

Band 7 Nestor R. Ahoyo Adjovi: Economie des Systèmes de Production intégrant la Culture de Riz au Sud du Bénin: Potentialités, Contraintes et Perspectives. 1996.

Band 8 Jenny Müller: Income Distribution in the Agricultural Sector of Thailand. Empirical Analysis and Policy Options. 1996.

Band 9 Michael Brüntrup: Agricultural Price Policy and its Impact on Production, Income, Employment and the Adoption of Innovations. A Farming Systems Based Analysis of Cotton Policy in Northern Benin. 1997.

Band 10 Justin Bomda: Déterminants de l'Epargne et du Crédit, et leurs Implications pour le Développement du Système Financier Rural au Cameroun. 1998.

Band 11 John M. Msuya: Nutrition Improvement Projects in Tanzania: Implementation, Determinants of Performance, and Policy Implications. 1998.

Band 12 Andreas Neef: Auswirkungen von Bodenrechtswandel auf Ressourcennutzung und wirtschaftliches Verhalten von Kleinbauern in Niger und Benin. 1999.

Band 13 Susanna Wolf (ed.): The Future of EU-ACP Relations. 1999.

Band 14 Franz Heidhues / Gertrud Schrieder (eds.): Romania – Rural Finance in Transition Economies. 2000.

Band 15 Katinka Weinberger: Women's Participation. An Economic Analysis in Rural Chad and Pakistan. 2000.

Band 16 Christof Batzlen: Migration and Economic Development. Remittances and Investments in South Asia: A Case Study of Pakistan. 2000.

Band 17 Matin Qaim: Potential Impacts of Crop Biotechnology in Developing Countries. 2000.

Band 18 Jean Senahoun: Programmes d'ajustement structurel, sécurité alimentaire et durabilité agricole. Une approche d'analyse intégrée, appliquée au Bénin. 2001.

Band 19 Torsten Feldbrügge: Economics of Emergency Relief Management in Developing Countries. With Case Studies on Food Relief in Angola and Mozambique. 2001.

Band 20 Claudia Ringler: Optimal Allocation and Use of Water Resources in the Mekong River Basin: Multi-Country and Intersectoral Analyses. 2001.

Band 44 Thomas Herzfeld: *Corruption begets Corruption.* Zur Dynamik und Persistenz der Korruption. 2004.

Band 45 Edilegnaw Wale Zegeye: The Economics of On-Farm Conservation of Crop Diversity in Ethiopia: Incentives, Attribute Preferences and Opportunity Costs of Maintaining Local Varieties of Crops. 2004.

Band 46 Adama Konseiga: Regional Integration Beyond the Traditional Trade Benefits: Labor Mobility contribution. The Case of Burkina Faso and Côte d'Ivoire. 2005.

Band 47 Beyene Tadesse Ferenji: The Impact of Policy Reform and Institutional Transformation on Agricultural Performance. An Economic Study of Ethiopian Agriculture. 2005.

Band 48 Sabine Daude: Agricultural Trade Liberalization in the WTO and Its Poverty Implications. A Study of Rural Households in Northern Vietnam. 2005.

Band 49 Kadir Osman Gyasi: Determinants of Success of Collective Action on Local Commons. An Empirical Analysis of Community-Based Irrigation Management in Northern Ghana. 2005.

Band 50 Borbala E. Balint: Determinants of Commercial Orientation and Sustainability of Agricultural Production of the Individual Farms in Romania. 2006.

Band 51 Pamela Marinda: Effects of Gender Inequality in Resource Ownership and Access on Household Welfare and Food Security in Kenya. A Case Study of West Pokot District. 2006.

Band 52 Charles Palmer: The Outcomes and their Determinants from Community-Company Contracting over Forest Use in Post-Decentralization Indonesia. 2006.

Band 53 Hardwick Tchale: Agricultural Policy and Soil Fertility Management in the Maize-based Smallholder Farming System in Malawi. 2006.

Band 54 John Kedi Mduma: Rural Off-Farm Employment and its Effects on Adoption of Labor Intensive Soil Conserving Measures in Tanzania. 2006.

Band 55 Mareike Meyn: The Impact of EU Free Trade Agreements on Economic Development and Regional Integration in Southern Africa. The Example of EU-SACU Trade Relations. 2006.

Band 56 Clemens Breisinger: Modelling Infrastructure Investments, Growth and Poverty Impact. A Two-Region Computable General Equilibrium Perspective on Vietnam. 2006.

Band 57 Meike Wollni: Coping with the Coffee Crisis. An Analysis of the Production and Marketing Performance of Coffee Farmers in Costa Rica. 2007.

Band 58 Franklin Simtowe: Performance and Impact of Microfinance. Evidence from Joint Liability Lending Programs in Malawi. 2008.

Peter Lang · Internationaler Verlag der Wissenschaften

John Kedi Mduma

Rural Off-Farm Employment and its Effects on Adoption of Labor Intensive Soil Conserving Measures in Tanzania

Frankfurt am Main, Berlin, Bern, Bruxelles, New York, Oxford, Wien, 2006.
XV, 135 pp., 13 fig., 14 tab.
Development economics and policy.
Series edited by Franz Heidhues and Joachim von Braun. Vol. 54
ISBN 978-3-631-54652-9 · pb. € 34.–*

This study analyzes two related aspects: households' participation in off-farm employment as a livelihood strategy and the effects of participation in off-farm employment on households' adoption of labor intensive soil conserving technologies. Several factors are significant but spatial econometric analysis reveals that model parameters vary substantially across space. In addition, households supplying labor off-farm are generally associated with reduced adoption of terraces, hedgerows and cut-offs. The negative impact of supplying labor off-farm can be moderately cushioned when households also hire labor to work on the construction or maintenance of soil conserving structures. However, it is shown that hired labor is not a perfect substitute for households' own labor and does not fully off-set the effect of a household's off-farm labor supply.

Contents: The Agricultural Sector and Rural Households in Tanzania · Farm Household Model: A Theoretical Framework · Households' Off-Farm Labor Allocation Decisions · Spatial Analysis of Village Level Labor Markets · Off-Farm Employment and Household's Decision on Soil Conservation Technologies

Frankfurt am Main · Berlin · Bern · Bruxelles · New York · Oxford · Wien
Distribution: Verlag Peter Lang AG
Moosstr. 1, CH-2542 Pieterlen
Telefax 00 41 (0) 32/376 17 27

*The €-price includes German tax rate
Prices are subject to change without notice

Homepage http://www.peterlang.de